Aquinas at Prayer

Aquinas at Prayer

The Bible, Mysticism and Poetry

Paul Murray OP

B L O O M S B U R Y

LONDON • NEW DELHI • NEW YORK • SYDNEY

First published in Great Britain 2013

Copyright © Paul Murray, 2013

The moral right of the author has been asserted

A Continuum book

Bloomsbury Publishing Plc
50 Bedford Square
London WC1B 3DP

www.bloomsbury.com

Bloomsbury Publishing, London, New Delhi, New York and Sydney

A CIP record for this book is available from the British Library.

ISBN 9781441107558

10 9 8 7 6 5 4 3 2 1

Typeset by Fakenham Prepress Solutions, Fakenham, Norfolk NR21 8NN
Printed and bound in Great Britain by CPI Group (UK) Ltd, Croydon CR0 4YY

MIX
Paper from
responsible sources
FSC® C013604
FSC
www.fsc.org

Contents

In Memory of
Maurice (Gerard) Fearon, OP
1943–2012

the well known is what we have yet to learn
T. S. ELIOT

Acknowledgements

The idea for the present work began with an invitation to deliver an Aquinas Lecture in England at Bristol University. To Dr Fernando Cervantes, therefore, who thought to invite me and who acted as my host, I am indebted in a most particular way. A book is never solely the work of one individual. Accordingly, it is both a pleasure and an obligation for me to record here my debt to those friends and scholars who generously read parts of the work or who responded to particular queries sent their way. Any errors that remain are, of course, my own. I thank, first of all, Dr Margaret Atkins OSA, Dr Bernard Blankenhorn OP, Dr Denis O'Brien, Dr Kevin E. O'Reilly OP, Monsignor Philip Whitmore, Archbishop Arthur Roche, Sr Helene Berger, and Dr Claire le Brun-Gouanvic. The German scholar, Professor Walter Senner, my Dominican colleague at the University of St Thomas ('Angelicum') in Rome, found time to read carefully through a number of the early chapters, and offered invaluable help and encouragement. A special word of thanks is also due to Adriano Olivo OP of the Leonine Commission in Paris not only for making available to me the text of a number of Aquinas's sermons as yet unpublished by the Commission, but also for making available the provisional Leonine text of a number of the *Lessons* composed by Aquinas for the Feast of Corpus Christi.

In conclusion, I want to thank my brothers of the Irish Dominican Province whose companionship and theological wisdom have taught me much of what is contained in this book. I especially thank Philip McShane OP and Vivian Boland OP for their close and critical reading of the manuscript at all its different stages. With these two wonderfully alert and generous friends 'at my elbow', I have been blessed, during the period of composition, to find happily fulfilled that brief but bright Dominican saying from the Middle Ages: '*in dulcidine societatis quaerere veritatem*' – in the joy of fellowship to search for truth together.

Chapter 1 of the present work, 'Aquinas *at* prayer: the interior life of a mystic on campus', appeared first in *Logos* (Winter 2001); Chapter 8, 'Aquinas on poetry and theology' in *Logos* (Spring 2013); Chapter 4, 'Prayer in practice: Aquinas on St Paul' in *Angelicum* (Spring 2013).

Translations into English. With respect to the *Summa theologiae,* of particular help has been the Blackfriars Latin/English edition published 1966–75, and also the version published by Benzinger Bros. in 1948. On occasion, these translations have been modified by the author. With regard to the translation of Aquinas's other works, when no name of a translator is given in the notes, the translation is by the author.

All biblical translations are taken from either the Douai-Rheims version or from the version published by CTS, 39 Eccleston Square, London, SW1, England.

Introduction

That Aquinas was an outstanding scholastic theologian, a man with a genius for abstract speculation, goes without saying. But what, over the centuries, has generally been ignored in the academic world, and is still today little known by many of our contemporaries, is that Thomas Aquinas was first and last a teacher of Scripture, a Master of the Sacred Page. And no less forgotten, no less strangely overlooked, are two other aspects of Aquinas's life and work: his quite remarkable genius as a poet, and the decidedly mystical or contemplative character of his theology. Jean Pierre Torrell, in his celebrated work, *Thomas Aquinas: Spiritual Master*, speaks of this 'unknown Thomas', and makes bold to declare that 'Aquinas's theology is clearly orientated towards contemplation and is as deeply spiritual as it is doctrinal.' In fact, he notes, it is 'even more spiritual than rigorously doctrinal ... a religious attitude that has no equivalent except that of a mystic wholly consumed by love of the absolute.'[1]

Historians of spirituality have tended, by and large, to exclude Thomas Aquinas from their considerations. The character of his writing, in marked contrast to that of celebrated saints and mystics such as Teresa of Avila and Bernard of Clairvaux, appears far too abstract and academic to be considered spiritual or devout. And, what's more, Aquinas's work has unfortunately come to be linked, and even sometimes confused, with later forms of Thomism and Scholasticism. This fact may well explain why, in modern times, St Thomas's work appealed so little to the generation of Ratzinger and von Balthasar. In

---

[1] Jean-Pierre Torrell, *Saint Thomas Aquinas*, vol. 2: *Spiritual Master*, trans., R. Royal (Washington 2003) p.viii. See also chapter entitled 'St Thomas Aquinas: Theologian and Mystic' in Torrell, *Christ and Spirituality in St Thomas Aquinas*, trans., B. Blankenhorn (Washington DC 2011) pp. 1–20.

his autobiographical study, *Milestones: Memoirs 1927–1977*, Joseph Ratzinger writes: 'I had difficulties in penetrating the thought of Thomas Aquinas, whose crystal-clear logic seemed to me to be too closed in on itself, too impersonal and ready-made.'[2]

Another scholar of a slightly earlier generation spoke in similar vein about the 'closed', impersonal character of Aquinas's work. He wrote: 'we are in the dark when we attempt to discover the man behind the scholar.'[3] But is this true? When reading the texts of Aquinas, are we always confronted by a great academic merely, and not by a man of prayer, not by a spiritual Master? Is there, in reality, no direct way of gaining access to Aquinas the contemplative?

The present work is divided into three distinct sections: (1) *Aquinas: man of prayer*; (2) *Prayer considered: soundings in the biblical commentaries*; and (3) *Poet of the Eucharist: The hymns and canticles of Aquinas*. Over the last few decades many books and articles have been written directly on the subject of St Thomas's teaching on prayer, his *theology* of prayer. But relatively little attention has been given to the interesting and important question of how he himself actually prayed. That question will be taken up in the first section of the present study, and explored further, and at greater length, in the third and final section when attention is given to the poems and canticles Aquinas composed for the Office and Mass of Corpus Christi. The middle section of the present work, *Prayer considered: soundings in the biblical commentaries*, consists of three chapters: 'Aquinas as exegete', 'Prayer in practice: Aquinas on St Paul', and 'Praying in time of need: Aquinas on the Psalms'.

---

[2] Joseph Ratzinger, *Milestones: Memoirs 1927–1977*, trans., E. Leiva-Merikakis (San Francisco 1998) p. 44.
[3] F. J. E. Raby, *A History of Christian-Latin Poetry: From the Beginnings to the Close of the Middle Ages* (Oxford 1927) p. 403.

Part One

Aquinas:
man of prayer

1

The interior life of a 'mystic on campus'

When glanced at for the first time, the title of this chapter might well appear not only somewhat surprising, but also decidedly presumptuous. For how, at this distance in time, can we hope to gain access to the interior life of a man, a medieval theologian, who was famously reticent when it came to talking about himself, and who, in all his writings, almost never spoke in the first person, almost never used the word 'I'. That Thomas Aquinas was a profoundly wise man goes without saying, but what evidence is there to suggest that his interior life was marked by that depth of spiritual experience, that contemplative intimacy we associate with the great Christian mystics?

1. Aquinas under Scrutiny: The judgment of von Speyr

Before attempting to answer this question, I would like, first of all, to draw attention to an extraordinary text, a truly unique and bizarre document in my opinion. Its author is the celebrated friend and confidant of Hans Urs von Balthasar, Adrienne von Speyr. The text contains a number of negative judgments regarding the contemplative life of Thomas Aquinas, judgments based not on any kind of ordinary intellectual reflection on the prayer-life of the saint, but rather on knowledge which von Speyr claims she received from a direct seeing – a direct *vision* – of Aquinas at prayer.[1]

Although not on principle suspicious of such alleged visions, I am by no means persuaded that, in this particular case, von Speyr gained access to the hidden truth concerning the prayer-life of Aquinas. I suspect, in fact, she gained access merely to her own unconscious thoughts and feelings regarding the saint.[2] Nevertheless, the comments von Speyr makes about Aquinas, although they are for the most part mistaken in my opinion, do at least possess the merit of being free from any kind of false unction. Von Speyr is clearly liberated from the need or the desire to appear over-pious with regard to the cult of Aquinas. And that is no bad thing. From start to finish, in fact, she casts a distinctly cold eye on the question of St Thomas's prayer life and contemplative experience. So, as we begin our own reflections on this matter, von Speyr's 'revelations', whether we judge them, in the end, to be basically accurate or almost wholly mistaken, can act as a sharp and immediate challenge to the idea suggested by the title of the present chapter, the idea that Aquinas was a great Christian contemplative.

Not one vision of Aquinas but two are reported by von Speyr. With regard to the first, she makes bold to declare that Friar Thomas, on those occasions when he turned his attention to prayer, was a man far too controlling and far too obsessively intellectual to surrender easily to the pressure of God's grace. The man, the theologian, whom she sees at prayer, was someone who seems to have resisted being led to the heights of contemplation. 'God,' she declared, 'is a concept for him, something to analyse, to take apart and put back together … Love is not there. Everything remains intellectual.'[3] Von Speyr notes further

---

[1] Adrienne von Speyr, *The Book of All Saints*, vol. 1, (ed.) Hans Urs von Balthasar, trans., D. C. Schindler (San Francisco 2008) pp. 240–1 and pp. 363–6.

[2] Von Speyr, while the 'vision' lasted, was actually describing what she saw to her friend, Hans Urs von Balthasar. It's not inconceivable, therefore, that she may have been unconsciously tapping into *his* decidedly negative attitude towards certain aspects of scholasticism. Referring on one occasion to the rage provoked in him, as a young Jesuit, by the utter 'dreariness' of the scholastic theology to which he was exposed at the time, von Balthasar remarked: 'I felt like tearing down, with Samson's strength, the whole temple and burying myself beneath the rubble'! See Adrienne von Speyr, *Erde und Himmel. Ein Tagebuch, II: Die Zeit der grossen Dikate*, (ed.) von Balthasar (Einsiedeln 1975) p. 195.

[3] *The Book of All the Saints*, p. 241.

that, for Aquinas, prayer is 'like a disputation with God or like a scholarly conversation.' 'But,' she goes on at once to say – and the qualification is truly damning – 'he does not let God speak. It remains a monologue.'[4] And again: 'It is as if love got stuck by the busyness of thinking.'[5]

That's the first vision of Aquinas, as reported by von Speyr. And the report she gives us of the second is just as negative. For, once again, Aquinas emerges as anything but impressive in his life of prayer. Von Speyr even goes so far as to suggest that the saint 'does not feel particularly attracted' to 'prayer and contemplation.'[6] 'He does not fly at a very high level,'[7] she declares: 'Everything in him is ultimately subordinated to the intellect.'[8]

> Wherever possible he always contemplates things that fit in with the work he is doing at the time. Here, too, he is the one who leads God, as it were, rather than allowing himself to be led by God. He lacks a certain magnanimity. He contemplates, as it were, with pen in hand. But then God has mercy on him and gives him a share in genuine contemplation.[9]

That 'share,' however, we are told by von Speyr, is a very modest share indeed. For, apart from his manifest gifts of wisdom and insight, in the end all that Thomas's contemplative life adds up is, we are led to believe, something narrow and ungenerous, a faith-experience of life in the spirit which hardly bears comparison with that of the great contemplatives of the Church: in von Speyr's words, 'a meagre subjective experience of grace.'[10]

---

[4] Ibid., p. 240.

[5] Ibid., p. 241. Questioned by von Balthasar concerning St Thomas's spiritual state, 'at the end of his life', the reply von Speyr gives, while being somewhat more positive in tone, is still basically negative in its overall judgment of the saint: 'When the intellectual power weakens, then something does emerge that is more like love. His meticulousness loses strength, so that a kind of goodnaturedness comes out that was basically missing beforehand', p. 241.

[6] Ibid., p. 364.

[7] Ibid.

[8] Ibid., p. 365.

[9] Ibid.

[10] Ibid., p. 366. I'm happy to say that one or two other aspects of von Speyr's report sound more plausible. She says, for example: 'His perseverance in work is hard to imagine … He has his heart set on bringing the whole, completed achievement to God. He overtaxes himself.' And again: 'you would have to say that he is holy because he placed his enormous intellectual gifts entirely in the service of the Church's truth, because he allowed himself to be taken up into a greater context', p. 365.

When we compare the writings of Aquinas with those of the mystics, von Speyr might seem to have a point. St Thomas is a scholastic theologian. He is an intellectual through and through. His style is measured, austere and impersonal. In contrast, the writings of the mystics possess a vocabulary and a style which, generally speaking, can be described as distinctly vivid and spontaneous, dynamic and affective. Their work is visionary in tendency, and is almost always of an immediate psychological interest; in contrast that of Aquinas is decidedly reserved, plain-spoken and ontological. No wonder, then, that both at a popular level and in the world of academe, although regarded as a great Christian philosopher, and an outstanding speculative theologian, Aquinas has not generally been thought of as a spiritual author, and has never been regarded as a Christian mystic with the distinctive character and genius of someone like St John of the Cross. Are we to conclude, then, that the insistently dogged and scientific nature of Aquinas's work as a theologian tended somehow to undermine his life as a man of prayer?

2. The dilemma of the intellectual: Aquinas and Charles Darwin

There has been for some years now in contemporary spirituality, a tendency to set up a contrast – an exaggerated contrast – between, on the one hand, the cold, abstract intellect and, on the other, the warm, sensitive heart. We are told that, in order to make progress in the spiritual life – and indeed in life in general – we must make a journey from head to heart, an exodus out of the arid 'Egypt' of dull, controlled reflection to the promised land of spontaneous, fresh and exuberant emotion. Needless to say, the unhappy dualism implicit in this way of thinking is something Dominicans have actively opposed over the centuries. Again and again in their writings we find an un-embarrassed enthusiasm for the role not only of the heart but also of the mind in contemplation: the mind in search of God, the mind in love with God.

That said, it would be naive to suggest there are no risks involved for the individual believer, whether man or woman, whose task in life is to be professional theologian, and who regards theology itself as a science. The kind of risks I have in mind here constitute a challenge not only for practising theologians but for all those who, in their different areas of research, are inclined to approach reality in an exclusively scientific spirit.

One example which illustrates this point with great vividness comes to mind. It is the unforgettable confession Charles Darwin makes in his autobiography concerning the unusual impact which a life-long dedication to science had on his sensibility and on his capacity to appreciate the finer things of life. Here is a small part of what he shared on that subject: 'Up to the age of thirty, or beyond it, poetry of many kinds ... gave me great pleasure ... even as a schoolboy I took intense delight in Shakespeare ... But now for many years I cannot endure to read a line of poetry; I have tried lately to read Shakespeare, and found it so intolerably dull that it nauseated me. I have also almost lost my taste for pictures or music.'[11]

Darwin is speaking here, and with an almost shocking self-penetration, of what he calls 'the atrophy of that part of the brain on which the higher tastes depend.'[12] 'My mind,' he writes, 'seems to have become a kind of machine for grinding general laws out of large collections of facts.'[13] What a devastating end, what a tragic fate for a scholar!

But the condition described here is not one peculiar to Darwin as a scientist. In the realm of theology, for example, since the time of Aquinas there have been, I have no doubt, more than a few neo-thomists and neo-scholastics whose minds were no less cold and machine-like but who lacked the honesty or the self-knowledge to admit to their condition. In the case of Darwin, an insistently scientific approach to nature, over so many months and years, rendered the man incapable, in the end, of enjoying what are acknowledged universally to be some of the highest and greatest gifts of life.

Is it possible that, in the case of Aquinas, a no less determined, no less scientific approach – this time to the mysteries of God – left the saint in some way bereft of the taste for prayer and contemplation, as von Speyr has

---

[11] *Charles Darwin: His Life told in an Autobiographical Chapter and in a Selected Series of his Published Letters,* (ed.) Francis Darwin (New York 1893) pp. 53–4.
[12] Ibid., p. 54.
[13] Ibid.

suggested? Can the great scholastic be accused, therefore, of being all head and no heart? In his practice of theology, did the mind of Aquinas become, in the end, like Darwin's, 'a machine for grinding general laws out of large collections of facts'?

To attempt some kind of answer to this question, it will be necessary to give attention to two important sources: first, the actual writings of Aquinas and, in particular, certain of his reflections which bear directly on the question of prayer and contemplation; and, second, the evidence concerning his own life of prayer and contemplation as reported by those of his contemporaries who knew him well.

3. Science and devotion: Aquinas and St Thomas Didymus

A good starting point for our reflections, I would suggest, is an incident to which St Thomas draws our attention in his commentary on the Gospel of John, chapter 20. The apostle, known as Doubting Thomas, or Thomas Didymus, is gazing with amazement and faith at the Risen Christ, and at the open wound in his side. This is the moment, according to Aquinas, when the Doubter is transformed into 'a theologian'.[14] Thomas, being himself a theologian, identified in a particular way, we may presume, with this moment of contemplative awareness in the life of the Apostle. So are we to think of him, then, as in some sense, 'another Thomas'?

This question, as it happens, was raised by a contemporary of Aquinas, Bernard Gui, in his biography of the saint. Answering his own question, Gui replies: 'Not indeed like [Thomas] Didymus in doubting, for our Thomas's hold on divine things was firm and sure; but resembling that Apostle in entering the abyss of the side of Christ … entering as one invited, and therein searching out and expressing the mysteries contained there, with such assurance that it is as if his hands had handled what the finger of his intellect

---

[14] St Thomas Aquinas, *In Joannem Evangelistas*, 20, lect. 6, Parma vol. 10, p. 634.

points to.'[15] The 'pointing' of the intellect is one thing, the fine brilliance of that kind of understanding, but Thomas, the theologian, was never content with an exclusively intellectual or merely scientific grasp of the mysteries of God. Something once said of St Dominic can be said equally here of his most famous son: 'he was able to penetrate the mysteries ... with the humble under-standing of his heart.'[16]

Bernard Gui, in his biography, notes that, on occasion, Friar Thomas would take time to read works which were in no way academic, devotional texts, for example, which speak more immediately to the heart than to the head. He undertook this practice, Gui tells us, 'in order to offset the aridity which is so often the result of abstract and subtle speculative thinking.'[17] And this practice, he says further, 'did both his heart good by increasing devotion and his intellect by deepening its considerations.'[18]

Clearly Thomas had no intention whatever of becoming a merely cold or abstract intellectual. In this context an observation he makes, in his commentary on *The Epistle to the Hebrews,* is highly significant. Theology, he notes, although it is indeed a science, is different from other sciences in the role it gives both to the head *and* to the heart. He writes: 'The doctrine of sacred scripture contains not only matters for speculation, as in geometry, but also matters to be accepted by the heart [*approbanda per affectum*].'[19] Accordingly, the discipline of theology cannot be undertaken in an exclu-sively academic spirit. 'In the other sciences, it is enough to be made perfect according to the intellect; in this one, however, it is required to be made perfect both intellectually *and* affectively [*secundum intellectum et affectum*].'[20]

In this sentence the word *affectum* alerts us to the *experiential* nature of

---

[15] Bernard Gui, *The Life of St Thomas Aquinas: Biographical Documents,* 13, (ed.) Kenelm Foster (London 1959) p. 36.

[16] Jordan of Saxony, [*Libellus*] *On the Beginnings of the Order of Preachers,* trans., Simon Tugwell (Dublin 1982) p. 2.

[17] Bernard Gui, op. cit., 15, p. 38. The one devotional work explicitly mentioned by Gui is a work ascribed to Cassian: 'Homilies of the Fathers' (*Collationes Patrum*).

[18] Ibid.

[19] St Thomas Aquinas, *Super epistolam ad Hebraeos lectura,* ch. 5, lect. 2, 273, in *Super epistolas,* Marietti vol. 2, p. 395.

[20] Ibid. In the same text Thomas also writes (p. 713): 'Perfection is of two kinds: one is of the intellect, when a person has the wisdom to discern and judge correctly about matters which have been

a genuinely engaged theology, an aspect of theology which, unfortunately, did not always receive due attention from the later scholastic tradition. But St Thomas, in his commentary *On the Divine Names,* declares: 'The learned person not only attains to knowledge of divine things, he also experiences [literally 'suffers'] them, i.e. not only does he receive them as knowledge into his mind, he also becomes one thing with them by love and by affection.'[21] The meaning Aquinas gives to the word 'experience' when speaking about God has provoked a great deal of debate. Some scholars argue that the word possesses an intellectual rather than an affective meaning. But, in the opinion of Jean-Pierre Torrell, Aquinas uses the word to describe a form of knowledge whose character is not merely speculative but is 'a knowing that also has a [frankly] experiential side (*quodammodo experimentalis*).'[22]

The word 'experience' itself Aquinas clearly borrows from the vocabulary of the senses. In his commentary on Psalm 33 he offers us, at one point, a description of the experience of God what might almost serve as a definition of mysticism. He writes: 'Experience of a thing comes through the senses ... Now God is not removed from us, nor outside of us, he is in us ...That is why experience of the divine goodness is called "taste" (*gustatio*) ...The effect of that experience is twofold: first, certitude of knowledge, second, the sureness of affectivity.'[23]

For Aquinas, the one who truly practises theology does not merely think about the mysteries of the faith at a safe, reflective distance. No – he or she is someone who, with profound regard, kneels down in spirit, as it were, before the mystery. That, I take it, is the reason why Jean-Pierre Torrell says of

---

proposed; the other is perfection of love, which charity produces, and is present when a person adheres entirely to God.'

[21] See *Expositio in librum b. Dionysii de divinis nominibus,* no. 191, Marietti edition, p. 59. See also *ST,* I II q.43; I II q.112, a.5; II II q.45 a.2.

[22] Jean-Pierre Torrell, *Saint Thomas Aquinas,* vol. 2: *Spiritual Master,* trans., Robert Royal (Washington 2003) p. 95.

[23] Cited in Torrell, *Saint Thomas Aquinas: Spiritual Master,* p. 96. For some reason this particular statement and others like it, in Aquinas's work, tend either to be ignored or overlooked by both modern and ancient authors. In the fifteenth century, for example, the Carthusian monk, Vincent Aggabach, impressed by the decidedly intellectual character of the saint's work, thought it wise to exclude Aquinas altogether from the history of Christian mysticism. On this point, see Martin Grabmann, *The Interior Life of Aquinas,* trans., N. Ashenbrener (Milwaukee 1951) p. 31.

Aquinas that when he attempts, as a speculative theologian, to reason about his faith, it is never simply 'a matter of logical rigour'. On the contrary, it always involves, Torrell insists, 'the totality of his person'.[24] Along, therefore, with the image of the theologian seated at a desk, and earnestly devoted to the study of truth, another necessary image for Aquinas is that of the apostle, St Thomas Didymus, falling to his knees at the feet of his Lord and God, and thereby acknowledging both the humanity and divinity of Christ, and becoming, in that moment, in the understanding of St Thomas, 'a *good* theologian' (*bonus theologus*).[25]

4. Dedicated scholar and man of prayer

Bernard Gui, in his biography of St Thomas, notes that 'In Thomas the habit of prayer was extraordinarily developed.'[26] One indication of this fact is that '[w]hen perplexed by a difficulty he would kneel and pray.'[27] In fact Gui tells us that 'he never set himself to study or argue a point, or lecture or write or dictate without first having recourse inwardly – but with tears – to prayer.'[28] And, what is more, he was prepared openly to acknowledge, according to Gui, that 'prayer and the help of God had been of greater service to him in the search for truth than his natural intelligence and habit of study.'[29] Clearly, what counted for Aquinas, as a theologian, was something far more profound than mere cleverness. In his commentary on Matthew's Gospel, he declares: 'Humility is what makes a man capable of God' (*humilitas facit hominem capacem Dei*).[30]

---

[24] Jean-Pierre Torrell, *Saint Thomas Aquinas*, vol. 2: *Spiritual Master*, trans., Robert Royal (Washington 2003) p. 371

[25] See *In Johannem Evangelistas*, 20, lect. 6, Parma vol. 10, p. 634.

[26] Bernard Gui, *The Life of St Thomas Aquinas*, 15, (ed.) Kenelm Foster (London 1959) p. 36.

[27] Ibid., p. 37.

[28] Ibid.

[29] Ibid. William of Tocco, who was one of the witnesses at the First Canonization Enquiry at Naples, remarked of St Thomas that 'all his writing began with prayer, and in all his difficulties he had recourse to prayer, with many tears.' See *From the First Canonization Enquiry*, LVIII, in *The Life of St Thomas Aquinas: Biographical Documents*, (ed.) K. Foster (London 1959) p. 98.

[30] *In Matthaeum Evangelistam expositio*, ch. 11, Parma vol. 10, p. 114.

That Thomas Aquinas turned to prayer in the way I have indicated will come as no surprise to anyone familiar with the lives of the saints. And the fact that humble and devoted prayer and dedicated, intellectual study should be regarded as two fundamentally different kinds of activity will also occasion no surprise. But what will perhaps seem strange, indeed may even astonish, is that Aquinas held fast to the view all his life that study – theological study – the passionate, unrelenting pursuit of divine truth, was itself somehow an actual form of prayer. Serious thinking about the Gospel was, for Aquinas, nothing less than a sacred activity. In the Prologue to the *Sentences* he states explicitly that, for the person who is actively engaged in it, theology takes on the form of prayer. It assumes what he calls the *modus orativus*.[31]

I have always been struck by a particular story about Aquinas which is recorded in one of the early biographies.[32] It reveals in an undoubtedly forceful but also I think amusing manner the emphatically intellectual character of the saint. Once, when he was praying in the Dominican convent at Naples, there appeared to Thomas in a vision a certain Brother Romanus whom he had last seen in Paris. Romanus said to Thomas: 'I have passed from this life, but I am allowed to come to you on account of your merits.' Thomas was shaken at first by the apparition, but summoning up his courage, he said to Romanus: 'If it be pleasing to God, I adjure you by God to answer my questions.'[33]

The saint then put to Romanus two rather straightforward questions, the first concerning himself, his work and the state of his soul, and the second, concerning the spiritual condition of his friend. But, with the third and final question we hear, all of a sudden, breaking into the story, as it were, the voice of Friar Thomas d'Aquino, the searching, indefatigable scholar and passionate scholastic. Without any preamble, he says to Romanus: 'On that question that we have so often discussed together concerning the dispositions of knowing which we acquire here [on earth]: do they remain with us in the fatherland?'[34] It was an unexpected question to put to an apparition, and certainly not the

---

[31] *In Sent. Pro.*, a.5; cited in J.-P. Torrell, *Saint Thomas Aquinas*, vol. 2, p. 17.
[32] *De visione fratris Romani*, in William Tocco, *Vita* XLV, pp. 118–19. A version of this story can also be found in Bernard Gui, *Vita* XIX, pp. 186–7.
[33] Ibid., p. 119.
[34] Ibid., p. 88.

sort of question we imagine saints, or those who have visions of this kind, are normally inclined to ask. The answer Brother Romanus gives is short and, perhaps, not surprisingly, negative. 'Brother Thomas, I see God,' he declares, 'and you may not question me further on that subject.'[35]

Now, that would seem to be that, with no more to be said. The end, it would appear, of a brief excursus into scholasticism. But Thomas returns at once to his point. Vision or no vision, he is a scholar with a question on his mind, and he is not going to be easily thwarted. 'Since you see God,' he says to Romanus, 'can you see Him directly, in an immediate way (*sine media specie*), or only by means of a likeness?' The ghostly visitant, at this stage, has clearly had enough. He chooses to bow out of the discussion at once and disappear, but not before delivering a short, mystical citation: 'As we have heard, so we have seen, in the city of our God!'[36]

It seems clear that Friar Thomas, in more than one respect, did not conform to the accepted model of a saint. He was pious certainly, but he was also a man obsessed with the desire for knowledge, and with the desire to know God. And, in the end, that obsession itself was part of his holiness. A.-D. Sertillanges, in his celebrated work, *La Vie intellectuelle*, writes: 'It is the thinker's special characteristic to be obsessed by the desire for knowledge.'[37] But study – the impulse to study – being like prayer rooted in *desire*, can itself become a form of prayer. Sertillanges calls it 'active prayer,'[38] a way of *praying without ceasing*. And that is precisely what study became for St Thomas.

Even, on those occasions, when St Thomas actually took time to go apart to pray, it was often connected with a particular intellectual challenge which was confronting him. He would withdraw, we are told, 'into secret prayer … in order to obtain understanding of the divine mysteries.'[39] So prayer, we can say, was *useful* to him in his vocation as a Dominican intellectual – a point, as

---

[35] Ibid.

[36] Ibid., p. 89. This brief reflection on the vision of Romanus appeared originally in Paul Murray, *The New Wine of Dominican Spirituality: A Drink Called Happiness* (London 2006) pp. 110–13.

[37] A.-D. Sertillanges, *The Intellectual Life,* trans., M. Ryan (Cork 1965) p. 71.

[38] Ibid., p. 70.

[39] See *Ystoria sancti Thome de Aquino de Guillaume de Tocco,* 30, (ed.) Claire le Brun-Gouanvic (Toronto 1996) p. 80.

it happens, which Adrienne von Speyr was concerned to stress in the second of her two reports. In fact, she even goes so far as to suggest that Aquinas 'uses his contemplation like practice for the clearer vision of his reasonings.'[40] 'His prayer', she tells us, is 'systematic practice for him'; 'He arranges it into his work, and it serves as preparation for the work.'[41]

The primary concern of the Dominican preacher is, or should be, to assist in some way the salvation of others. Accordingly, intellectuals in the Order such as St Thomas Aquinas have never been afraid to manifest, even with regard to the life of prayer and contemplation, a certain healthy pragmatism. Aquinas would no doubt, for example, have agreed with the eminently practical advice offered, on one occasion, by Pope St Gregory the Great: 'When preachers are resting, they should absorb in contemplation something they can give out later in their sermons, when they are busy again for the good of others.'[42]

In this passage, the act of contemplation is seen, first and last, as an outstanding aid towards better preaching. It is not regarded, therefore, as an end in itself. But such an exclusively pragmatic approach to the life of contemplation, wise though it certainly is on occasion in view of the preacher's vocation, does not represent the whole of St Gregory's, or indeed of St Thomas's thinking on the subject.[43] The determined pragmatism of these two preachers of the Word is more than balanced, I would say, by a comment Aquinas makes in one of his lesser known works regarding the contemplation of wisdom. There St Thomas insists that contemplation possesses something of the happy *uselessness* – the sheer, self-delighting quality of a game. He writes:

---

[40] Adrienne von Speyr, *The Book of All Saints*, p. 364.

[41] Ibid.

[42] Pope St Gregory the Great, *PL* 75:761A. This text is cited by Humbert of Romans in his *Treatise on the Formation of Preachers*, no. 236. See *Early Dominicans: Selected Writings*, (ed.) Simon Tugwell, (New York 1982) p. 252.

[43] In the *Summa theologiae*, II II q.180, a.1, Thomas writes: 'Gregory makes the contemplative life to consist in the love of God, inasmuch as through loving God we are aflame to gaze on his beauty.' According to Thomas the individual at prayer can be so overwhelmed at times by the immensity of the power of God, the ecstasy experienced can literally sweep the individual off his standing (II II q.175, a.1 and a.2). A number of Thomas's own contemporaries reported that he himself, on occasion, experienced rapture of this kind. See Bernard Gui, *The Life of St Thomas Aquinas*, 23 and 24, pp. 42 and 44.

We should observe that the contemplation of wisdom is fittingly compared to a game by reason of two features that are found in a game. First, a game is enjoyable in itself and the contemplation of wisdom provides the greatest enjoyment … Second, the activities of a game are not ordered to anything else, but are sought for their own sake. And this same feature belongs also to the delights of wisdom.[44]

5. The scholastic among the mystics

When, as students, we first encounter the work of Aquinas, the scholastic form of his writing can be distinctly off-putting.[45] What we have before us, it would appear, are a series of doctrinal insights merely: the thoughts a man had, not a man *having* thoughts, not the language of experience. Yes, we have evidence in full of a vast speculative wisdom, of a manifestly intellectual 'knowing', but no clear evidence, it would appear, of any kind of deep interior or mystical experience, no evidence, in other words, of 'knowing with all one's soul'.[46]

Carl Gustav Jung, when he first 'took a dive into St Thomas'[47] – to use his own vivid expression – found that the plunge was hardly worth the trouble. In a letter to a friend he confessed his disappointment, saying that he 'did not feel refreshed afterwards'.[48] Almost certainly, I would say, it was the impersonal, scholastic nature of Aquinas's work which was the most immediate

---

[44] Prologue, *Expositio libri Boetii de ebdomadibus*, Leonine vol. 50, pp. 267–8. The term 'contemplation', in this passage, does not refer specifically to a form of *Christian* contemplation but rather to a *simple* act of gazing at the truth. A comparable statement by St Thomas can be found in *Contra gentiles*, III, ch. 2, no. 9.

[45] Not every student, it should be said, has this experience. For some, the first encounter with the work of Aquinas is a decidedly positive experience, a graced discovery.

[46] This distinction between 'knowing' and 'knowing with all one's soul' is noted by the French philosopher, Gustav Thibon, when speaking about the mysticism of his friend, Simone Weil. 'Such mysticism,' he writes, 'had nothing in common with those religious speculations divorced from any personal commitment which are all too frequently the only testimony of intellectuals who apply themselves to the things of God. She actually experienced in its heart-breaking reality the distance between "knowing" and "knowing with all one's soul", and the one object of her life was to abolish that distance.' See Thibon's 'Introduction' to *Gravity and Grace* by Simone Weil (London 1962) pp.viii–ix.

[47] Letter to Victor White OP, 31 December 1945, in *C. G. Jung Letters*, vol. 1: *1906–1950*, (eds), G. Adler and A. Jaffes (Princeton 1973) p. 540.

[48] Ibid.

cause of his disappointment. Those, like Jung, who have had some familiarity
with mystical texts, and with their impressively experiential and personal
character, will find it difficult at the beginning, if not impossible, to recognize
in Aquinas's work its strong, contemplative character.

In contrast, a devoted reader of Aquinas, like the great contemporary
scholar, Jean-Pierre Torrell, is prepared to speak openly about the 'mystical'
dimension of Aquinas's theology.[49] And Étienne Gilson, a figure from the
receding past but a no less eminent Thomist in his day, after a lifetime's reading
of the work of Aquinas, did not hesitate to declare: 'The burning desire of God
which in a John of the Cross overflows into lyric poems is here [in Aquinas]
transcribed into the language of pure ideas.'[50] The end result is not, of course,
a kind of exalted or burnished metaphysics, a wonderfully inspired but purely
intellectual phenomenon. No – according to Gilson, the *Summa theologiae,*
for example, 'with its abstract clarity, its impersonal transparency, crystallizes
before our very eyes and for all eternity his [Aquinas's] interior life.'[51]

That statement is, I think, both authoritative and illuminating. It invites us
to continue to contemplate, as best we can, what we might call the 'content' of
that interior life. But the very *form* of Aquinas's writing is, I would suggest, a
revelation of its basic, contemplative character. The vision expressed – the *way*
it is expressed – is something utterly plain. Here, there is nothing whatever
esoteric or mandarin. And yet that very plainness is, in the end, no small
part of its appeal, and part also of its secret. A line from a prose passage by

---

[49] Jean-Pierre Torrell, *Saint Thomas Aquinas,* vol. 2, p. 3. Since Torrell's book appeared, A. N. Williams
published an important and illuminating article on the subject of Aquinas as mystical theologian.
Aquinas's theology, she argued, although 'not concerned specifically with mystical experience –
visions, revelations, ecstasy and such', was at core directly concerned 'with the conditions of the
possibility of union with God.' She writes: 'I am proposing that we look at one of the greatest of all
systematic theologies, Thomas's *Summa Theologiae,* as both an exhortation to contemplation and an
act of contemplation.' See 'Mystical Theology Redux: The Pattern of Aquinas' *Summa Theologiae',
Modern Theology,* 13:1 (January 1997) p. 56.
[50] Étienne Gilson, *The Christian Philosophy of St Thomas Aquinas* (New York 1956) p. 375. A no less
striking remark regarding the contemplative basis of Aquinas's teaching was made by the saint's early
biographer, Bernard Gui. Very soon after Thomas began to teach, Gui reports, people were at once
aware that here was a mind possessed by 'a new light from God': 'The divine splendor hitherto hidden
in his soul was now shining out, and all were amazed at the glory and lucidity of his utterance.' See *The
Life of St Thomas Aquinas: Biographical Documents,* 11, p. 33.
[51] Ibid., p. 376.

the English poet, Ted Hughes, comes at once to mind: 'Not the plainness of a white marble floor, but of deep, clear water, open and immediate.'[52] This simple image I have lifted out of its original and altogether different context. But I can hardly think of a better phrase to describe the distinctive quality and character of Aquinas's writing: *Not the plainness of a white marble floor, but of deep, clear water, open and immediate.*

6. Portrait of a mystic?

Over the years, scholars and readers of Aquinas have been inclined to base the notion or image they have of the Dominican Master almost exclusively on his philosophical and theological writings. Relatively little attention, as a result, has been given to the accounts of his life and character handed down to us by those of his contemporaries who knew him at first hand. Of these witnesses, one of the most important was William of Tocco, St Thomas's first biographer.[53] Claire le Brun-Gouanvic, who edited the *Life* by Tocco, writes: 'More than the philosopher and theologian, it is the mystic who emerges from the portrait by Tocco.'[54]

The astonishing energy which marked St Thomas's intellectual and academic life was, in Tocco's presentation, almost indistinguishable from an abiding passion that was fundamentally mystical in its manifestations. Tocco speaks, for example, of 'the almost continual state of abstraction in which he lived,' and of the frequency with which he would get 'caught up in the things of heaven.'[55] But such a marked capacity for abstraction, it could be argued, does not in itself constitute a decisive portrait of a Christian mystic. St Thomas may indeed have been habitually withdrawn, but was that not, perhaps, due to

---

[52] Ted Hughes (ed.), *A Choice of Shakespeare's Verse* (London 1971) p. 202. Hughes is describing here one of the sonnets of Shakespeare.
[53] Writing in 1911, as editor of *Fontes vitae S. Thomae*, D. Prümer regarded the biography composed by Peter of Calo as the earliest, but this view has not found favour with later scholars.
[54] See *Ystoria sancti Thomae de Aquino,* (ed.) Claire le Brun-Gouanvic (Toronto 1996) p. 40.
[55] Ibid., 63, p. 203.

the fact that 'he was an intellectual entirely given over to the inner life of the mind'?[56]

Needless to say, a more complete portrait of a mystic would have to include at least one or two other elements such as mystical locutions, visions, the gift of tears, prophecy, miracles, or levitation – things which most readers are certainly not inclined to associate with the great Aquinas. But all these elements – *all* these extraordinary phenomena – are in fact included by Tocco in his *Life* of the saint.[57] How, then, are we to understand this decision, on the part of Tocco, to highlight the mystical traits in St Thomas's life and character? Is it possible that the portrait he gives us is no more than a medieval exaggeration, a pious attempt to fit Aquinas into a traditional, hagiographical framework?[58] Or is there, perhaps, on the contrary, a genuine and surprising likeness to Thomas in the Tocco portrait, an essential veracity?

That Tocco was inclined to a certain exaggeration, I have no doubt, and for the reason suggested above. But, while being wary of the medieval bias of someone like Tocco, we must be at least as wary of our own modern bias in the way we are inclined to approach the subject of holiness and the manifestations of holiness.[59] To dismiss out of hand, therefore, as mere fiction or invention all the stories reported by Tocco would surely be a mistake on our part, and betray a lack of objectivity. Tocco was by no means alone among the contemporaries of Aquinas in giving prominence to a wide range of mystical phenomena in the life of the saint.[60]

---

[56] A comment by Simon Tugwell in *Albert and Thomas: Selected Writings* (New York 1988) p. 262.

[57] Tocco's *Ystoria sancti Thome de Aquino*: for *visions*, see 17, pp. 127–8; 31, p. 159; 32, p. 160; 44, pp. 176–7; 45, p. 178; for *mystical locution*, see 24, p. 162; for *the gift of tears*, see 29, p. 154; 24, p. 162; for *prophecy*, 46, pp. 179–80; 57, pp. 195–6; for *miracles*, see 50, pp. 185–6; 51, pp. 186–7; 53, pp. 189–90; for *levitation*, 33, pp. 160–1; 34, p. 162.

[58] William of Tocco, when engaged in writing Aquinas's life, was involved, at the same time, in collecting materials to be submitted to the Holy See with the intention of bringing about, as quickly as possible, the canonization of Aquinas.

[59] 'When modern biographers treat his visions and miracles,' according to Joseph Goering, 'they do so uneasily, and are often quick to use the reigning canons of historical criticism to dismiss them, or to interpret them in ways that are acceptable to contemporary tastes.' See Goering, 'The Miracles and Visions of Thomas Aquinas,' in *Mystics, Visions, and Miracles* (New York 2002) pp. 127–39.

[60] Note, for example, the reported comments of his friend, Brother Reginald, and other comments made by contemporaries at *The First Canonization Enquiry*, in *The Life of Saint Thomas Aquinas: Biographical Documents*, (ed.) K. Foster, pp. 82–126.

And, of course, Aquinas himself is not unwilling, on occasion, to speak of such things.[61] But, compared to the focus given in his work to the most fundamental aspects of spiritual life, St Thomas devotes very little time or attention to extraordinary phenomena. Unlike the great Carmelite mystics of the sixteenth century, he manifests no interest whatsoever in analysing the inner workings of his own mystical or contemplative experience. His mysticism has, in that sense, a decidedly *objective* character. His most pressing concern is not with the communication of certain spiritual and psychological states and stages, but rather with the attainment of an intimate and final union with God, and the attainment also of that wisdom which comes from living knowledge of God.

7. Herman Hesse reading Aquinas

So solemnly monumental, and indeed almost a-historical, has the achievement of Aquinas become in the popular imagination, his work can impress the uninitiated, as nothing more than a great marble edifice, a temple of answers, a closed structure of hard and fixed dogma. But Herman Hesse, a representative figure of the twentieth century, encountering for the first time one of Aquinas's most famous works, would seem to have received a more positive impression. He gave an account of this experience in a poem entitled 'After Dipping into the *Summa Contra Gentiles*'.[62] Bewildered by the chaos of the world's suffering, and by what is named in the poem as 'strife, / Obsessions, and longings for a better life',[63] Hesse, as soon as he begins to dabble in the work of Aquinas, finds himself in a world which appears to be free of all strife

---

[61] Aquinas speaks, for example, about different states of mystical rapture and vision in the *Summa theologiae*, II II q.174 and q.175.

[62] The poem is one of a batch of poems attributed to a fictional character in Hesse's novel *The Glass Bead Game*. But since the voice we hear in the poem is much closer to the troubled, searching voice of a poet like Hesse, living in the twentieth century, than to the voice of the young, serene Master of 'the Game', Joseph Knecht, I have taken the liberty of attributing a number of the statements in the poem to Hesse himself. This is not, of course, to deny the objective distance which still remains between Hesse, the living poet, and the fictional author of his poem. See *The Glass Bead Game*, trans., R. and C. Winston (Harmondsworth 1974) pp. 412–13.

[63] Ibid., p. 412.

and anguish, a serene uncomplicated realm, a universe of luminous clarity.
He writes:

> Whenever we entered the temple of Aquinas,
> The graceful *Summa contra Gentiles,*
> A new world greeted us, sweet, mature,
> A world of truth, clarified and pure.
> There all seemed lucid, Nature charged with Mind,
> Man moving from God to Him, as He designed.
> The law in one great formulary bound,
> Forming a whole, a still unbroken round.[64]

Though these lines certainly capture something of the atmosphere of the
Contra Gentiles, the poem overall does not present an accurate picture of
Aquinas's work or indeed of Aquinas's world. Later, towards the end of the
poem, Hesse briefly evokes an image – *his* image – of the sweet, blissful world
he imagines 'blessed' people like Aquinas were privileged to inhabit – people,
he writes,

> Who never suffered anguish or knew fear,
> Whose times were times of glory and good cheer,
> Who lived like children, simple happy lives.[65]

Now it has to be said at once that the description given here bears no
resemblance whatever to the world of the thirteenth century into which
Thomas d'Aquino was born, and lived for nearly fifty years. And it also fails
utterly to represent the day-to- day experience of Thomas as a theologian 'on
campus' at the University of Paris. Marie-Dominique Chenu, with typical
accuracy, warns us not to be taken in by the romantic image of Thomas as
a man so 'abstracted' and 'solitary' as to be effectively removed from 'the
conflicts and squabbles of his century.'[66] That medieval world, Chenu explains,

---

[64] Ibid.
[65] Ibid., p. 413.
[66] M.-D. Chenu, *St Thomas d'Aquin et la théologie* (Paris 1959) p. 113.

was one 'where a manifest violence of spirit, even among believers, intensified the roughness of people's behaviour.'[67]

Even the members of Thomas's own immediate family were not immune from the violence of the period. His own brother, Reginaldo, was involved in a plot, in the year 1246, to assassinate the deposed Emperor Frederick II. The attempt failed, and the young man was subsequently caught and executed.[68] It should come, of course, as no surprise to encounter 'violent spirits' in the world of politics. But Thomas's experience of university life as a young theologian in Paris was not, as it happens, that much different. One or two examples of life on campus at the time will serve, I think, to dispel once and for all 'the simple, happy lives' scenario proposed by Herman Hesse's poem.

8. Aquinas 'on campus'

When Thomas arrived in Paris in 1252, he found himself in an atmosphere which was decidedly hostile to the Friars Preachers, that small group of revolutionary mendicants who were just then beginning to enjoy great influence at the university. Needless to say, the drama entailed a lot more than a mere struggle for certain coveted academic positions. 'It may virtually be taken for granted,' writes Josef Pieper, 'that a revolutionary movement which had risen up out of criticism of the existing state of affairs ... would naturally not be treated with joy by the powers representative of the existing order. And it might be anticipated that the antagonism would grow all the stronger as the revolutionary movement exerted an ever more potent spell over "the younger generation" – which, amazingly, is what the mendicant orders did.'[69]

As time passed, the atmosphere within the university got so bad that, by 1255, it became actually dangerous for the friars to walk out into the streets. On more than one occasion, in the immediate vicinity of the Dominican Priory of San Jacques, there were riots and demonstrations. And, by the spring

---

[67] Ibid.

[68] See James Weisheipl, *Friar Thomas d'Aquino: His Life, Thought and Works* (Washington 1983) p. 48. At the time of his brother's execution St Thomas was already a member of the Order of Preachers.

[69] Josef Pieper, *Guide to Thomas Aquinas,* trans., R. and C. Winston (New York) p. 64.

of 1256, things came to such a head that, according to Humbert of Romans, as soon as a friar was seen out in public, he was likely to be surrounded on all sides by an aggressive mob, the air filled with the loathsome sounds of mockery and yelling: 'tumult of shoutings, the barking of dogs, the roaring of bears, the hissing of serpents.'[70] What's more, all kinds of filth would be deliberately dumped down from above onto the cowled heads of the friars!

Fortunately, at least so far as we know, Thomas was not himself subject to any such form of physical violence. But he did, on one occasion, have to endure the sudden, rude interruption of a heckler in church when he was trying to preach. The heckler, a certain Guillot, while making his dramatic protest, held up for all to see a tract written against the friars, denouncing them in the strongest possible terms as dangerous fore-runners of the Anti-Christ.[71] So Thomas d'Aquino lived, as the Chinese would say, in 'interesting times'!

Given the atmosphere within the university during these years it's not surprising to learn that St Thomas on occasion also came under determined and severe *intellectual* attack. In 1270, for example, he was accused of contaminating his philosophy with naturalism. And, because of a number of suspect propositions which were then in circulation and which, mistakenly, came to be linked with his thought, he was constrained for a number of years to live under threat of public censure if not indeed condemnation.[72] Nevertheless, our young Dominican Master seems to have taken it all in his stride. He was never the kind of intellectual who invited opposition or controversy for its own sake. When, however, he found himself confronted by blatant lies or by manifest stupidity in an opponent, St Thomas did not hesitate to assume the role of a fierce advocate and stout defender of the truth.

Once, for example, addressing a number of his Parisian adversaries, he declared: 'If anyone glorifying himself with false knowledge, dares to argue against what I have just written, let him not babble in corners, or in the company of youngsters, who are incapable of judging such a difficult subject,

---

[70] Humbert of Romans, *Chart. U. P.,* I, 311–12, n.273; cited in Weisheipl, *Friar Thomas d'Aquino,* p. 93.
[71] This incident took place on Palm Sunday, 6 April 1259. See Jean-Pierre Torrell, *Saint Thomas Aquinas,* vol. 1: *The Person and His Work,* trans., R. Royal (Washington 1996) pp. 71–2.
[72] See M.-D. Chenu, *St Thomas d'Aquin et la Théologie* (Paris 1959) pp. 111–12.

but let him write against this book – if he dares.'[73] And again: 'Those who defend that position must confess that they do not understand anything at all and that they are not even worthy of discussion with those whom they attacked.'[74]

Students of the work of Aquinas may be inclined to ignore these alarming, historical details as irrelevant. After all, when we turn to the actual writings of St Thomas, the spirit we encounter there, line by line, paragraph by paragraph, is one of great calmness and quiet order. The world of thought in which we find ourselves is one far removed, it would seem, from the 'conflicts and squabbles' of a century long passed. But that serenity of thought, which so distinguishes the work of Aquinas, has not been achieved by ignoring, in any sense, the challenge of his own century. No – his theological vision is one which has been tested in the fires of immediate historical circumstance, and is all the more authoritative for that fact. Speaking of St Thomas's last great work, the *Summa thelogiae*, Josef Pieper writes: 'The very fact that a work of such unperturbed objectivity and such deep, radiating peace could grow from a life which, far from being untroubled, consumed itself in strife, gives us an insight into the special quality of the man.'[75] And, in the same book, Pieper speaks of 'the noisy and disgraceful tempest of strife and jealousy in which he had to work.'[76]

9. Aquinas and the unknown God

The wide calm which impresses us, as soon as we read any of the works of Aquinas, is not a calmness born of a cold solipsism but rather that of an open,

[73] *De unitate intellectus contra Averroistas*, 5, II. 434–41; cited in J.-P. Torrell, *Saint Thomas Aquinas*, vol. 1: *The Person and His Work*, p. 93.

[74] Ibid., 3, II. 315–17. Other caustic remarks – indicative of life 'on campus' – can be found in Aquinas's work, but they are few and far between. What most characterizes St Thomas's reaction to intellectual opponents, even those who were decidedly intransigent, is a surprising openness of spirit to anything they might say that was true. Again and again he is spoken of by his contemporaries as a man 'wonderfully kind' (*miro modo benignus*).

[75] Josef Pieper, *The Silence of St Thomas*, trans., D. O'Connor (London 1957) p. 12.

[76] Ibid., p. 20.

easeful, and living relationship to all things. What the German poet, Rainer Maria Rilke said, on one occasion, when praising the sculptor, Auguste Rodin, can also be said here, I believe, and with the same authority of recognition, regarding the life and work of Aquinas:

> He has left nothing in uncertainty ... he has made things and has placed them about him, things and things; so a reality grew around him, a wide calm relationship of things that linked him with other and older things, until he himself seemed to stem from a dynasty of great things; his quiet and his patience comes from thence, his fearless enduring age, his superiority over people who are much too mobile, too vacillating, playing too much with the equilibrium in which, almost unconsciously, he rests.[77]

Of all the works of Aquinas the one which, I think, best communicates this sense of wide calm is the *Summa contra Gentiles*. Page by page, the text reveals to us an ordered universe of ideas, in which, as Herman Hesse notes in his poem, 'Wisdom and knowledge were not yet divided.'[78] But such an impressively achieved vision, both doctrinal and spiritual, does not represent, on the part of Aquinas, a bland, complacent hold on the mysteries of God. No, in fact, the opposite is the case. Had Herman Hesse been able to do more than merely 'dip' into the *Contra Gentiles*, had he persevered in his reading up to Book 4, Chapter 1 for example, he would, I think, have been startled into a very different perception of Aquinas. For, from the very beginning of the chapter, St Thomas is concerned to emphasize the radical limitation of all human knowledge of God, even when informed by faith. 'Job,' Thomas notes, 'rightly names it a droplet.'[79]

Side by side with the undeniable authority which shines through the many pages of Aquinas's work, there is another quality which is equally radiant but somehow less known, and that is the open *questio* of his approach to reality, his profound humility before the mystery of things. In his theological writings

---

[77] Letter to Lou Andrea-Salomé, 10 August 1903, in *Letters of Rainer Maria Rilke: 1892–1910*, trans., J. B. Greene and M. D. Herter Morton (New York 1945) p. 123.
[78] Hesse, 'After Dipping into the Summa Contra Gentiles', p. 412.
[79] *Summa contra Gentiles*, Bk 4, ch. 1, Leonine vol. 15, p. 4.

there is even a certain 'loose-endedness' at times when it comes to final conclusions, a way of thinking about God and about reality which is the very opposite of a closed system.[80] On this subject Han Urs von Balthasar writes: 'despite his will to clarify, he is a master in the art of leaving questions open.' Thomas displays, in fact, 'an astonishing breadth, flexibility, and mutablility of perspectives which allow quite automatically the aporetic element in his thinking to emerge.'[81]

Believing Christians today seldom hear from preachers and teachers about the incomprehensibility of the divine nature. So the notion that the height of our human knowledge of God, far from being a remarkable fountain of wisdom, is no more than a mere 'drop' in the ocean relative to the awesome mystery of God, might well sound alarming. But St Thomas, in his work, shows not the least hesitation in making clear to us, and over and over again, the true depth of our 'ignorance'. Thus, in the *Summa theologiae,* he writes: 'Neither a Catholic nor a pagan knows the nature of God as he is in himself.'[82] And, in a commentary on Boethius on the Trinity: 'at the end of our knowledge, God is ultimately known as unknown.'[83]

Such forceful language might seem to suggest that Aquinas is of the opinion we can make no true statements whatever about the nature of God. But, in reality, as Brian Davies points out, according to St Thomas we can know many things about God – that he is loving, good, powerful and so on.' So what, then, does it mean to assert 'We cannot know what God *is*'? Davies explains: 'To grasp his position, we need to understand that according to him we know what something is when we can define it. More precisely, we know what something is when we can locate it in terms of genus and species.'[84] But to 'locate' God in that way, to imagine that we could comprehend God as a

---

[80] See Fergus Kerr's reflections on this aspect of Aquinas's work in *After Aquinas: Versions of Thomism* (Oxford 2002) p. 210.

[81] Hans Urs von Balthasar, 'On the tasks of Catholic Philosophy in our Time,' *Communio* 20 (1963) p. 173; cited in Kerr, *After Aquinas,* p. 15.

[82] *ST,* I, q.13, a.10, ad 5.

[83] *Super Boethium de Trinitate,* 1.2. ad 1, Leonine vol. 50, p. 84.

[84] See Brian Davies, *The Thought of Thomas Aquinas* (Oxford 1993) p. 41.

scientist comprehends objects in the known world, would be knowledge not worth having. *Un dieu défini est un dieu fini.*

St Thomas is, of course, well aware of the marvellous knowledge that comes to us through faith. So important, however, is the point he wants to make regarding our mind's inability to grasp the unutterable mystery of God, he is prepared, at times, to risk sounding almost like an agnostic. Not for a moment, of course, is he forgetting the fullness of God's revelation to us in Christ. But what makes that final revelation so astonishing is the fact that, at its core, there is not simply a cold handful of dogmas proposed for our acceptance, but rather a living Divine Person present to us in all his mystery. With regard to the 'agnosticism' of St Thomas, the Dominican Victor White asks, 'If St Thomas is right when he says we cannot know what God is then are we not driven back to stark agnosticism?' And he replies:

> St Thomas's position differs from that of modern agnostics because while modern agnosticism says simply, 'We do not know, and the universe is a mysterious riddle', a Thomist says, 'We do not know what the answer is, but we do know that there is a mystery behind it all which we do not know, and if there were not, there would not even be a riddle. This Unknown we call *God*. If there were no God, there would be no universe to be mysterious, and nobody to be mystified'![85]

No small part of the contemplative strength of Aquinas's theology is the purposefulness with which he is determined to explore, as far as humanly possible, the depths of that mystery and yet, at the same time, to acknowledge himself defeated in the end, mastered by the sheer wonder of what he is contemplating. At one point in the *Contra Gentiles,* he writes: 'If we contemplate the mystery of the Incarnation earnestly and reverently, we find there such a depth of wisdom that our human knowledge is overwhelmed by it

---

[85] See Victor White, *God the Unknown* (London 1956) pp. 18–19. Because St Thomas was centrally concerned with the unknown in God, with that ineffable mystery, he can be regarded, in the view of Herbert McCabe, as 'a mystical thinker'. McCabe writes: 'in what is sometimes misunderstood as his dryly rational approach ... he is in fact engaged in, and inviting the reader to be engaged in, a mystical exploration, which is not at all the same as a mystical experience.' See McCabe, *God Still Matters,* (ed.) Brian Davies (London 2005) p. 13.

... That is why to all those who consider things reverently the reasons for this mystery appear ever more marvelous (*semper magis ac magis admirabiles*).'[86]

10. The collapse, the silence

In the last year of Aquinas' life it was remarked by those closest to him that he was becoming more and more abstracted, more and more absorbed in contemplation. Of course, for years, Thomas had been given to bouts of absent-mindedness. But this was something different. It was certainly different in intensity. At Compline, during the singing of the *Media vita*, his face was now bathed in tears. And, during Mass, he would appear completely overwhelmed at times by the mystery he was celebrating. On Passion Sunday 1273, with a large group of people present at the Mass, it was noticed that tears were flowing from his eyes, and, so profound was his ecstasy, at one point he had to be shaken so that he might return to himself and continue with the celebration.[87] On 6 December, several months later, finding himself once again rapt in prayer during Mass, something happened, an event of grace so truly overwhelming it was to mark a change in him forever.

There were, it would seem, two aspects to this extraordinary event, a 'physical' as well as a 'mystical' aspect. According to James Weisheipl, 'The physical basis for the event could have been ... an acute breakdown of his physical and emotional powers due to overwork.'[88] That a profound mystical

---

[86] *Summa contra Gentiles,* Bk 4, ch. 54, Leonine vol. 15, p. 173.

[87] See Bernard Gui, *The Life of St. Thomas Aquinas,* 28, p. 46. And see also William of Tocco, *Vita S. Thomae Aquinatis,* in *Fontes vitae S. Thomae,* (eds), D. Prümer and M. H. Laurent, in facsimiles attached to *Revue Thomiste* (1911–1937) p. 103. Many times during his life St Thomas was seen weeping at prayer, a fact which rather contradicts the notion of the saint as a cold and unemotional contemplative. See the reports in Bernard Gui's biography, and also the reports given by the witnesses at the first Canonization Enquiry: *The Life of St Thomas Aquinas: Biographical Documents,* pp. 34, 37, 87, 98 and 100. On the subject of tears, Thomas made an observation which would seem to have come straight from the depth of his own contemplative experience: 'Tears are caused not only through sorrow, but also through a certain tenderness of the affections, especially when one considers something that gives joy mixed with pain ... In this way tears arise from devotion.' *Summa theologiae* II II, q.82, a.4, ad 3.

[88] See Weisheipl, *Friar Thomas d'Aquino,* p. 322. I am indebted to Weisheipl for the helpful phrase 'mystic on campus'. See his article, 'Mystic on Campus: Friar Thomas', in *An Introduction to the Medieval Mystics of Europe,* (ed.) P. Szarmach (New York 1984) pp. 135–59.

experience can, on occasion, be accompanied by a complete physical collapse is noted, in one place, by the Dominican preacher and mystic, Johannes Tauler. He writes: 'a man may die of a broken heart because God works in him so vehemently that it is more than he can bear.'[89] And again: 'many a man has died of this, giving himself up so utterly to these wondrously great works that his nature could not endure it and collapsed under the strain.'[90]

After Mass that morning, 6 December 1273, Thomas, we are told, 'hung up his instruments of writing.' He never completed the *Summa*. Asked by his bewildered assistant, Brother Reginald, 'Father, are you going to give up this great work?', Thomas replied: 'I can't go on … Everything seems as so much straw in comparison with what I have seen and what has been revealed to me.'[91]

St Thomas – the '*bonus theologus*' – leaves us with a final, unexpected word. And the word is silence. This does not mean, of course, that he had no more to say. It means simply that what he had glimpsed, in his ecstasy, was utterly beyond the reach of human thought and human speech.[92] Years earlier, in a treatise on the Trinity, he had written: 'God is honoured by silence, not because we may say or know nothing about him, but because we know that we are unable to comprehend him.'[93]

In the light of all the different texts and stories contained in the present chapter, I have no doubt that St Thomas was both a great intellectual *and*

---

[89] See Tauler, Sermon 11, in *Sermons*, trans., M. Shrady (New York 1985) p. 58.

[90] Ibid.

[91] This account was shared by Brother Reginald with a friar who then passed on the story to Bartholomew of Capua. See the First Canonization Enquiry at Naples, in *Fontes vitae S. Thomae*, (eds), D. Prümmer and M. H. Laurent, in facsimiles attached to *Revue Thomiste* (1911–37) p. 376. 'Straw', in the Middle Ages, was a common term for Scripture's literal sense. As an image it evoked, therefore, something distinctly limited and yet of manifest value. So, although St Thomas was compelled, at the end, to acknowledge the radical limitation of his life-time's work, he was not dismissing all of it as rubbish. See 'Foreword' by Aidan Nichols in *The Silence of Thomas* by Bruno Forte (London 2003) p. 10.

[92] According to the report of William of Tocco, St Thomas, speaking on one occasion about the 'revelation' he received when in ecstasy on 6 December 1273, remarked to his friend, Brother Reginald: 'it has pleased the Lord to impose on me the silence of not being able to teach (*docendi silentium*).' See *Ystoria sancti Thome de Aquino de Guillaume de Tocco*, 63, (ed.) Claire le Brun-Gouanvic (Toronto 1996) p. 204.

[93] *Super Boetium de Trinitate*, 2, 1, ad 6, Leonine vol. 15, p. 94.

a great, albeit discreet, mystic. That is the reason, I am persuaded, why the 'silence' of which he speaks – the silence which *honours* God – can be detected between the lines and words of almost everything he wrote. It is a silence, first and last, of attention to the Word of God, the silence of the grace of listening, the silence of a mind continually amazed at the radiant fullness of truth revealed in Christ. It is a silence of willing obedience to the will of the Father, and to the least movement of the workings of the Spirit. It is a silence of love, of Trinitarian communion, a silence of day-to-day intimacy and friendship, a silence which denotes the very opposite of a mere intellectual monologue. It is a silence which, though contemplative of the fact that God is beyond all human thoughts, all human words, is never for a moment disdainful of the humble words we use when we try to speak of God. It is the silence of a mind utterly at rest in the contemplation of truth, and yet ever restless in its search for a deeper understanding. It is a silence which breathes with that freedom of spirit which comes from the contemplation of eternal things, and yet remains committed always to the immediate task of the hour. It is the silence of a man, living for years in the midst of the ordinary squabbles and conflicts of academe, who was yet able to be somehow at ease, and to live a quite extraor- dinary interior life. It is the silence of a mystic on campus.

2

*Four prayers:
the influence of Humbert
of Romans*

1. Introduction

Of the many descriptions of St Thomas's life which have survived, by far the most moving and vivid, I would say, are the accounts of his last hours and days, and in particular the unforgettable account of the final words he spoke before dying. According to Peter of Montesangiovanni, who was present at the monastery of Fossanova when Thomas passed away, and who was also one of the witnesses at *The First Canonization Enquiry*, St Thomas bore his final illness 'most patiently', and he 'received the sacraments of the Church reverently and devoutly, and especially the Body of Christ.'[1] What's more, 'in the presence of the whole community of monks and many Dominicans and Friars Minor', St Thomas, though he was manifestly ill and dying, said 'many beautiful things' concerning the real presence of Christ in the Eucharist.[2] A number of these 'things' we find recorded in some of the early biographies of St Thomas. Here, for example, is the account given by Bernard Gui:

---

[1] 'From the First Canonization Enquiry,' XLIX, in *The Life of Saint Thomas Aquinas: Biographical Documents,* (ed.) Kenelm Foster (London 1959) p. 94.
[2] Ibid.

Feeling his strength ebbing away, he devoutly asked for the most holy body of Christ: and when the abbot, accompanied by the monks, brought it to him, he did reverence to it, prostrate on the ground; weak in body, but with his mind, as it were, running strongly to meet his Lord. And being asked, as the Church discipline requires, whether he believed that this was indeed the body of the Son of God which was born of the Virgin and hung on the cross for our sake and on the third day rose again, Thomas answered with a strong voice and alert devotion and shedding tears ... 'I truly believe and most certainly know that this is indeed true God and Man, Son of the eternal Father, born of the Virgin mother, the Lord Jesus Christ. This I sincerely believe and confess.' Then with tears and devotion he received the life-giving sacrament. But first (according to report) he said also these words: 'O price of my redemption and food for my pilgrimage, I receive you. For your love I have studied and toiled and kept vigil. I have preached you, and taught you. Never consciously have I said a word against you.'[3]

That St Thomas should express such a firm belief in the Real Presence at this point in his life is no surprise. But to those readers familiar only with the impersonal, scholastic language and discourse of Aquinas, the direct, personal manner with which Thomas now addresses Christ in the Eucharist, will come as something of a shock. Here, the great theologian is not thinking speculatively – in the abstract, as it were – about the mystery of the Eucharist. No, with a rapt, contemplative immediacy his whole attention is, we can say, fixed on the Bread of Life. And he is speaking so intimately and so directly to Christ that, when we read his words, we are in effect overhearing a saint at prayer.

Other prayers, with the same immediacy and directness, have been attributed to St Thomas over the centuries, and a few have become reasonably well known (*The Prayer before Study*, for example). But, for the most part, the

---

[3] Bernard Gui, *Vita s. Thomae Aquinatis*, in *Fontes vitae s. Thomae Aquinatis*, (ed.) D. Prümmer (Toulouse 1911) p. 205. Bernard Gui's account here, including as it does an actual prayer spoken by St Thomas, is much more elaborate than the account recorded by Peter of Montesangiovanni. Except for one small word – 'love' – the translation of the Gui text is by Kenelm Foster OP. The phrase '*pro cujus amore*' Foster translates as 'for your sake'. See Foster's edition of *The Life of Saint Thomas Aquinas*, pp. 55–6.

Piae preces, the prayers attributed to the saint, have received relatively little attention.[4] How, then, are we to assess their actual character and status today? Is it possible that these prayers really are the work of Aquinas?

The first thing to note is that the *Piae preces* are not to be found in the official catalogue of the works of Aquinas prepared at the time of the canonization process. This fact would seem to argue against their authenticity. But the catalogue is concerned only with what it calls 'works', and it is not obvious that short prayers fit under that particular rubric or category. The celebrated prayer, *Adoro te devote,* though now generally accepted as one of Aquinas's finest achievements, was also excluded from the canonization catalogue. And that's of no small significance. I say this because the *Adoro te* was not composed as a hymn (as people nowadays are inclined to think) but rather as a private *prayer.*[5] We have, therefore, impressive evidence to suggest that Aquinas was by no means averse to the composition of short, devotional texts or prayers in the manner of the *Piae preces.*

None of the manuscripts which attribute the *preces* to Thomas Aquinas are earlier than the fourteenth century. When, however, the prayers appear in manuscript form they are almost always attributed to Aquinas: never to any other author. This fact, in itself, is not of course a definite proof of authenticity. And, inevitably, doubts of one kind or another will persist in the minds of scholars with regard to the question of authorship. But it is worth noting here that an impressive number of commentators, over the last one hundred years, have had no difficulty in acknowledging Aquinas as the author or probable author of the *Piae preces.*

Otto Hermann Pesch, for example, commenting on the *Piae preces* in 1998, remarked: 'The texts are worthy of being studied in order to see how all the theology of Thomas is reflected in a lived piety.'[6] Many years earlier,

---

[4] The prayers can be found in both the Busa and Marietti editions of Aquinas's work: Busa, vol. 6 (*Reportationes*) pp. 584–5; Marietti, *Opuscula theologica,* vol. 2, *De re spirituali,* pp. 283–9.
[5] See Robert Wielockx, 'Poetry and Theology in the *Adoro te deuote*: Thomas Aquinas on the Eucharist and Christ's Uniqueness,' in *Christ Among the Medieval Dominicans,* (eds), K. Emery and J. P. Wawrykow (Notre Dame, Indiana 1998) pp. 157–74.
[6] Otto Hermann Pesch, *Thomas von Aquin: Grenze und Gröe mittelalterlicher Theologie* (Mainz 1988) pp. 105–6.

the Dominican scholar, A.-D. Sertillanges, published in French a translation of the *Piae preces* and, when introducing the work, made clear his conviction that the *preces* deserved to be grouped 'under the high signature' of Aquinas: 'The depth and structure of these writings correspond so well with the doctrine, style, and natural movement of thomistic thought that those readers, most familiar with the works of Aquinas, are those least able to doubt the mark of Aquinas.'[7]

In more recent years, the *Piae preces* have attracted the attention of the German scholar, Lydia Maidl.[8] Although basically negative in her assessment, Maidl is tentatively open to the possibility that Aquinas might indeed be the author of the *preces*. Nevertheless, for a number of stated reasons, Maidl finds herself much less impressed than A.-D. Sertillanges by the 'depth and structure' of some of the prayers.[9] The points she raises are both challenging and of very considerable interest. I will take the opportunity, therefore, when commenting on the individual prayers, to reflect on what she has to say.

The *Piae preces* are works of prose not poetry. But in the original Latin there is, at times, beneath the surface bareness of the language, such a clear bronze-like pattern of thought and image, such a decided sense of *form* as well as content that the overall effect is not unlike that of good verse. And that's one of the reasons why, in translating the prayers into English, I have relied on the use of line-breaks and indentation to suggest something of the controlled structure and rhythmic energy of the original texts.

*   *   *

What has greatly impressed readers of Aquinas, over the years, is the consonance of thought and expression, of image and idea, which seems to exist between the prayers attributed to Aquinas and the theological vision

---

[7] See A.-D. Sertillanges, *Prières de Saint Thomas d'Aquin* (Paris 1920), p. 8. Another Dominican, Pierre Mandonnet, writing around the same time, expressed an equal confidence with regard to the question of Aquinas's authorship: 'Les *Piae preces,* ou collection de diverses prières attribuées au Docteur angélique ... se présentent dans des conditions d'authenticité très acceptables.' See P. Mandonnet and J. Destrez, *Bibliographie thomiste* (Kain, Belgium 1921) p.xviii.
[8] Lydia Maidl, *Thomas von Aquin* (Freiburg 1994). This collection of texts from Aquinas, with commentary by Maidl, was introduced by Otto Hermann Pesch.
[9] Ibid., pp. 90–2.

expressed in his other works. Lydia Maidl, for example, draws attention to the fact that the themes expressed in '*Concede michi*' (the Prayer for Wise Ordering) are themes 'dear to Thomas's heart'.[10] And she goes on to say: 'Virtues characteristic of Thomas's personal manner of life (obedience, poverty, chastity) and of his teaching on the virtues are considered in turn'.[11] In spite of such an impressive acknowledgement, however, Maidl decides in the end that Aquinas is probably not the author of *Concede michi*, and nor, in her opinion is he the likely author of any of the other prayers attributed to him.

Among the reasons she puts forward to explain this decision, one stands out in particular: 'Linguistically', she writes, 'all these prayers are differentiated from the scholastic conceptual world that Thomas uses in his theoretical works'.[12] But is this true? And are we constrained, therefore, in the name of serious scholarship, to go against the tide of tradition, and take the prayers out of the hands of Aquinas, as it were, surrendering ownership and authorship to some anonymous medieval Dominican?

At first glance, it might seem like basic common sense to expect the prayers of a notable scholastic such as Thomas Aquinas to be marked by the distinctive language of medieval scholasticism. And it might be thought a no less natural expectation to find, in the sermons attributed to Aquinas, the same clear linguistic mark. But, in the case of the sermons, there is a noteworthy absence of scholastic discourse, a tendency to avoid the academic language we normally associate with thomistic philosophy and theology. On this point Mark-Robin Hoogland writes: 'Thomas uses hardly any theological terms in his academic sermons. He could have done so, since the main part of his audience would have understood it. Yet Thomas's language in these sermons is strikingly plain and simple; he did not want to show off, it seems, as some of his contemporaries did'.[13]

What Hoogland says here about the sermons can be applied, I believe, with

---

[10] Maidl, pp. 106–7.

[11] Ibid., p. 107.

[12] Ibid., p. 92.

[13] See 'Introduction' by Mark-Robin Hoogland (ed.), in *Thomas Aquinas: The Academic Sermons* (*The Fathers of the Church: Medieval Continuation*, vol. 2), (Washington 2010) p. 13.

at least equal force to the *preces* attributed to St Thomas: we should in no way expect them to be weighed down by scholastic terminology. What we can expect, however, is to find, in the prayers, ideas and themes corresponding to the core vision of Aquinas's theology, themes dear to his heart. And that is precisely what we discover, and over and over again, in the *Piae preces*.

2. The influence of Humbert of Romans

But what of the sources that lie behind the prayers? Is it possible that, from within the tradition, one author stands out as having had a particularly telling influence on some of the *preces*? As it happens, on this subject, Lydia Maidl draws attention to something of great interest. It concerns a source – an unexpected source – behind a number of the prayers: a letter, an *epistola*, sent to all the friars of the Dominican Order during the lifetime of St Thomas, and composed by the then Master of the Order, Humbert of Romans.[14] The extent of the influence of this text on the prayers is quite remarkable. In four of the prayers we find not only small phrases but entire sentences taken over and absorbed into the later text. So the question needs to be asked: is it likely that Aquinas would have allowed himself to be influenced by his older and revered contemporary in this way?

The first thing to note here is that Aquinas, in his various writings, was always open to being influenced by many different sources and voices. Once in a homily given in Paris, he remarked: 'we should not just open our ears to one person only, but to many people.' And, in the same homily, he cited Sirach 6.34: *Stand in the midst of prudent elders, and dwell in the wisdom of their hearts.*[15] These 'elders' are not, of course, likely to be present *physically*. But, in

---

[14] *Epistola beati Humberti, Opera de vita regulari,* vol. 1, Marietti edition (Rome 1956). Maidl expresses gratitude to Dr Marianne Schlosser for directing her attention to the influence of Humbert on the prayers.

[15] See Sermon 8, *Puer Jesus: Sermon on the First Sunday after Epiphany,* in *Thomas Aquinas: The Academic Sermons* (*The Fathers of the Church: Medieval Continuation,* vol. 2) (ed.) M-R Hoogland (Washington 2010) p. 100.

the end, as St Thomas explains, that makes no difference: 'If you do not have an abundance of people, you still have an abundance of texts.'[16]

The *Epistola* of Humbert of Romans was no ordinary text. Not only was it rather well written in a distinctive epigrammatic style, it possessed a depth of understanding about the character of religious life and of religious observance which would certainly have inspired many of the young Dominicans who read it. The letter was sent out to all the Provinces of the Order at a time when Aquinas was either in his thirties or late twenties. Naturally, at this distance in time, it's impossible for us to know exactly what impact the letter made on the young theologian. But what we do know for certain is that the letter had a profound influence on the individual who wrote the *preces*. And, with regard to the identity of this individual, one thing is clear: he was a Dominican friar, and a Dominican with manifest intellectual gifts.[17]

But was St Thomas the friar in question? Maidl seems to make a telling point when she says that the prayers represent what might be called 'original Dominican bedrock'.[18] What she means by this is that, although the prayers 'express requests that were also those of the Dominican Thomas Aquinas, at least in broad terms … one may not expect to find the issues that moved him personally and in a particular way.'[19] But is this, in fact, the case? And is Maidl correct when she goes on to state that certain 'popularizing tendencies and images (*vulgarisierende Tendenzen und Bilder*) emerge in the prayers which can be found also in a similar form in Humbert, but which Thomas doesn't use, not even in his sermons'?[20]

---

[16] Ibid., p. 102.

[17] There is a reference to a religious 'Order' in one of the prayers attributed to Aquinas. The author, addressing Mary, asks for strength to serve 'you and your beloved Son in your Order'. Given the general character of the *Piae preces*, and the fact that they have always been attributed to Aquinas, it is presumed that the Order referred to is the Dominican Order, and that the author is a Dominican friar. Further confirmation of Dominican authorship comes from a comment made by Humbert of Romans. He describes Mary as the 'special patron' of the Order of Blessed Dominic. 'She is,' he writes, 'the special mother of that Order which exists to praise, bless, and preach her Son, developing, advancing, and defending the Order.' See *Super constitutiones Fratrum Praedicatorum*, XLII, *De vita regulari*, vol. 2, Marietti edition (Rome 1956) p. 136.

[18] Maidl, p. 91.

[19] Ibid.

[20] Maidl, p. 92.

To attempt an answer to this question it will be necessary to examine, in some detail, the few prayers which show the unmistakable influence of Humbert. There are four of them:

1   *Concede michi*: Prayer for the Wise Ordering of One's Life

2   *O Deus omnipotens*: Prayer to Obtain the Virtues

3   *Laudo, glorifico, benedico*: Prayer of Praise

4   *Te Deum totius consolationis*: Prayer for the Attainment of Heaven

What Maidl calls 'popularizing tendencies and images' is something, we are assured, one cannot expect to find *even* in St Thomas's sermons. But is that the case? The tone of the sermons, it's true, is for the most part highly controlled and dispassionate. But there are occasions, and more than a few, when St Thomas, in his concern to communicate the Gospel message, makes clear that he is by no means unwilling to manifest a certain 'popularizing tendency'. On occasion, in fact, he doesn't hesitate to employ rather vivid *exempla* and images to help bring home the force of his message.[21] One colourful example he gives is that of man's foot growing unnaturally longer than the other and, as a result, requiring medical attention. The point St Thomas is trying to make is that, in order to grow in wisdom, the development of the human mind must not be stunted, but must keep pace with the rest of the person's growth.[22] But the image chosen, it has to be said, is certainly an unexpected one!

On another occasion, half way through a sermon delivered on 1 December 1269, St Thomas, unable or unwilling to hide his frustration at the phenomenon of actual heresies being preached in the place where he lives, suddenly abandons his customary calm and impersonal mode of utterance, and speaks out loud and clear, and in the first person singular: 'About certain matters I am astonished (*Miror de quibusdam*). Once it was said that it was an evil thing

---

[21] In this matter Thomas is, perhaps, consciously following the example of Humbert of Romans who went so far as to compose a collection of *exempla* for the use of preachers. See *Early Dominicans: Selected Writings*, (ed.) S. Tugwell, (New York 1982) p. 373.

[22] *Puer Jesus: Sermon on the First Sunday after Epiphany, S. Thomae Aquinatis, Opera Omnia*, Busa vol. 6, 083, n. 1 (1980) p. 34 c.

that heresies were preached in Lombardy, but nowadays they are preached in this very house!'[23]

The 'popularizing tendencies and images' which Lydia Maidl claims to find in the *Piae preces* persuade her that the work is probably not by Aquinas. But what exactly does she mean by this particular phrase (*vulgarisierende Tendenzen und Bilder*)? It goes without saying, of course, that the *preces* will have a different character from that of any of the other works attributed to Aquinas. Prayers are, by their very nature, more immediately engaging, and more personal than, say, an academic treatise or a public sermon. Accordingly, the personal character of the *preces* in itself cannot be taken as a mark against Aquinas's possible/probable authorship. If that were the case, one would be forced to deny authenticity to the wonderfully direct, personal character of the brief but unforgettable prayer Aquinas makes to Christ just before his death.

The original text in Latin of the four *Piae preces* with which we are concerned here can be found in 'Appendix 1' at the end of the book. What follows now is a new translation into English of all four prayers with an extended commentary on each of them in turn. There are, of course, other *Piae preces* attributed to Aquinas – some of them remarkable in their own right – but attention in this chapter will be given exclusively to the four prayers already mentioned.

(1) Prayer for the Wise Ordering of One's Life

O merciful God,
>> whatever is pleasing
> to you,
>> may I ardently desire,
>> wisely pursue,
>> truly recognize,
>>> and bring
> to perfect completion.

---

[23] See *Osanna filio David: A Sermon on Advent*, line 253 (Complete text by Louis Jacques Bataillon). I am indebted to Adriano Oliva OP of the Leonine Commission for kindly making available to me the Provisional Leonine text of this sermon.

For the praise
                    and glory of your name
            put order into my life,
                                    and grant
that I may know
what it is you require me to do,
                        and help me
        to achieve
                        whatever is fitting
and necessary
for the good of my soul.

        May my way, Lord,
be yours entirely,
                        upright and perfect,
    failing
    in neither prosperity
                    nor adversity
so that, in prosperity, I give you thanks,
            and in adversity
                    serve patience,
neither exalted
in the former
            nor dejected in the latter.

        May I not rejoice
                            in anything
unless it leads me to you,
            nor be saddened
                        by anything
unless it turns me from you.

        May I not desire
                    to please

or fear to displease
> anyone but you.

> May all passing things
become worthless to me
>> on your account,
> and all things
>> that are yours
be dear to me,
>> and you, God,
>> above all things.

> May all joy
>> without you
leave me tired and weary,
> and may I not desire anything
apart from you.

> May all work
that is done for you
>> delight me, Lord,
and all repose
> not centered
> on your presence
be wearisome.

> Let me, my God,
direct my heart to you
>> often
and let me
> grieve over my failure
with determination to change.

Make me, my God,

    humble without pretense,
    cheerful without frivolity,
    sad without dejection,
    mature without heaviness,
    quick-witted without levity,
    truthful without duplicity.

Let me fear you
    without despair,
and hope in you
    without presumption.

Let me correct my neighbour

    without hypocrisy, and
    without pride
      edify him
by word and example:
      obedient
without contradiction,
patient without murmuring.

Give me, dearest God, a vigilant heart
    which no distracting thought
      can lure away from you.

Give me a noble heart
    which no unworthy desire
      can ever debase.

Give me an unconquered heart
    which no tribulation
      can fatigue.

Give me a free heart
> which no violent temptation
>> can enslave.

Give me an upright heart
> which no perverse intention
>> can hold fast.

Grant me, Lord my God,

> intelligence in knowing you,
> diligence in seeking you,
> wisdom in finding you,

conversation pleasing to you,
perseverance in confidently waiting for you,
and confidence in finally embracing you.

Grant that
> as penance
I may be afflicted with your hardships,
> as grace, make use
along the way, of your favours,
> as glory, delight
in your joys in the fatherland.

Amen.

Prayer for the Wise Ordering of One's Life
A commentary

A. The Search for Wisdom

This is undoubtedly the finest of the four prayers under consideration. From first phrase to last, it makes manifest a quiet yet urgent determination of both mind and heart to surrender everything to God. The prayer is said by a man asking for living knowledge of God. But, although it is a prayer clearly composed by an intellectual, the wisdom that is being sought is no mere intellectual knowledge. Rather it is that wisdom of spirit which impacts on every aspect of life, both interior and exterior.

Put order into my life,

and grant

that I may know

what it is you require me to do,

and help me

to achieve

whatever is fitting

and necessary

for the good of my soul.

If I were asked to choose one phrase or sentence from this prayer which, more than any other, stands out as typical of Aquinas, I would, without hesitation, select the following: '*ordina statum meum*' (put order into my life). What the prayer is asking for is, first and last, the gift of wisdom. And a bed-rock conviction of St Thomas is that it is the special gift or capacity of the wise man to set things in order: '*sapientis est ordinare*'[24]. For Thomas, as a theologian and philosopher, the truly wise individual is the person who knows God as the 'Highest Cause', and is able as a result, in the light of that knowledge, to view and understand other 'causes', both in relation to each other and to God, and so begin 'to place things in order'.[25] This capacity, however, when it comes to the question of supernatural knowledge, is never achieved by human effort alone. It is, Thomas repeats over and over again, always a gift of the Spirit. And that explains, no doubt, the quiet insistence and humility of the repeated phrases and sentences of petition.

Because Christian prayer, on occasion, takes the form of asking God for help, and at times even pleading for divine assistance, it can easily be caricatured as a demeaning, slavish form of behaviour, an activity that in some way undermines

---

[24] Thomas, in his commentary on the *Nicomachean Ethics*, Bk 1, lecture 1, 1, writes: 'As the Philosopher says, at the beginning of the *Metaphysics*, it is the business of the wise man to order. The reason for this is that wisdom is the most powerful perfection of reason whose characteristic is to know order.'

[25] See *ST*, II II q.45, a.1. Thomas R. Heath writes: 'The Aristotelean teaching is accepted that wisdom is the knowledge of the highest cause, or the most fundamental reality, that its major activities are: (1) contemplating that reality, (2) making judgments both of a theoretic and practical nature in the light of that contemplation, and (3) putting things in order.' See 'Appendix 4' in *Summa theologiae*, Blackfriars Edition, vol. 35, pp. 200–1.

the dignity of the human person. But the author of this particular prayer, although by no means unwilling to reveal the depth of his need for grace, stands before us, and stands before God, with an unmistakable strength of presence and strength of character. Something of that character, I would suggest, is revealed in the strong, radiant adjectives he chooses when describing, at a particular stage in the prayer, the kind of person he would most wish to become with God's help: namely, vigilant, noble, unconquered, free and upright.

> Give me, dearest God, a vigilant heart
> > which no distracting thought
> > > can lure away from you.
> Give me a noble heart
> > which no unworthy desire
> > > can ever debase.
> Give me an unconquered heart
> > which no tribulation
> > > can fatigue.
> Give me a free heart
> > which no violent temptation
> > > can enslave.
> Give me an upright heart
> > which no perverse intention
> > > can hold fast.

Reading over these five short petitions one is made aware not only of a devoted man of prayer, but also of someone well-schooled in the knowledge of the human heart, acquainted with its virtues and vices, its weaknesses and its wounds, its fears and longings, and its irrepressible capacity for greatness. What the author desires are – yes – the gifts of God, but what matters for him even more, it would seem, than life itself is the Author of Life. The section in the prayer beginning with the phrase, 'May I not rejoice in anything unless it leads me to you …' is eloquent of this fact. Here, the insistent statements of desire, repeated over and over again, betray a contemplative passion which is, I would suggest, as radical in its urgency and longing as that of the great mystical theologian and poet, St John of the Cross. The author writes, for example:

> May all passing things
> become worthless to me
> > on your
> account,
> > and all things
> > > that are yours
> be dear to me,
> > and you, God,
> > above all things.

What comes immediately to mind, when I read these lines, is the famous reply St Thomas made to the voice he heard speaking to him from the crucifix in Naples: 'Thomas, you have written well of me; what reward will you take from me for your labours?' And the reply: '*Nil nisi te, Domine*': 'Lord, nothing but yourself.'[26] The 'nothing' here – the '*nil*' – worth setting alongside the '*nada, nada, nada*' of the Spanish mystic. When such undistracted, contemplative attention is given to God it does not, of course, negate for a moment the ordinary capacity to live a full human life. On the contrary, it makes that life more complete, more satisfying. But, for the author of the prayer, what matters even more than life itself is the Author of life. And that may, perhaps, be the reason why the prayer goes on at once to speak of both human labour and human rest in relation to God.

The question of labour is, of course, discussed elsewhere by St Thomas. In the *Summa,* one of the 'objections' raised with regard to the subject claims that, unlike the easefulness of contemplation, in which there is 'no toiling under a load' and one can therefore enjoy a life informed by wisdom, in active life, in contrast, all work is decidedly 'wearisome' (*taedium*): 'we labour under a great burden of wants', and we find no rest.[27] St Thomas, taking issue with this idea, insists that work does not have to be experienced always as something 'bitter'. It can be transformed from within by the grace of wisdom, because wisdom, properly understood, is not just for contemplation, but is a necessary aid and guide for the active life as well, for the life of labour.

---

[26] See *Albert and Thomas: Selected Writings,* (ed.) S. Tugwell (New York 1988) p. 265.
[27] *ST*, II II q. 45, a.3, obj 3.

He writes: 'The guidance of human acts by wisdom does not bring bitterness or toil; on the contrary, the effect of wisdom is to make the bitter sweet, and labour a rest.'[28] A tiny but significant echo of this teaching can be heard midway through the prayer for wisdom: 'May all work that is done for you delight me, Lord, and all repose not centered on your presence be wearisome.'

When, later, the prayer begins to draw to a close, there is a notable repetition of the words 'you' and 'yours'. The focus of both mind and heart is on God and God alone. And if it was not already obvious earlier in the prayer, it now becomes abundantly clear: the mind behind the prayer is a mind in continual search of knowledge of God, a mind in love with God.

> Grant me, Lord my God,
>
> > intelligence in knowing you,
> > diligence in seeking you,
> > wisdom in finding you,
>
> conversation pleasing to you,
> perseverance in confidently waiting for you,
> and confidence in finally embracing you.

B. The question of authorship

Maidl, in her book, as already noted earlier, speaks of 'issues that moved St Thomas personally and in a particular way', adding that we should *not* expect to find evidence of these precise issues in the prayers since, in her opinion, the *preces* were most probably composed by some anonymous Dominican author or authors unknown to us. Against this theory, it is worth noting that the actual passages in the prayers, which most betray the influence of Humbert, are passages which touch directly on questions or 'issues' of a very particular and personal interest to Thomas: first, the passionate search for knowledge of God; second, the attempt in the Christian life of virtue to find the golden mean; and, third, the longing of heart and mind to attain to the joys of heaven, the desire for eternal life. The author of the prayers, it seems to me, is a man

---

[28] *ST*, II II q.45 a.3 ad 3.

decidedly careful and discriminating with regard to the passages he decides to incorporate into his text. None of the florid rhetoric of Humbert, for example, finds a home in the prayers.[29] Instead, the passages the author chooses to 'borrow' from the *Epistola* are, without exception, passages of a manifest wisdom and of undoubted strength and beauty.

Take, for example, the following brief exhortation from the *Epistola* in which Humbert, with plain but impressive eloquence, exhorts his brethren to seek living knowledge of God: 'As far as it is in your power, always strive to possess a mind that knows God, a will that loves God, an eagerness that seeks Him, a wisdom that finds him, a conversation that pleases Him, a perseverance that confidently awaits Him.'[30] The author of '*Concede michi*', the Prayer for Wise Ordering, turns this preacherly exhortation into the form of a solemn petition, incorporating into his text almost all the images of Humbert. What might shock us today, and indeed look like a form of plagiarism was, in the Middle Ages, a practice found entirely acceptable. Thomas, in one of his homilies, encourages his listeners to 'pick the flowers' (*carpere flores*) from as many teachers as possible.[31] And he may well have been more than happy, therefore, to regard the words and ideas in Humbert's letter as a harvest waiting to be gathered.

The poet Goethe, on one occasion, reflecting on this subject but thinking in particular of the case of the poet, remarked: 'Do not all the achievements of a poet's predecessors and contemporaries rightfully belong to him? Why should he shrink from picking flowers where he finds them? Only by making the riches of others our own do we bring anything great into being.'[32]

One of the fundamental desires, expressed in both the Prayer for Wise Ordering (*Concede michi*) and the Prayer for Virtues (*O Deus omnipotens*),

---

[29] Here is an example of that rhetoric: 'Let each one try, therefore, to possess a heart which is like a garden flourishing with the trees of virtues, like a storehouse fragrant with the perfumes of holy affection, like a sky radiant with the stars of Divine brightness, like a flower receiving heavenly dew', Humbert of Romans, *The Religious Vows and Virtues*, (ed.) J. Harrison (London 1922) pp. 73–4. For the original Latin text, see *Epistola beati Humberti*, LI, p. 33.

[30] Humbert of Romans, *Epistola beati Humberti*, XLVII, *Opera de vita regulari*, vol. 1, Marietti edition (Turin 1956), p. 30.

[31] *Puer Jesus: Sermon on the First Sunday after Epiphany*. See Sermon 1, in 'Appendix: *Sermones*,' *Opera omnia sancti Thomae*, Parma vol. 24, p. 223a.

[32] Cited by Harold Bloom in *The Anxiety of Influence: A Theory of Poetry* (Oxford 1973), p. 52.

is the desire to attain to a way of living that avoids unnecessary extremes, and keeps to a middle path, to what has been traditionally referred to as 'the golden mean'. In the *Summa theologiae* St Thomas writes: 'The good for both intellectual and moral virtue consists in a mean by reason of conformity with a measure'.[33] And so, when people go to extremes, there is discordance from the rule or measure, and 'this can happen either by their exceeding the measure or by their falling short of it'.[34]

In the *Epistola* of Humbert we find a sustained insistence on the importance of attaining, in life and in religious life, to the golden mean. He writes: 'In all your actions fly from extremes, and always hold yourselves to the middle (*semper in medio vos tenete*)'.[35] Then, by way of illustration of what he means, he goes at once to say: 'My brothers, be humble without deception, mature without heaviness, quick without levity, fearful without despair, hopeful without presumption, merry without frivolity, patient without murmuring'.[36] The passage is so clearly insightful, and is such a sharp and fine illustration of the golden mean, and is so succinctly expressed by Humbert, it is no wonder the author of *Concede michi*, felt drawn to incorporate it, and almost word for word, into his prayer.

One other short passage from the prayer deserves, in this context, to be quoted. It manifests, once again, a profound desire to find, in the midst of all the pleasures and pressures of life, the golden mean: 'May my way, Lord, be yours entirely, upright and perfect, failing in neither prosperity nor adversity, so that, in prosperity, I give you thanks and, in adversity, serve patience.' The subject of how best to cope with adversity and prosperity is addressed a number of times in the *Epistola*. Humbert writes for example: 'Let your way of going to God be by adversity as well as by prosperity, so that you may be humble and grateful in your successes and patient in trouble and ill-hap'.[37]

With regard, therefore, to the question of 'prosperity' and 'adversity', the influence of Humbert of Romans is clear. But the author of the prayer is not

---

[33] *ST*, I II q.64, a.4, ad 1.
[34] *ST*, I II q.64, a.1.
[35] *Epistola beati Humberti*, LIII, *Opera de vita regulari*, vol. 1, p. 37.
[36] Ibid.
[37] Humbert of Romans, *The Religious Vows and Virtues*, (ed.) J. Harrison (London 1922) p. 63. For the original Latin text, see *Epistola beati Humberti*, XLVII, p. 29. See also *Epistola*, XLII, p. 25.

content simply to take over a number of phrases, and repeat them without at least some modest effort at transformation. In this case what he does is not, as it happens, to develop or change the idea, but rather to express that idea in a new, controlled pattern of words. He writes, in effect, a new sentence, complete in itself, with its own distinct cadence and rhythm, and possessing something of the quality of a prose-poem. The sentence opens with a strong exclamation: 'May my way, Lord, be yours entirely' (*Via mea, Domine, ad te tuta sit*), and ends, referring briefly to '*prospera*' and '*adversa*' with two superbly balanced phrases: '*ut in illis non extollar, et in istis non deprimar*' (neither exalted in the former, nor dejected in the latter).

One clear hint that the author of the prayer we are considering is not, as has been suggested, an anonymous Dominican author but rather Aquinas himself, is the fact that an explicit reference to the theme of adversity and prosperity can be found in one of the authentic sermons of St Thomas. There, with words reminiscent of the words used in the prayer, Thomas speaks of those 'who are elated in a time of prosperity, but murmur in a time of adversity' (*qui sunt elati tempore prosperitatis, et mumurant tempore adversitatis*).[38] In the same sermon Thomas also speaks of the unhappy result that can ensue when a proper perspective on life is not maintained in both good times and bad: 'It can even happen,' he notes, 'that sometimes a man, in a time of prosperity, can keep a curb on his mouth but, in a time of adversity, he blasphemes and murmurs.'[39]

So what, then, are we to conclude? Are there grounds, in the light of the research presented so far in this chapter, for believing that Thomas Aquinas really is the author, or at least the probable author, of *Concede michi*? Different readers will inevitably come to different conclusions, but it is my own conviction that, already, we do indeed have sufficient grounds for making this assertion.

And there is something else as well. Shortly after I had completed my research on this topic, and composed the present pages, I came upon a vital piece of information regarding Aquinas's authorship of the prayer which happily confirms my conviction that Aquinas is indeed the likely author

---

[38] *Lux orta est: Sermon on the Feast of the Birth of the Blessed Virgin Mary*, Busa vol. 6, 37 b, p. 37.
[39] Ibid.

of this profound and beautiful prayer. What I discovered was that *Concede michi,* the Prayer for Wise Ordering, was included in the first *Life* of Aquinas by his Dominican contemporary, William of Tocco,[40] and attributed to St Thomas.[41] This manifestly important detail was not known to scholars until 1996 when a new authoritative edition of the *Life* was published by Claire Le Brun-Gouanvic.[42] And that means, presumably, that even a scholar as distinguished as Lydia Maidl, when working on her book, would not have been made aware of the new information regarding the Aquinas prayer. Her work was published two years earlier in 1994.[43]

Concerning Le Brun's scholarly edition of the *Life,* Torrell writes: 'One of the author's most interesting results is establishing the evidence on the basis of late but trustworthy manuscripts, for four successive versions of the text, which William [of Tocco] reworked up to the last moment, i.e. until Thomas's canonization, 18 July 1323.'[44] The fourth version, Torrell notes, 'carries numerous additions that have remained unpublished until the present.' One of these 'additions' is the prayer *Concede michi.*[45] Given the inclusion of the prayer in Tocco's *Life,* it now seems practically certain that the *Concede michi* is indeed a work of Thomas. And, if that's the case, it reveals something of very

---

[40] Tocco knew Aquinas towards the end of his life at Naples (1272–4). He was a devoted disciple of the saint, and his *Life* is generally regarded as our chief source of information about St Thomas Aquinas.

[41] See Claire le Brun-Gouanvic, *Ystoria sancti Thome de Aquino de Guillaume de Tocco,* 29 (Toronto 1996) p. 156. The two original manuscripts which include the prayer with the attribution to Aquinas are located in Germany. They are listed by Le Brun on pages 61–3. For information concerning other manuscripts of *Concede michi,* see A. I. Doyle, 'A Prayer attributed to Aquinas' in *Dominican Studies* 1 (July 1948), pp. 229–38.

[42] Claire Le Brun-Gouanvic's edition began life as a doctoral thesis presented at the University of Montreal in 1987. Prior to her edition of the *Life,* the most authoritative edition available was that published by Dominique Prümmer in 1912. See *Ystoria sancti Thome de Aquino',* p. 71.

[43] One clear indication that Maidl was unaware of Le Brun's innovative research is the fact that the version of *Concede michi,* included in her book, differs in a number of respects from the version of the prayer which William of Tocco included in his *Life,* and attributed to St Thomas.

[44] Jean-Pierre Torrell, *St Thomas Aquinas: The Person and His Work,* vol. 1, trans., R. Royal (Washington 1996), p.xvi.

[45] The 'addition' which particularly interests Torrell, and interests also many other scholars, is the presence in Tocco's *Vita* of the prayer *Adoro te devote.* The fact of its inclusion by Tocco has greatly encouraged the attribution of this work to Aquinas. Unfortunately, however, little or no attention has been given to the inclusion by Tocco of the other prayer, *Concede michi,* even though in the opinion of Le Brun-Gouanvic the attribution of this prayer to St Thomas enjoys exactly the same status as that of *Adoro te devote.* See *Ystoria sancti Thome de Aquino',* 53–4, p. 156.

great interest: a manifest regard, on the part of Brother Thomas of Aquino, for his older contemporary, Humbert of Romans. Generally speaking, when the question of Aquinas's sources is discussed by scholars, the tendency is to focus attention on figures from the distant past, on famous authors such as Aristotle and St Augustine. But here what is at issue is an influence much closer to home: the wise and humble *Epistola* of Blessed Humbert.[46]

*   *   *

The prayer '*Concede michi*' is a prayer for wisdom and for wise ordering. 'But where can we find wisdom,' Thomas asks in one of his sermons. And his reply: 'First, from a *magister* or from people who are wiser [than you are]. Hence it says in Deut. 32.7: 'Ask your father,' that is, a *magister*. Because just as a father has brought you forth physically, a *magister* brings you forth spiritually.'[47] One of the eminently wise pieces of advice Blessed Humbert offers to his fellow friar preachers, in the *Epistola,* is 'to seek opportunities for secret prayers (*Orationes furtivas quaerite*).'[48] Friar Thomas took this advice to heart, it would seem, and then went one step further. If the evidence we have gathered so far is not mistaken, Thomas decided to compose (for the sake of devotion, no doubt) a 'secret prayer' inspired to a remarkable degree by the wisdom of his revered contemporary, Blessed Humbert of Romans.

---

[46] This 'borrowing' may not mark the only occasion on which Thomas's work betrayed the influence of Humbert of Romans. Leonard Boyle OP has suggested that St Thomas's brief Prologue to the *Summa theologiae* was itself directly influenced by a text from Humbert. In his *Liber de instructione officialium,* Humbert cautions the Lector, for the sake of his listeners, to refrain 'from annoying prolixity which occurs when there is too much repetition.' Thomas likewise, in his Prologue, declares that 'frequent repetition has provoked annoyance and confusion in the minds of listeners.' See Leonard Boyle, *Facing History: A Different Thomas Aquinas* (Louvain-La-Neuve 2000) pp. 81–2. I am grateful to Conor McDonough OP for bringing this passage in Boyle's work to my attention.

[47] *Puer Jesus: Sermon on the First Sunday after Epiphany,* in *Thomas Aquinas: The Academic Sermons (The Fathers of the Church: Medieval Continuation),* trans., M. R. Hoogland (Washington 2010) p. 102. See Busa vol. 6, 083, no. 1, p. 34b. It is worth noting that Humbert of Romans was known personally to Thomas. Both of them were present at the general chapter of the Order held at Valenciennes in 1259.

[48] *Epistola beati Humberti,* XLVIII, *Opera de vita regulari,* vol. 1, p. 30.

(2) Prayer to Obtain the Virtues

O God,

> you who are all-powerful
> and all-knowing,

> > without beginning or end,

the giver
and sustainer of the virtues,

> > deign to establish me

on the firm ground of faith,
and be protected
by the impregnable shield of hope,
and be adorned
with the wedding garment of charity.

Give me the grace

> through justice
> > to be subject to you,
> through prudence
> > to avoid the deceptions of the devil,
> through temperance
> > to hold fast to the middle way,
> through fortitude
> > to bear adversity with patience.

Give me the good
> I do not have, and the grace
> > humbly to seek from others
> > who have.

May I reproach myself
    honestly for the evil of the wrong
        I have done

and bear calmly
    the evil of the punishment
        brought upon myself.

May I not begrudge
    what my neighbour possesses,
        but always give thanks
           for your good things.

May I always be disciplined
    in the way I dress,
        the way I walk,
           and the gestures I use.

Restrain my tongue
        from idle talk,
prevent my feet
        from running this way and that,
keep my eyes
        from wandering glances,
protect my ears
        from rumours.

Lower my gaze in humility,
    raise my mind
        to heavenly things,
let me disdain all that passes
    and yearn
        for you only.

Grant that I may

    subdue my flesh,
        purify my conscience,
    honour the saints,
        praise you worthily,
    make progress in doing good,
        and end a life of good works
    with a holy death.

Plant in me, Lord,
        the virtues
so that I may be
    devout in divine matters,
    prudent in human affairs,
and burdensome
        to no one
in the care of my own body.

Grant me, Lord,

    fervour in contrition,
    integrity in confession,
    and complete reparation.

Deign to set in order
        my inner self
by a good life
so that I may do what is right
        and what will be meritorious
for me
and be an example for others.

Grant that I may never be
    over-hasty

in undertaking tasks

or lazy

in avoiding them

lest I try to begin things

too soon

or try to abandon them

before they are completed.

Amen.

Prayer to Obtain the Virtues
A commentary

A close reading of the Prayer for Virtues reveals one thing very clearly: its author is either a dedicated Thomist, a scholastic, writing in the spirit of St Thomas, or else, and perhaps more likely, St Thomas himself. This judgment is, I believe, well founded. For, with respect to scholasticism, although the words of the prayer are plain and straightforward, and are not weighed down with scholastic terminology, nevertheless what one might call the 'architecture' of the prayer, its inner structure, is manifestly scholastic through and through.

A. Major and minor virtues

The prayer can helpfully be divided into three sections: first, a section on the principal virtues ('O God, you who are all powerful' to 'adversity with patience'); then a section concerned with avoiding evil and doing good ('Give me the good' to 'holy death'); and, finally, a brief section concerned with the wise ordering of one's life, both interior and exterior ('Plant in me' to 'they are complete').

The prayer opens with an address to God, the 'all-powerful and all-knowing', the God 'without beginning or end', who alone is 'the giver, sustainer and rewarder of the virtues.' The things asked for are, first of all, the three theological virtues of faith, hope and love, and, second, the four cardinal virtues of justice, prudence, temperance and fortitude. The graces, which the author links here with temperance and fortitude, recall at once to mind two particular needs or concerns noted earlier in the Prayer for Wise Ordering, namely: through temperance, 'to hold fast to the middle way' and, through fortitude, 'to bear adversity with patience'. This opening section is distinguished by an almost scientific clarity of expression and by a fine symmetry of form.

In the second section, the key word is 'good' or '*bonum*'. It opens with a prayer asking for grace to use well the *good* things of life, and it concludes with a prayer to 'make progress in doing *good*' and to 'end a life of *good* works with a holy death.' The word '*bonum*', in this section, is found in a number of different forms, and is twice placed in contrast with the word 'evil' or '*malum*'. The prayer speaks first of the '*malum culpae*', 'the evil of wrongdoing', and then goes on to speak of '*malum poenae*', 'the evil of punishment'. Since, in the actual context of the prayer, this latter term refers to divine punishment, the question arises: in what sense can God's punishment be said to be 'evil'? St Thomas, writing in the *Summa*, offers a thoughtful answer to this question. And, in the process, he makes use of the very same phrase, '*malum poenae*', distinguishing it from '*malum culpae*'. He writes: 'The evil that can threaten us from God is the evil of punishment (*malum poenae*), an evil not outright but evil in a qualified sense; absolutely speaking it is a good.'[49]

The third and final section is less structured than the two preceding sections, but it does refer directly, at one point, to the 'good life' ('*bonam vitam*'), and it gives voice also to a few plain and practical desires regarding the attainment of wisdom in everyday life. In this third section, the importance of the virtue of penance is underlined and with clear, scholastic exactitude. The 'three parts' of penance declared by St Thomas in the *Summa* to be integral to the Sacrament ('contrition', 'confession' and 'reparation') are included in the prayer, and are placed in exactly the same order as in the *Summa*[50]:

> fervour in contrition,
> integrity in confession,
> and complete reparation.

But is St Thomas the likely author of the Prayer for Virtues? The German scholar, Lydia Maidl, although willing to acknowledge that, in the prayer, 'a theme is addressed which belongs to the core concerns of Thomas', nevertheless decides in the end against the probability of Aquinas's authorship. 'The prayer,' she writes, 'lacks Thomas's clarity and breadth in both content

---

[49] *ST*, II II q.19, a.1.
[50] *ST*, III q.90, a.2 and a.3.

and language.'[51] If we compare the quality and overall pattern of the prayer under consideration with that of the Prayer for Wise Ordering, the former is, without question, less strictly ordered, less 'inevitable', perhaps, than the latter. That said, however, the Prayer for Virtues ('*O Deus omnipotens*') does have its own very considerable merit, its own honest expression of desire for right order and virtue, its own wise knowledge of the way to perfection. And, added to that, unless I am much mistaken, in phrase after phrase, in image after image, it does read and sound like Aquinas.

*   *   *

One notable characteristic of the Prayer for Virtues is the simplicity of its form of address. No reference is made to the three Persons of the Holy Trinity. Instead, God is addressed simply as 'God' or 'Lord'. Elsewhere, in some of the other prayers attributed to St Thomas, we find the Trinity invoked and, on occasion, very powerfully. Thus in *Adoro te devote*, for example, the prayer, from beginning to end, is addressed to Christ Jesus. And we know that *Adoro te* was included by Tocco in his *Life* of St Thomas. But, in that same work, Tocco also included *Concede michi* (The Prayer for Wise Ordering) which makes no reference to any of the three Persons of the Trinity. It would seem, therefore, that Thomas was content, when at prayer, either to address God simply as 'God', or to address God as one or all of the Persons of the Trinity. I make this point here because Lydia Maidl appears to judge the absence, in the *Piae preces*, of explicit reference, on occasion, to the Holy Trinity as a mark against the likelihood of Aquinas as author.[52]

At the opening of the third section of the prayer a request is made for those virtues which will enable our author to be 'devout in divine matters' and 'prudent in human affairs'. This request touches on one of the most challenging aspects of spiritual life. How, in practice, is it possible to balance a whole-hearted attention to the things of God and, at the same time, a responsible and devoted attention to the things of earth? Enormous weight is given in the prayer to the first of these two aims. Not only do we read, 'raise

---

[51] Maidl, p. 92.
[52] See Maidl, pp. 91–2.

my mind to heavenly things', we read also, 'let me disdain all that passes, and yearn for you only.'

The language of the prayer, at this point, may sound like language too extreme for Aquinas to have used. But, in fact, it corresponds almost exactly with language employed elsewhere by St Thomas.[53] Here, for example, is a representative passage from one of his sermons: 'let us apply ourselves to renouncing earthly things and to loving heavenly things in such a way that we disdain the worldly life and embrace the heavenly life, that we may pass over from labor to rest, from the world to glory.'[54] When, in the Prayer for Virtues, the names of the four cardinal virtues are listed, one after the other, the first of them is introduced as follows: 'Give me the grace through justice to be subject to you.' The focus is on God alone. Likewise, in the *Summa,* when the four cardinal virtues are introduced, they are spoken of as 'perfecting virtues': 'virtues of men and women' who are on their way, and tending towards the divine similitude.'[55] It is, in other words, their *contemplative* character that receives the greatest emphasis:

> Thus prudence, by contemplating the things of God, scorns all the things of the world, and directs all the thoughts of the soul only to divine truths; temperance, so far as nature allows, sets aside the needs of the body; fortitude prevents the soul from being afraid of losing the body in rising to heavenly things; and justice consists in the soul giving a whole-hearted consent to following the way thus proposed.[56]

What is being described here is a radical form of Christian asceticism, a discipline shaped not by hatred of the world or hatred of the body, but by a deep, insatiable longing for 'the things of God'. And it is that same longing

---

[53] The fact that, on occasion, St Thomas apparently expresses 'contempt for this world' is discussed helpfully by Torrell in relation to Thomas's fundamental 'position on the goodness of things'. See Torrell, vol. 2, pages 241–5. And, on this question, see also pages 227–8, 234–5 and 238.

[54] *Caelum et terram transibunt: Sermon on the First Sunday of Advent,* in *Thomas Aquinas: The Academic Sermons (The Fathers of the Church: Medieval Continuation),* p. 84. This particular passage is not found in either Marietti or Busa, but is included in the Provisional Leonine text prepared by L.-J. Bataillon. I am grateful to Adriano Oliva OP for making available to me the Leonine text.

[55] *ST,* I II q.61 a.5.

[56] Ibid. This particular text reflects a Plotinian division of virtue, something Thomas knew about through Macrobius. The passage, however, by no means represents Thomas's complete view of the cardinal virtues. See Vivian Boland, *St Thomas Aquinas* (London 2007) pp. 197–200.

which explains the strong impulse towards detachment and self-control evident in the prayer.

B. The influence of Humbert of Romans

In the prayer's second section we read: 'May I subdue my flesh and purify my conscience.' And again: 'May I always be disciplined in the way I dress, the way I walk, and the gestures I use. Restrain my tongue from idle talk, prevent my feet from running this way and that, keep my eyes from wandering glances, protect my ears from rumours, lower my gaze in humility, raise my mind to heavenly things.' Every single one of these images of radical self-discipline can be traced to Humbert's *Epistola*. In fact, all or almost all of them can be found together in one particular paragraph.[57] The author of the Prayer for Virtues, like the author of the Prayer for Wise Ordering, was quite obviously impressed by Humbert's letter, and by parts of it in particular. One clear indication of this fact is that the first part of the last petition is nothing other than a statement of Humbert transformed into a prayer.[58]

At this point, however, a question needs to be asked: are the references to dress and comportment, to gait and to gesture (which can all be traced directly to the *Epistola*) are these images, are these preoccupations, likely to find themselves included in a Prayer for Virtue composed by a speculative theologian such as Aquinas? The answer to this question is, as it happens, an unqualified 'yes'. St Thomas, in the *Summa*, makes it clear that the question of what is becoming in movement and behaviour, the way one dresses, for example, or the way one walks, are matters of minor but real importance, things well worth considering, therefore, in the context of virtue. 'There is,' he writes, 'a virtue about the style of outward movement,'[59] and there is also 'a virtue that moderates outward dress.'[60]

Outward movements are signs of the inward disposition, according to Ecclesiasticus 19.27, *The attire of the body, and the laughter of the teeth, and*

---

[57] *Epistola beati Humberti*, LIV, *Opera de vita regulari*, vol. 1, p. 38. See also p. 39.

[58] Humbert writes: '*Nolite non fienda insipienter appetere, aut facienda per accidiam fastidere.*' *Epistola*, LIV, p. 38. And the phrase in the prayer reads: '*Da mihi ut numquam ea quae fiunt insipienter appetam.*'

[59] *ST*, II II q.168, a.1, *sed contra*.

[60] *ST*, II II q.169, a.1, ad 1.

the gait of a man, show what he is. And Ambrose says that the habit of mind is seen in the gesture of the body, and that the body's movement is an index [literally, the voice] of the soul.[61]

The way we present ourselves in society, the way we choose to walk or to dress, will inevitably make some kind of impact, however minor, on the people with whom we live. Accordingly, since ways of comportment and dressing are, at one level, signs of our inward disposition towards others, their moderation, Thomas notes, will require help from the virtues. And, in this context, Thomas speaks of two virtues in particular: first, the virtue of 'friendliness or affability',[62] and second, 'the virtue of truthfulness, whereby, by means of words and deeds, we reveal what we are inwardly'.[63]

The two virtues mentioned here are clearly related to what St Thomas names in the prayer as 'human affairs' (*humana*). Earlier, in these pages, I noted how an enormous weight is given, in the prayer, to 'divine matters' (*divina*), and to a way of life that would make possible the contemplation of 'heavenly things'. But, in a number of the petitions, concern is also shown for the neighbour. Thus we read, for example: 'May I not grudge what my neighbour possesses', and 'may I do what is right and what will be meritorious for me and be an example for others.'[64]

One of the prayer's distinguishing marks is the generous number of virtues actually referred to at different stages, though not always mentioned explicitly by name. These include devotion, perseverance, liberality, detachment, humility, repentance, wisdom, gratitude, justice, prudence, temperance, fortitude and the three theological virtues: faith, hope and love. One is frankly amazed to find such an extensive list included in a single prayer, and to find them described in language that is both clear and unmistakably thomistic. Aquinas may or may not be the actual author of this prayer, but one thing at least is undeniable: the language *is* his language, the content *is* his content. And there is one further

---

[61] *ST*, II II q.168, a.1, ad 1.
[62] On the virtue of friendliness, see *ST*, II II q.114, a.1.
[63] *ST*, II II q.168, a.1, ad 3.
[64] Concern for the neighbour's good is made even more explicit in one of the surviving manuscripts of the Prayer for Virtues. There we read: 'Grant that the good I have I may share generously with those who have not.' See '*Piae preces*' in *Opuscula theologica*, vol. 2, Marietti edition, p. 288.

thing to note: the text we are considering is a prayer, not a scholastic treatise. We cannot expect it, therefore, to have the full range of thought and expression which exists in a lengthy theological work. That said, however, the Dominican who composed this prayer clearly desired to include in it as many allusions to the Christian virtues as possible, a decision which may, in the end, have placed too great a strain on the modest and simple prayer-format.

If we consider the different links and likenesses that exist between the two prayers we have been considering so far – the Prayer for Virtues and the Prayer for Wise Ordering – the link between them that is most immediately noteworthy is that both prayers are influenced by the same text of Humbert of Romans. And not only influenced. Both prayers contain entire sentences and phrases 'borrowed' from the same *Epistola*. This fact points, I would suggest, to the likelihood, or at least to the very real possibility, that it was the same medieval author, the same Dominican, who composed both prayers. And since we now know that the Prayer for Wise Ordering (*'Concede michi'*) was almost certainly the work of Thomas, being directly attributed to him in the *Life* by his contemporary William of Tocco, it would seem not unreasonable to conclude that he, Thomas, is also the likely author of the Prayer for Virtues.

(3) Prayer of Praise and Thanksgiving

I praise,
   glorify and bless you,
                              my God,
for the immeasurable
   favours shown to me
      who am unworthy.

I praise
   your kind forbearance,
      waiting on me for so long

and your gentleness
   appearing in the guise of a
      sharp reprisal.

I praise
   your tenderness
      calling out to me,

   your kindness
      supporting me,

   your mercy
      forgiving my sins.

I praise
   your goodness for giving me
      more than I deserve
and your patience
   for not remembering
      past injuries.

   I praise your humility
         that consoles me,
   your patience
      that protects me,
   your eternity
      that preserves me,
   your truth
      that rewards me.

      What can I say,
my God, about your ineffable generosity?

For you call back the fugitive,
   you welcome the one who returns.

You support the one who falters.

   You gladden the despondent,
      you urge on the negligent.

You arm the warrior,
  you crown the victor.

You spurn not the repentant sinner,
  you do not remember past crimes.

You set us free from many perils,
  you soften our hearts for penitence.

You frighten us with chastisements,
  you entice us with promises.

You correct us with scourges,
  you guard us with a ministering angel.

Temporal things
you supply for us, eternal things you keep for us
in reserve.

You inspire us with the grandeur of creation.

You draw us forward
with the mercy of redemption. You promise us
blessings in reward.

For all these things
I cannot give sufficient praise.

I give thanks, however,
  to your Majesty,
for the abundance of your immense goodness.
  May you always
  increase your grace in me,
preserve that increase,
  and reward what you have preserved.

Amen.

Prayer of Praise and Thanksgiving
A commentary

The writing of this prayer of praise was directly inspired by two short passages from Humbert's letter. Both texts refer, first of all, to the overwhelming majesty and beauty of God's nature, and then to the 'innumerable benefits' all of us have received from God:

> For God himself enlightens our hearts with his wisdom, governs them by his tenderness, feeds them with his sweetness, entices them by his beauty, changes them by his power, allures them by his promises, trains them by stripes, terrifies them by threats and softens them by his favours.[65]

With these thoughts in mind, Humbert encourages his fellow Dominicans to strive, with all their heart, to 'serve the Lord, and give him praise.'[66] And the same message is repeated once again in another part of the letter:

> Let us adore the power of God, let us marvel at his wisdom, let us love his tenderness, let us desire his beauty, let us be drawn by his sweetness, let us venerate his eternity, let us imitate his humility, let us discover his greatness, let us praise his perfection, let us hope in his mercy, let us fear his justice.[67]

What we are hearing, or reading, in this passage of Humbert is, of course, the language of exhortation, and it is very fine. But as soon as the preacherly discourse is transformed into the form of a prayer, the result is a work far more immediately engaging and far more personal. All of a sudden, the words appear to catch fire with a new flame of intimacy, a new sense of personal indebtedness to God for his unfailing kindness and compassion.

I praise
your kind forbearance,
waiting on me for so long,

and your gentleness

---

[65] *Epistola beati Humberti*, LI, *Opera de vita regulari*, vol. 1, p. 34.
[66] Ibid.
[67] Ibid., p. 30.

appearing in the guise of a
　　sharp reprisal.

I praise
　　your tenderness
　　　　calling out to me,

　　your kindness
　　　　supporting me,

　　your mercy
　　　　forgiving my sins.

At different points in the prayer, the author is not slow to acknowledge his own earlier failures, his 'sins' and 'past injuries'. But this humble acknowledgement is, by no means, the principal focus of the prayer. In fact, the effect of his acknowledgement is to underline, over and over again, the depth of God's extraordinary goodness and kindness. The prayer recites the different ways in which God intervenes over time to help and instruct fallen humanity, an instruction that is, needless to say, not always easy. It's true, of course, we are again and again 'enticed by promises' and 'freed from many perils'. But we are also, it has to be said, 'corrected with scourges' and frightened 'with chastisements'. 'God,' Lydia Maidl tellingly remarks, with regard to this prayer, 'proceeds pedagogically in his steering of the world and humanity, something that's strongly emphasized by Thomas when writing on salvation history.'[68]

*　　*　　*

No small part of the prayer's appeal, in the original Latin, is the repeated consonance of clause endings, a trick of style which reveals undoubted talent in its author. And something of the same bright workmanship can be seen also in *O Deus omnipotens*, the Prayer for Virtues. This way of writing, this rather stylized form of prose, the medievals called *ars rithmica*. They thought

---

[68] Lydia Maidl, *Thomas von Aquin* (Freiburg 1994), p. 109. Fears and threats, Thomas explains in his sermon *Beata gens*, are God's way of drawing us away from sin in order to lead us to happiness. 'It is necessary for us,' he declares, 'that God corrects us.' And again: 'The fact that God corrects us is a sign of love.' *Beatus vir: Sermon on the Feast of St Martin*, Busa vol. 6, p. 41 a.

of writing as having three main forms and not merely two (prose and poetry) as we think of writing today. The three forms were 'the prosaic', 'the metrical' and 'the rhythmical'.[69] The aim of 'the rhythmical' was close, in some ways, to that of poetry. It was 'formed for the delectation of the ears of the hearer',[70] and consisted in a repeated series of 'clause endings', a kind of taut, lyrical prose. Of course, none or almost none of this can be conveyed in a literal English translation. And that's a pity. The lift that these repeated 'endings' give to the prayer can be seen – or *heard* – in the following representative passage:

Tu enim vocas fugientem,	For you call back the fugitive,
suscipis reverentem,	you welcome the one who returns,
adjuvas titubantem,	you support the one who falters,
laetificas desperantem,	you gladden the despondent,
stimulas negligentem,	you urge on the negligent,
armas pugnantem,	you arm the warrior,
coronas triumphantem.	you crown the victor.

The impression the prayer leaves is one of wonder at the energy of God's love and, along with that, a sense of overwhelming gratitude. It is a song of praise, a psalm of the New Covenant.

(4) Prayer for the Attainment of Heaven

O God of all consolation,
you who see in us nothing
but your own gifts,
I entreat you
to give me, at the close of this life,
knowledge
of the First Truth,
and enjoyment of your divine majesty.

---

[69] See James J. Murphy, *Rhetoric in the Middle Ages: A History of Rhetorical Theory from St Augustine to the Renaissance* (Berkeley 1981) p. 157.

[70] This was the opinion expressed by the thirteenth century author, Thomas of Capua. See *Rhetoric in the Middle Ages*, p. 159.

Most generous Rewarder,
give to my body also
the beauty of lightsomeness,
responsiveness of
flesh to spirit,
a quick readiness and delicacy,
and the gift of
unconquerable strength.

And add to these

an overflow of riches,
a spate of delights,
a confluence of all good things,

so that I may rejoice

in your consolation
above me,
in a place of loveliness
below me,
in the glorification of body and soul
within me,
in the delight of friends and angels
all around me.

Most merciful Father,
being with you
may my mind
attain the enlightenment of wisdom,
my desire,
the fulfilment of its longing,
my courage
the praise of triumph.

For where you are

is avoidance of all danger,

plenitude of dwelling places,

harmony of wills.

Where you are is

the pleasantness of spring,

the radiance of summer,

the fecundity of autumn,

and the repose of winter.

Give, Lord God,

life without death,

joy without sorrow,

that place where reigns

sovereign freedom,

free security,

secure tranquillity,

delightful happiness,

happy eternity,

eternal blessedness,

the vision of truth

and praise, O God.

Amen.

Prayer for the Attainment of Heaven
A commentary

Concerning heaven we read in the New Testament, *Eye has not seen nor ear heard … the things God has prepared for those who love him* (I Cor. 2.9) – a statement highlighting the near impossibility of describing what heaven will be like for those found worthy to enter into everlasting joy, those who will witness with their own eyes the unimaginable glory of the divine light. What I find moving and impressive about this short prayer is that, against all expectation, it is somehow able to offer a glimpse, a hint, of that untold beauty and radiance.[71]

A. The glorification of soul and body

The first request made by the author of the prayer is, 'at the close of this life', to have living knowledge of God, and also to have enjoyment of the divine presence. What that divine presence will mean for those privileged to come close to God is suggested later in the prayer when the name of God the Father is expressly invoked. 'My mind', the author notes, and 'my desire' – the deepest longing of the heart – will then find fulfilment:

> For where you are
> is avoidance of all danger,
> plenitude of dwelling places,
> harmony of wills.

> Where you are is
> the pleasantness of spring,
> the radiance of summer,
> the fecundity of autumn,
> and the repose of winter.

For the author of *Te Deum totius consolationis* a major part of the joy of heaven will consist in possessing an intimate and profound knowledge of God, 'the first Truth'. And thus, with manifest desire, the Dominican is looking forward to that final 'vision of truth', to what he calls 'the enlightenment of intellectual wisdom'. But the delight of heaven is not, in his understanding, restricted merely to forms of spiritual and *intellectual* joy. The body also, in an extraordinary way, will be transfigured. In fact, no small part of the miracle of the life of heaven will consist in what the prayer calls 'the glorification of the *body*'. Accordingly, just after asking for 'the enlightenment (or manifestation) of wisdom' – the

---

[71] The Last Judgment painting by Beato Angelico, which is in San Marco, Florence, offers the same kind of vision. And the painting actually includes, among the radiant company of saints and angels, the figure of Aquinas. It may just be possible that this particular vision of future joy – 'in the delight of friends and angels' – directly inspired the Angelico masterpiece.

fulfilment of the *mind* – the prayer appeals for a comparable fulfilment of the two most basic forms of human passion as understood by Aquinas and by the scholastic tradition: passion (*concupisciblis*) that has to do with desire, and passion (*irascibilis*) that has to do with spirited resistance.[72]

In the *Summa theologiae* St Thomas explains that our inclination to seek what appeals to us, 'what is suitable according to the senses,' constitutes concupiscible passion.[73] Irascible passion, in contrast, is active when we find ourselves faced with a challenge which is either arduous or threatening, and we seek to overcome the challenge. The fact that the two technical terms for the passion of desire and for that of spirited resistance ('*concupiscibilis*' and '*irascibilis*') are both used in the prayer underlines the thoroughgoing scholastic character of the author of this tiny prayer: 'Abiding with you, most merciful Father, may my mind attain the enlightenment of wisdom, my desire (*concupiscipilis*) the fulfilment of its longing, my courage (*irascibilis*) the praise of triumph.'[74]

With regard to the body, the prayer asks for four wondrous gifts: 'the splendor of *claritas* ... the promptitude of *agilitas* ... the penetration of *subtilitas* ... the strength of *impassibilitas*.' These four dowries or gifts (*dotes* of the glorified body) are included in the *Epistola*, but we find them referred to also by St Thomas in a work composed when he was still a young man.[75] And he referred to them once again in his *Lectures on Matthew*.[76] The wonderful *claritas* of the transfigured body will mark a clear fulfilment of the promise made in The Book of Wisdom 3.7: *The virtuous will shine, and will run to and fro like sparks among the stubble*, and of the promise made in Matthew 13.43: *The virtuous will shine as the sun in the kingdom of their Father.*[77] Owing to the overflow of grace from the resurrected soul into the body,[78] there will be

---

[72] See *ST*, 1 q. 81, a. 2.

[73] Ibid.

[74] Courage, in scholastic understanding, comes under the rubric of *irascibilis*. It has to do with a threatening but conquerable evil. So authors and translators such as R. Anderson and J. Moser are not mistaken when they translate *irascibilis* as 'courage'. See *The Aquinas Prayer Book* (Manchester, New Hampshire 2000) p. 55.

[75] *Commentary on the Sentences* [of Peter Lombard], Book III, d. 16, q. 2, a. 2, and d. 21, q.2, a.3, ad 5.

[76] *Lectures on St Matthew*, 17, 1.1.

[77] See *Commentary on the Sentences*, Book IV, d. 44, q. 2, a. 4.

[78] Ibid. Compare *ST*, I II q.4, a.6: 'The soul's beatitude redounds to the body so that it too may taste of its perfection.'

no strain or labour in the movements of the saints; a new-found *agilitas* will enable them to travel vast distances at the speed of thought.[79]

The third gift, that of *subtilitas,* refers to a certain ease and subtlety of movement, a lack of density in the body, whereby the body, while remaining flesh, will acquire such a delicacy of spirit, it will be able to pass through every obstacle even as Christ, after the resurrection, was able to pass through walls of stone.[80] Finally, because of the saints' unchangeable and everlasting enjoyment of God, they will receive the gift of *impassibilitas,* an unconquerable strength which will mean not only freedom forever from the dominion of the passions but also immunity from all suffering.[81]

At this point, in the prayer, the language is both direct and personal, the appeal being made to God at once bold and humble: 'Give to *my* body', the Domincan prays: *Da corpori meo.* And, then, after listing the four desired and amazing qualities of the resurrected body, he writes:

> And add to these
>
>> an overflow of riches,
>> a spate of delights,
>> a confluence of all good things,
>
> so that I may rejoice
>
>> in your consolation
>>> above me,
>> in a place of loveliness
>>> below me,
>> in the glorification of body and soul

---

[79] *Commentary on the Sentences,* Book IV, d. 44, q. 2, a. 3.

[80] Ibid., Book IV, d. 44, q.2, a.2.

[81] Ibid., Book IV, d. 44, q.2, a.1. It's almost impossible to provide a succinct and precise translation into English of the Latin phrases Aquinas uses to describe the four gifts of the resurrected body. That said, however, the translation by John Finnis of two of these tiny phrases ('*claritatis pulchritudem*' and '*agilitatis promptitudinem*') in the light of St Thomas's own teaching, I find to be particularly helpful. Accordingly, I have presumed to incorporate both phrases into my own translation: 'the beauty of lightsomeness' and 'responsiveness of flesh to spirit'. See Finnis, *Aquinas: Moral, Political, and Legal Theory* (Oxford 1998) p. 333.

within me,
in the delight of friends and angels
all around me.[82]

B. The influence of Humbert of Romans

The prayer for the attainment of heaven, relative to its size, shows more traces of the influence of the *Epistola* of Humbert than is apparent in any of the three prayers attributed to Aquinas we have been considering so far. Almost all the images in the prayer, in fact, including the references to the transformed state of the human body in heaven, can be traced to a single paragraph in the *Epistola*.[83] That said, however, the ideas and images 'borrowed' are taken up into the new prayer-form with such complete and quiet authority, the prayer impresses at once as a fully integrated and achieved work in its own right. The author of *Te Deum totius consolationis* was apparently not concerned with originality, but simply with the making of a prayer.

The key paragraph from the *Epistola,* to which reference has just now been made, is distinguished by an intense longing for eternal life, and so with the freedom, rest, beauty, communion and joy that come with eternal life. It is unquestionably one of the finest short passages ever composed by Humbert. And it's not difficult, therefore, to imagine the extract making a very particular impact on someone like the young Aquinas when he first read it. I say this because the theme which it explores – the longing for eternal life – is one which held for Aquinas a unique attraction all his life. So strong, in fact, was that orientation – that 'straining toward the vision of God' – one commentator, Pierre-Marie Gy, has observed that it was a distinguishing mark of his 'theological and spiritual personality',[84] something – in the opinion of Gy – of which 'we will hardly find an equivalent among contemporary theologians [of the same period].'[85]

---

[82] In the original Latin text, the last phrase reads: '*iuxta de angelorum et hominum delectabili associatione*'. By '*hominum*' Aquinas intends, of course, to include both men and women. And that's why, rather than translate '*angelorum et hominum*' as 'angels and men,' I have presumed to introduce the word 'friends'.

[83] *Epistola beati Humberti*, LVII, *Opera de vita regulari*, vol. 1, p. 41.

[84] Cited by Jean-Pierre Torrell in *Saint Thomas Aquinas: The Person and His Work*, p. 136.

[85] Ibid. The comment of Pierre-Marie Gy refers particularly to the link between St Thomas's eucharistic theology and his eschatology.

The final sentence of the prayer appears to be an almost exact echo of the final sentence in Humbert's paragraph. Concerning eternal life, Humbert writes: 'There shall be, I say, life without death, certainty without doubt, day without night, freedom without fear, joy without sadness, rest without labour, royal sovereignty without end.' Two of these phrases are repeated almost verbatim in the prayer itself: 'life without death' and 'joy without sadness'. But, when the lines are looked at more closely, we discover that a few significant changes have been made to Humbert's original text. For example, the author of the prayer, instead of continuing to repeat the word 'without', as in phrases such as 'rest *without* labour' and 'freedom *without* fear', decides instead to employ a tiny but manifestly effective literary device in order to emphasize his own deep longing for eternal life. The words he uses are very nearly the same as those used by Humbert. But, in this case, with a quite deliberate artistry, the Dominican transforms what is already a fine prose passage into something closer to poetry. At the close of the prayer, he asks to be given entry to that place 'where reigns'

sovereign freedom,	*summa libertas,*
free security,	*libera securitas,*
secure tranquility,	*secura tranquillitas,*
delightful happiness,	*jucunda felicitas,*
happy eternity,	*felix aeternitas,*
eternal blessedness	*aeterna beatitudo*[86]

What we find here, and what is not to be found in Humbert, is a deliberate *play* on four key words: freedom, security, happiness and eternity. Each of these words appears, first of all, in the sentence as a noun, but it is then immediately followed in the form of an adjective. And the effect is magical. The exquisite phrasing and formal balance of the lines allow us not merely to *think* of eternity but almost to *feel* something of its joyous atmosphere. Clearly, the Dominican who composed this brief prayer was a man gifted with no small literary talent.

But was that Dominican, Thomas Aquinas? Do we have any evidence that

---

[86] *Epistola beati Humberti*, LVII, *Opera de vita regulari*, vol. 1, p. 41.

this particular play on words would have appealed to him? As it happens, there does exist, in St Thomas's work, convincing evidence regarding precisely this point. In his sermon, *Beata gens,* for example, when reflecting in similar vein on the nature of an achieved eternal joy, Thomas asks: 'But what will be in that end? We will be free without end, and being free we will see, and seeing we will love, and loving we will praise.'[87] Here, even in a rough English translation, the manifest delight in word play is unmistakable. But the original Latin itself is superb. The text reads:

> *Sed quod erit in illo fine?*
>
> > *Sine fine vacabimus,*
> > > *vacando videbimus,*
> > *videndo amabimus,*
> > > *amando laudabimus.*[88]

Thomas claims here to be quoting from St Augustine but his own words are not, in fact, an exact echo of Augustine.[89] (Perhaps he was quoting from memory?) In any case, the end result is a happy one: Aquinas's further play on words rendering the statement by Augustine even more powerful, even more eloquent.

Conclusion

From the Middle Ages until modern times the four prayers we have been considering have been attributed to St Thomas Aquinas and to no one else. And that's no surprise. Both in terms of language and content, the prayers explore themes wholly characteristic of Aquinas. At a first reading, however, students who are familiar only with the philosophical and theological works of St Thomas may find it hard to believe that the urgent, personal voice we hear in the prayers is really that of the great speculative theologian. St Thomas,

---

[87] *Beata gens: Sermon on the Feast of All Saints,* Busa vol. 6, p. 40 c.

[88] Ibid.

[89] The original passage in Augustine reads: '*Ibi vacabimus, et videbimus; videbimus, et amabimus; amabimus, et laudabimus. Ecce quod erit in fine sine fine.*' *City of God,* vol. 10: 22.

as we know, almost never uses the word 'I' even when engaged in preaching. He would no doubt, therefore, have wholeheartedly agreed with the following statement of Humbert of Romans from the *Epistola*: 'You will arrive at perfect humility ... if you leave out of your speech the pronoun *I*.'[90] Private or personal prayers are not, however, theological tracts or philosophical treatises. Prayers arise from the heart as well as from the mind, and the required humility of a prayer demands, in fact, the use of the personal pronoun.

After our examination of all four prayers in this chapter, one thing has become clear: these texts are not merely fervent expressions of pious devotion but also literary compositions in their own right, works of considerable 'subtlety and design'.[91] A. I. Doyle writes: 'Prayers of this kind and length are developed spiritual exercises, found especially in compilations made by or for contemplative religious, those who followed the "mixed life" as well as those strictly enclosed.'[92] And Doyle refers in passing to 'verbal changes usual in such a process of literary tradition, "improving" as often as "corrupting".'[93] What is especially noteworthy about all four of the prayers under consideration is that rather than demonstrating the influence of a number of earlier prayers which, in some way, they transform, they betray instead – and most unexpectedly – the influence of phrases and sentences belonging to a very different kind of text, a letter, in fact, *not* a prayer – the *Epistola* of Humbert of Romans.

Speaking on the subject of *Concede michi*, the first prayer to which we gave attention, Lydia Maidl notes that whoever composed the work was someone clearly moved by themes 'dear to Thomas's heart'.[94] And she notes further: 'The petitions are formulated very clearly and in a way that is easy to understand.'[95] Nevertheless, in spite of this commendation, and it spite of the fact that *Concede michi* has always been attributed, within the tradition, to Thomas Aquinas, Maidl decides in the end that Aquinas was probably not the author. It

---

[90] '*Ad perfectum humilitatem ... pervenietis ... si singularem sensum reliquatis*'. *Epistola beati Humberti*, XXXV, *Opera de vita regulari*, vol. 1, p. 21.
[91] The phrase is used by A. I. Doyle, 'A Prayer attributed to Aquinas', in *Dominican Studies* 1 (July 1948), p. 229.
[92] Ibid.
[93] Ibid.
[94] Maidl, pp. 106–7.
[95] Ibid., p. 107.

is 'perhaps more likely', she suggests, that the prayers were ascribed to Thomas but were actually composed by some anonymous Dominican or Dominicans.[96] Maidl is a scholar of undoubted repute, but I can see no compelling reason – based on *internal* evidence alone – for coming to this conclusion.

Fortunately, as indicated earlier, there is now available to us also strong *external* evidence which points to the near certainty, or at least to the probability, of Aquinas's authorship. I am referring here, of course, to the attribution of the prayer to St Thomas by his contemporary and first biographer, William of Tocco, and to the fact that the prayer itself was actually included by Tocco in his life of the saint. This information, as I have already noted, was not available to scholars until recently. The great scholar, Dom A. Wilmart, writing as long ago as 1932, chose to keep an open mind regarding the question of St Thomas's authorship of *Concede michi*. While acknowledging the possibility of an anonymous attribution, he wrote: 'Nevertheless, I intend still to reserve judgement on this point until more information is available.'[97] Happily, that information has now come to light, and is available to scholars, thanks to the work of Claire le Brun-Gouvanvic.

Of all the different prayers attributed to Aquinas, only the four we have been considering betray the clear influence of Humbert's *Epistola*. The first prayer, *Concede michi*, was almost certainly, we now know, composed by St Thomas, a fact which suggests that Thomas was also the likely author of the three other prayers. This suggestion is greatly strengthened, I find, by a small but probably significant detail. When we consider the influence of the *Epistola* on the second of the three prayers, *O Deus omnipotens*, we find that the particular sections of the *Epistola*, which made the greatest impact on the prayer, are almost without exception the very parts of the work which impacted so decisively on the composition also of *Concede michi*.[98] And that

---

[96] Ibid., p. 91.

[97] A. Wilmart, *Auteurs spirituels et textes dévots du Moyen A ̆ge latine. Etudes d'histoire littéraire* (Paris 1932) p. 380, note (1).

[98] In the Marietti edition of the *Epistola*, the text, in its entirety, takes up 41 pages. The principal pages containing phrases 'borrowed' by *Concede michi* are the following: 29, 30, and 37. The pages containing phrases 'borrowed' by *O Deus omnipotens* are pages 31 and 38. Similarly, the passages in *Laudo, glorifico, benedico*, which most betray the influence of Humbert, are from the very same section of the *Epistola*, pages 30 and 34.

detail, though small, lends further credence to the suggestion that one and the same individual composed both prayers.

If Thomas Aquinas is indeed the author of the prayers we have been considering, it would appear that, at a certain stage in his life, the *Epistola* became a significant text for his meditation. 'What is the fruit of meditation?' he asks in one of the Paris sermons, and he replies: 'I say that meditation is the key to the memory of someone who can read and listen to many things, but cannot retain it unless he meditates.'[99] Then he goes on to say: 'For just as food does not nourish unless it is first chewed, so you cannot advance in knowledge except by chewing, through frequent meditation, the things you have heard.'[100] But why would someone like St Thomas, after having read over the *Epistola* of Humbert of Romans (a text which has a decidedly hortatory and preacherly character) decide to make it the basis for the composition of private or 'secret prayers'?

A remark made in passing by Humbert of Romans in the *Epistola* may suggest an answer to this question. After first advising his reader, 'Seek opportunities for secret prayers', Humbert goes on to say: 'And use more freely those prayers which seem most to excite your heart to fervour.'[101] Engaging in the composition of personal or secret prayers (*orationes furtivas*) may well have been a way, for St Thomas, of not only 'chewing' on the wisdom of the revered *Magister*, Humbert of Romans, but also of allowing his own heart to be in some way quickened to a state of fervour.

There are indications in the *Life* composed by Bernard Gui, that St Thomas was well aware of how he needed, on occasion, to rely on devotional texts 'in order to offset the aridity which is so often the result of abstract and subtle speculative thinking.'[102] Desire is fundamental in prayer. And that's why St Thomas judges it both wise and necessary to 'call our minds back to the

[99] *Puer Jesus: Sermon on the First Sunday after Epiphany*, in *Thomas Aquinas: The Academic Sermons* (*The Fathers of the Church: Medieval Continuation*), trans., M-R Hoogland (Washington 2010) p. 104. See Busa vol. 6, 083, no. 1, p. 34c.

[100] Ibid.

[101] *Epistola Beati Humberti*, XXXV, in *Opera de vita regulari*, vol. 1, p. 30.

[102] Bernard Gui, *The Life of Saint Thomas Aquinas: Biographical Documents,* 15, (ed.) Kenelm Foster (London 1959), p. 38.

business of praying at certain times to make sure that desire does not freeze up entirely, once it has begun to cool.'[103] Thomas, in the *Summa*, asks the question: 'Should prayer last a long time?', and he replies: 'it should last long enough to arouse the fervour of interior desire.'[104]

*   *   *

To summarize: with regard to the question of authorship, I have little doubt that Thomas Aquinas wrote the four prayers which have been the object of our reflection in this chapter. And since all four betray the clear influence of the *Epistola* of Humbert of Romans, that would seem to indicate that, in the composition of the prayers, Aquinas allowed himself to be directly influenced by one of his own contemporaries.

When questions are raised regarding the sources of Aquinas's work, attention quite naturally goes to important figures of the ancient past such as St Augustine and Aristotle. Here, in this particular case, if I'm not mistaken, there are compelling indications of a probable use, and indeed of an imaginative transformation, by St Thomas, of a contemporary Dominican text, the *Epistola* of Humbert of Romans. Reflecting on the different sources of St Thomas's spirituality, J.-P. Torrell remarked: 'We certainly have to take the Dominican heritage into account.'[105] Should it prove to be the case that Aquinas did, in fact, allow himself to be influenced by Blessed Humbert in the composition of the prayers under consideration, then what we have, in the four Dominican prayers before us, are documents of the rarest kind: prayers not merely composed with considerable artistry and care by the Angelic Doctor, but work actually based on an earlier Dominican text, an *Epistola* composed by one of the Order's greatest leaders and saints, St Thomas's older contemporary, Blessed Humbert of Romans.

---

[103] *Commentary on the Sentences* [of Peter Lombard] Bk 4, dist. 15, q.4, II, (c). See *Albert and Thomas*, p. 383. Thomas is quoting a passage from St Augustine: *Ep.* 130. 9.18 (PL 33:501).

[104] *ST*, II II q.83, a.14.

[105] J.-P. Torrell, *Saint Thomas Aquinas: Spiritual Master*, p. 377.

Part Two

Prayer considered: soundings in the biblical commentaries

3

Aquinas as exegete

The most famous work of Aquinas which has come down to us is a work of speculative theology: the celebrated *Summa theologiae*. But, in his life as teacher, St Thomas seldom held classes on the *Summa* or, for that matter, delivered regular lectures on philosophy.[1] He was a Master of the Sacred Page (*Magister in Sacra Pagina*): his assigned task, as friar and scholar, to give classes on the Bible. That said, however, in the Middle Ages, no clear-cut distinctions were made between what today we call scriptural exegesis and dogmatic theology. Accordingly, as a theologian, Aquinas was expected to be conversant with all the different aspects of Christian faith and Christian tradition.[2]

1. The young master

The task of becoming a fully-fledged teacher of Scripture was, in the Aquinas's opinion, impossible to achieve without years of dedicated preparation. He wrote: 'The truth of faith is contained in Sacred Scripture diffusely, under various modes [of expression], and sometimes obscurely. The result is that in order to draw out the truth of faith from sacred Scripture, one needs long

---

[1] J.-P. Torrell, following the lead of Leonard Boyle, suggests that Thomas when living and working in Rome, may just possibly have taught the *Prima pars* of the *Summa* and a portion of the *Prima secundae*. See Torrell, *Saint Thomas Aquinas*, vol. 1, *The Person and His Work*, pp. 145–6.
[2] See Thomas Prügl, 'Thomas Aquinas as Interpreter of Scripture,' in *The Theology of Thomas Aquinas*, (eds), Rik Van Nieuwenhove and Joseph Wawrykow (Notre Dame, Indiana) p. 386.

study and practice.'[3] Owing, no doubt, to his own manifest giftedness as a student, St Thomas, at an unusually young age, was awarded the title *Magister in Sacra Pagina*. When, however, the moment came for him to be established in his new role, the young friar at first hesitated, feeling both unable and unworthy. In the end, what gave him the courage to go forward was, it is reported, nothing less than an inspiration received in a dream.

Apparently Thomas gave an account of the dream to the Prior of Fossanova, a conversation recalled at the canonization process by Peter of Montesangiovanni.[4] And Peter of Caputio, another witness at the Naples process, declared that the story of the dream was common knowledge among the friars at the Priory of San Jacques in Paris.[5] In light of these facts, and since the witnesses seem happily to agree among themselves on the basic facts, Jean-Pierre Torrell concludes: 'historians have every reason to believe that we have here a personal confidence that goes back to Thomas himself.'[6] With regard to the manifest distress of the young Thomas prior to the dream, and on the dream itself, we read in the *Vita* by Bernard Gui:

> With tears he begged for that understanding of divine things which had become so rare among men, and also for inspiration as to the theme he should choose for his inaugural lecture. Then he fell asleep and dreamed. He seemed to see an old man, white-haired and clothed in the Dominican habit, who came and said to him: 'Brother Thomas, why are you praying and weeping?' 'Because,' answered Thomas, 'they are making me take the degree of Master, and I do not think I am fully competent. Moreover I cannot think what theme to take for my inaugural lecture.' To this the old man replied: 'Do not fear: God will help you to bear the burden of being a Master. And, as for the lecture, take this text, *'Rigans montes de superioribus*

---

[3] *ST*, II II q.1 a.9. For a clear outline of the preparation involved in becoming a Master of the Sacred Page, see James Weisheipl, *Friar Thomas d'Aquino: His Life, Thought, and Works* (Washington 1983) pp. 6–7.

[4] Naples Canonization Process, 49, in *Fontes vitae s. Thomae Aquinatis*, (ed.) D. Prümmer (Toulouse 1911) p. 331.

[5] Ibid., 92, pp. 398–9.

[6] Jean-Pierre Torrell, *Saint Thomas Aquinas*, vol. 1, *The Person and His Work*, trans., R. Royal (Washington, DC 1996) p. 51.

suis, de fructu operum tuorum satiabitur terra' (From your heights you water the mountains, the earth is filled with the fruit of your works') Ps. 103.13. Then he vanished, and Thomas awoke and thanked God for having so quickly come to his aid.[7]

That would seem to mark the end of the young man's difficulties. But, at this point, Thomas was confronted with a new challenge, and one that was truly unexpected. The academic year in which he made his inception (1255–6) was, as it happens, the year when his fellow Dominican friars endured unusually sharp opposition within the university. So intense, in fact, was the opposition, attempts were made at one point, on the very day of Thomas's inception, to prevent students and teachers from attending his opening talk. As a result Pope Alexander IV felt constrained to write a letter to the university (17 June 1226) in which he spoke of the 'unworthy manner' in which the authorities had behaved, noting how they had 'opposed those who desired to attend the lectures, disputations and sermons of the friars, in particular those who wished to be present at the inception of our beloved son, frater Thomas Aquinas.'[8]

The young Aquinas, in his inaugural lecture, spoke of the unique character of Scripture. Nowhere on earth, he declared, was there a teaching or doctrine higher in wisdom or more sublime. In light of that fact, he went on to say that all teachers of Sacred Scripture ought themselves to be 'high' (*elevati*) in the conduct of their lives, 'despising earthly things' and cleaving to 'heavenly things alone' (Phil. 3.25).[9] What's more, they ought also to be 'illumined' (*illuminati*) like high mountains, being the first to catch the sun's rays, the first that is to be enlightened by 'the rays of divine wisdom'.[10] But how, in fact, was this ideal to be realized in practice? To Thomas it must have seemed a

---

[7] Bernard Gui, *Vita s. Thomae Aquinatis*, 12; translation from *Biographical Documents*, (ed.) K. Foster, p. 34. William of Tocco, in his biography of Thomas, also speaks about the dream. See *Ystoria sancti Thome de Aquino*, 17, (ed.) Claire le Brun-Gounaanvic (Toronto 1996) pp. 127–8.

[8] See '*Alexandre IV réprouve l'attitude prise à l'égard des frères Prêcheurs, et principalement de fr. Thomas d'Aquin*', in *Fontes vitae s. Thomae Aquinatis*, XII, (ed.) M. H. Laurent (Saint-Maximin 1937) p. 549.

[9] *Breve principium fratris Thomae de Aquino*, 2, 1212: '*Rigans montes de superioribus suis*,' in *Opuscula theologica*, vol. 1, Marietti edition (Turin 1954) p. 442.

[10] Ibid.

near impossibility. And so, after first listing all the different things required of a teacher of Sacred Scripture, the young Master brought his lecture to an end with a simple, heart-felt prayer:

> But *who is capable of this?* (2 Cor. 2.16). What God requires are ministers who are innocent ... intelligent ... fervent ... and ... obedient. Nevertheless, although no one by himself is sufficient for such a ministry, he can hope to have this sufficiency from God. *Not that we are capable, on our own, of a single thought, as if it came from us, but our sufficiency is from God* (2 Cor. 3.5). He [the teacher of Scripture] should ask it of God. *If anyone is wanting in wisdom, let him ask for it from God, who gives abundantly, and it will be given to him* (James 1.5). Let us pray. May Christ grant this to us. Amen.[11]

2. Master of the sacred page

Before Aquinas had delivered his inaugural lecture in Paris, he had already commented on at least two books from the Old Testament, Isaiah and Jeremiah, and very possibly also on Lamentations.[12] Later, he would go on to comment on the Book of Job, the Letters of St Paul, the Gospels of St Matthew and St John and the book of the Psalms. He was not, therefore, Master of the Sacred Page merely by name. And yet, for many years, indeed until fairly recently, the nature of his contribution as biblical theologian has been strangely overlooked within the world of academe and beyond.

One rather striking acknowledgement of Aquinas's importance as a commentator on Scripture came from Pope Pius XII in a talk he delivered, on 14 January 1958, to students and professors of the 'Angelicum' (The Pontifical University of St Thomas in Rome). With regard to the different works which Thomas wrote on Scripture, the Pope remarked: '[these commentaries] shine with such authority, such keen insight and such precision, they can be

---

[11] Ibid., 4, 1215, p. 443.
[12] See Thomas Prügl, 'Thomas Aquinas as Interpreter of Scripture', p. 388.

numbered among his greatest theological works.'[13] And he went on to say: 'If anyone, therefore, should neglect them, that person can hardly be said to enjoy a full and clear familiarity and knowledge of the Angelic Doctor.'[14]

But how could it happen that, for such a long time, Aquinas's stature as commentator on Scripture received so little recognition from readers and scholars within the academic community? Here, the first thing to note is that even for those people already familiar with Aquinas's work as a theologian, his commentaries on Scripture make for decidedly difficult reading. And, what's more, the actual texts of the commentaries are not, generally speaking, available in a satisfactory form. In fact, the critical editions of almost all Thomas's commentaries on Scripture are still lacking, and very nearly half of them – amazing fact – were not translated into English until recently, or were not readily available.[15]

How can we explain this extraordinary situation? No doubt there are a number of different factors in play, but the key point at issue is one which has already been quietly but forcefully noted by the Dominican Fergus Kerr. He writes: 'The lack of decent texts, it has to be admitted, is entirely due to the fact that Thomists themselves have never read the biblical commentaries much. The Aquinas often criticized for being unbiblical is the creation of his self-styled admirers.'[16]

Many years ago, assessing the general character of St Thomas's Scripture commentaries, Beryl Smalley remarked: 'Reading these against a background of modern exegesis, one naturally finds the medieval element in them startling; [but], approaching them from the twelfth and thirteenth centuries, one is more startled by their modernity.'[17] She then went on to note that sometimes Aquinas will 'put fresh life into old conventions', and sometimes

---

[13] Pope Pius XII, 'Allocutio: *Moderatoribus, docentibus, atque alumnis Pontificii Athenaei, quod "Angelicum" nuncupator*', *Acta Apostolicae Sedis* 50 (1958) p. 152.

[14] Ibid.

[15] A translation of St Thomas's commentaries on St Paul has recently been made available in a handsome six-volume set by The Aquinas Institute for the Study of Sacred Doctrine. The translation is based largely on work done by F. R. Larcher.

[16] Fergus Kerr, 'Recent Thomistica 1', *New Blackfriars*, vol. 83 (May 2002) p. 248.

[17] Beryl Smalley, *The Study of the Bible in the Middle Ages* (Oxford 1952) p. 301.

simply 'ignore' the conventions.[18] What, I think, for the modern reader, is most 'startling' is the scholastic method employed by Thomas, a method which demands, at almost every turn, the creation of a whole algebra of divisions and distinctions, imposing on the text of Scripture an Aristotelean structure which, it could be argued, risks obscuring rather than revealing the true meaning of the text.

Why Aquinas chose to rely on this particular method can, in large part, be explained by the academic context in which his writing took place, a context very different from that in which the Fathers of the Church, for example, composed their texts. This decidedly academic way of approaching Scripture, though manifestly limited, did all the same have considerable usefulness, as James Weisheipl explains:

> St Thomas' commentaries on the Sacred Text are typically *medieval,* that is they lack the unction, colloquialism and engaging informality of Patristic commentaries (which were largely homilies) … In other words, it is easier to read St Augustine's commentary on John than it is to read St Thomas' or that of any other medieval writer addressing students in the 'schools' of Paris and elsewhere. The big difference is between the Patristic and Monastic commentaries, which were largely homiletic, pastoral, personal, and mystical, on the one hand, and Scholastic commentaries aimed at teaching students in the university or *studium* the literal meaning of the text. The style of medieval Scholastic commentaries is rather formal, literal, student-orientated, and bookish. This style often makes such commentaries difficult for a modern reader to follow, and to some extent hinders him from deriving the greatest benefit for his mind and heart. At first glance, such a 'commentary' – with its definitions, divisions, arguments, footnotes and concern for the orthodox meaning of the sacred message – may seem like searching for a needle in a haystack. But in the case of Thomas' commentaries the reader may be confident that his efforts at discovering that needle will prove to be both intellectually and spiritually

---

[18] Ibid.

rewarding; once discovered, it will be valued as 'the pearl of great price'. (Mt. 13.46)[19]

3. A new context, a new way of reading

Weisheipl speaks here of the academic context in which Aquinas was working. But there is another context – a wider social and ecclesiastical context – which helps explain the particular method and style of teaching and of reading Sacred Scripture favoured by Aquinas and by his contemporaries. In the century prior to the birth of Thomas, the Church found itself confronted by a major doctrinal crisis. New, unorthodox movements, inspired by Gnostic and dualistic understandings of Sacred Scripture, had begun to flourish, and thousands of people were being drawn away from basic Catholic teaching and Catholic practice. In time, and not surprisingly, these movements were condemned by the hierarchy, but such condemnations, no matter how firm they were, or how insistent, made little or no impact. What was needed was some kind of spiritual and intellectual response from within the body of the Church. And the one group which, of course, possessed the resources for such a response were the many hundreds of men and women living in the monasteries at that time. But their chosen vocation was not to go out and preach the Gospel to the world, but rather to retreat from the world and, in a spirit of repentance and humility, to pray and intercede for their own and others' salvation.

In time, the challenge of the hour was met by the foundation of two new Orders, the Friars Preachers (the Dominicans) and the Franciscans. For the Dominicans, the most important task was not simply to contemplate the mysteries contained in Scripture, but first to contemplate, and then to pass on to others the fruits of contemplation. Thomas's basic desire, as an exegete, therefore, was to be of use to the Church of his time. He approached his

---

[19] James Weisheipl, 'Introduction' in *Commentary on the Gospel of St John* (Albany, NY 1980) pp. 5–6. For further reflection on the usefulness of thomistic exegesis for the reading of Scripture today, see Margherita Maria Rossi, 'L'Attenzione a Tommaso d'Aquino esegeta, *Angelicum*, vol. 76 (1999) pp. 73–104.

task from a perspective that was, in the phrase of Olivier-Thomas Venard, 'resolutely ecclesial'.[20] Scripture in its fullness, for Thomas, was not realized merely in a single moment of past history – at the time of Christ's Incarnation – but realized also, and in incarnate form, within his Body, the Church.[21] And the Church, as Venard points out, is always 'moving forward in history'.[22] Thomas's approach as an exegete, therefore, 'should find fruitful echoes with the exegetes of our time, who are rediscovering, *via* philosophical hermeneutics, the essentially communitarian character of the biblical canon and of biblical interpretation.'[23]

The particular brand of scholasticism and of biblical commentary practised by Aquinas arose within the framework of what was, we can say without exaggeration, 'an evangelical movement'.[24] Thomas belonged to a group of Friars Preachers who read Scripture in a way that was significantly different from the way the monks did. According to Nicholas M. Healy, 'The visible surface of the text, its "literal" sense, was regarded [by the monks] as of secondary importance compared with its invisible depths.'[25] The 'depths', of course, were by no means overlooked or ignored by the Friars Preachers. In fact, Albert the Great gave notable weight to the allegorical sense, as indeed did Aquinas. But St Thomas, and other friars after him, tended to give much greater importance to the literal and historical sense of Scripture. And, with unembarrassed enthusiasm, they chose to use logic and reason in their approach to the sacred text, the purpose being 'to raise difficulties and questions that, once resolved, would deepen understanding of the text', and also result in the end 'in better preaching of the Gospel'.[26]

The medieval commentators at that time – many friars and scholastics

---

[20] Olivier-Thomas Venard, 'Croire en savant: saint Thomas bibliste,' in *Thomistes ou de l'actualité de saint Thomas d'Aquin,* Serge-Thomas Bonino et al. (Toulouse 2003) p. 42.

[21] Ibid.

[22] Ibid.

[23] Ibid.

[24] See Otto Hermann Pesch, 'Paul as Professor of Theology: The Image of the Apostle in St Thomas's Theology', *The Thomist,* vol. 38 (July 1974) pp. 584–605. See also M.-D. Chenu, 'L'évangélisme de saint Thomas d'Aquin', *Revue de sciences philosophiques et théologiques,* vol. 58 (1974) pp. 391–403.

[25] Nicholas M. Healy, 'Introduction' in *Aquinas on Scripture: An Introduction to His Biblical Commentaries,* (eds), T. G. Weinandy, D. A. Keating, J. P. Yocum (London 2005) p. 7.

[26] Ibid., p. 9.

among them – with their new commitment to public proclamation of the Word, and a new dependence on logic and philosophy, had little or no hesitation in replacing the monastic way of reading with a more scientific exegesis. One scholar of the period, for example, Robert of Courçon, made bold to declare: 'Whoever reads Scripture publicly has undertaken a road to perfection superior to that of the Clairvaux monk.'[27] What, however, these commentators did not always realize was that their scientific approach, for all its thoroughness, risked overlooking the wonderful depth of wisdom and insight contained in monastic *lectio.*

In the Middle Ages, the intense focus within the monasteries on the *spiritual* meaning, or meanings, of Scripture was, in some considerable measure, inspired by the high spirituality of Neo-Platonism. The text of Scripture became largely an instrument for the contemplative journey, a crucial aid for the mystical ascent. Thomas Aquinas did not abandon outright this method or practice of Scripture reading. Far from it. But, being an attentive student of Aristotle, he modified it significantly in light of the alternative ontology proposed by the Philosopher. According to Nicholas Healy, in the work of Thomas and his contemporaries at this time, there was 'a demonstrably greater interest in the visible realities of the world.'[28] Ordinary tangible things, therefore, 'could now be understood as good and true and beautiful in themselves, without having to look to that of which they were merely the image.'[29]

Correspondingly, for readers such as Aquinas, 'the "surface" of the text of Scripture, its literal and historical meaning, was more readily accepted as the truthful witness to the revelation of the Word of God.'[30] This traditional and yet clearly new way of responding to Sacred Scripture was summarized by

---

[27] Robert of Courçon, *Summa*, in *Paris ms., Bibl. Nat. lat.* 14524, fol. 74r; cited in Chenu, *Toward Understanding Saint Thomas*, p. 237.

[28] Nicholas M. Healy, 'Introduction' in *Aquinas on Scripture: An Introduction to His Biblical Commentaries*, p. 8.

[29] Ibid.

[30] Ibid., pp. 8–9. This point should not be exaggerated. Aquinas, in his reading of the psalms, for example, remains clearly fascinated by the different levels of spiritual meaning in the text. In fact, so traditional and 'monastic' is his interpretation, on occasion, scholars were generally inclined to regard *Super Psalmos* as an early work of Aquinas.

Peter the Chanter in a text composed towards the end of the twelfth century. It is a passage which could well have been written by Aquinas himself:

> The practice of Bible study consists in three things: reading (*lectio*), disputation, and preaching ... Reading is, as it were, the foundation and basement for what follows, for through it the rest is achieved. Disputation is the wall in this building of study, for nothing is fully understood or faithfully preached, if it is not first chewed by the tooth of disputation. Preaching, which is supported by the former, is the roof, sheltering the faithful from the heat and wind of temptation. We should preach after, not before, the reading of Holy Scripture and the investigation of doubtful matters by disputation.[31]

For the modern reader it can sometimes be disconcerting to find, in Thomas's commentaries, the text of Scripture being chewed over so relentlessly by 'the tooth of disputation'. The text, as a result, can begin to appear fragmented: the living Word reduced to dry-as-dust formulations, and to a plethora of minute distinctions, divisions and sub-divisions. That said, however, the manifest shortcomings of Aquinas's method are happily outweighed, I believe, by his overall achievements as a biblical theologian and commentator.

What his method ably demonstrates – both in what he writes on Scripture and on philosophy – is what Kenelm Foster has named, in an illuminating passage, as Aquinas's 'power of active discrimination', his remarkable 'depth of mind':

> Where his mind seems most distinctively and outstandingly great is in its sense of proportion, in its tact. He leaves out nothing, he blurs nothing. Each facet of reality is isolated, focused, regarded and then *placed*; and once placed, it is henceforth related, rid of its isolation. Other thinkers have been orderly and unhurried, but surely none have so respected the tiniest fibres and connections in the order of life as they knew it; and even more than the active power to order, it is this respect for the factors in

---

[31] *Verbum abbreviatum*, PL, 205, col. 25; cited in Beryl Smalley, *The Study of the Bible in the Middle Ages*, p. 208.

the order that I call tact … In itself it may perhaps be best regarded here as the humility of a truly great intellect thoroughly accepting the human and therefore limited, more precisely the embodied, condition of our knowledge.[32]

*   *   *

That humility is much in evidence in Thomas's biblical commentaries and, with regard to prayer, two commentaries are of particular importance: Aquinas on Paul and Aquinas on the Psalms. The focus of attention in the chapter which follows (Chapter 4) will be on Thomas's understanding of prayer in general. A more specific question will be discussed in Chapter 5 namely Thomas's understanding of prayer in a time of grave need. The book of Psalms and St Paul's Epistles, these two biblical texts – one from the Old and one from the New Testament – occupy in St Thomas's understanding a unique place within the Church and within the Liturgy. He writes:

> Just as the most frequently used writings of the Old Testament in the Church are the psalms of David, who obtained pardon after his sin, likewise the most frequently used writings of the New Testament are the epistles of Paul, who obtained mercy so that, by these examples, sinners might be aroused to hope.[33]

What is impressive about this quotation is, first of all, the connection made between the two texts and the manifestly encouraging emphasis on pardon for the sinner. But also worthy of note is St Thomas's awareness of the unique importance afforded to both of these texts by the Church, the fact that the Epistles of Paul and the Psalms occur more often than any other texts of the Bible within the Sacred Liturgy.[34] That simple fact – the privileged role they

---

[32] Kenelm Foster, *God's Tree: Essays on Dante and Other Matters* (London 1957) pp. 148–9.

[33] Prologue, 6, *Super epistolas s. Pauli lectura*, Marietti edition (Rome 1953) p. 2.

[34] Thomas never composed an independent, autonomous treatise on the Liturgy, but the prayer of the Liturgy was fundamental in the shaping of his theological vision. Unfortunately, this fact was not generally recognized for many years – another instance, I would say, of the 'unknown Thomas'. For one of the most insightful acknowledgements of this dimension of St Thomas, see Liam G. Walsh, 'Liturgy in the Theology of St Thomas', *The Thomist* 38 (1974) pp. 557–83. See also David Berger, *Thomas Aquinas and the Liturgy*, trans., C. Grosz (Ann Arbor MI 2004); Matthew Levering, 'Aquinas on the

both enjoy within the solemn prayer of the Church – is one of the reasons why, in a study of St Thomas on prayer, I have thought it wise to give particular attention to his commentaries on these two unique texts.

Liturgy of the Eucharist', in *Aquinas on Doctrine: A Critical Introduction,* (ed.) Thomas G. Weinandy et al. (London 2004) pp. 183–97; Aidan Nichols, 'St Thomas and the Sacramental Liturgy', *The Thomist* 72 (2008) pp. 571–93.

4

Prayer in practice: Aquinas on St Paul

1. Introduction

Exactly when and where St Thomas lectured on the letters of St Paul has been a matter of considerable debate among scholars.[1] According to the report of William of Tocco: 'He wrote on all the epistles of Paul, which he valued above all writings, the Gospels alone excepted.'[2] This clear acknowledgement, in the thirteenth century, of the importance of the Apostle to the Gentiles for St Thomas has found an echo, I am happy to say, in the work of more than a few modern and contemporary scholars.[3] What has begun to emerge, since about the middle of the last century, is an increasing awareness that Thomas's commentaries on the Pauline letters are 'major works of his

---

[1] It used to be generally believed that there were two separate teachings of St Thomas on the Pauline corpus. In the light, however, of the complete manuscript tradition, that particular view has been shown by Robert Wielockx to be mistaken. See Wielockx, 'Au sujet du commentaire de Saint Thomas sur le "Corpus Paulinum" Critique Littéraire,' *Doctor Communis* (2009): L'Interpretazione di San Tommaso delle Dottrine di San Paolo' (Proceedings of the IX Plenary Session, 19-21 June 2009) pp. 150–77.

[2] William of Tocco, *Vita s. Thomae Aquinatis*, 17; translation in K. Foster (ed.) *The Life of St Thomas Aquinas: Biographical Documents* (London 1959) p. 70.

[3] See, for example, the impressive collection of papers, in 'L'Interpretazione di San Tommaso delle Dottrine di San Paolo,' *Doctor Communis* (2009). See also *Aquinas on Scripture*, published in 2005, and edited by Weinandy et al. Five of the eight papers are devoted to the Pauline epistles.

theology'.[4] M.-D. Chenu, in his book *Toward Understanding Saint Thomas*, remarked:

> The case of this commentary is more complex and more important all the while, not only because the text of it alone represents a third of all the exegetical writings of Saint Thomas, but especially because it deals with the book of Scripture that, by its subject matter, is the most propitious to theological exegesis.[5]

Ceslaus Spicq, writing in the *Dictionnaire de théologie catholique*, went even further declaring that what we find 'in the commentaries of St Thomas on St John, and especially on St Paul, is the most mature fruit and the most perfect realization of scholastic medieval exegesis'.[6]

2. Introducing Paul the Apostle

Aquinas, in the impressive 'Prologue' to his commentary on Romans, a text which serves to introduce all his commentaries on St Paul, quotes from Acts 9.15: *This man is to me a chosen vessel to carry my name before the Gentiles and kings and the sons of Israel.*[7] This sentence, though brief, provides Thomas with an opportunity to ring the changes on all the possible meanings of the word 'vessel' when applied to Paul. The character of a vessel, he notes, is known by the sort of things which it pours out. And St Paul poured out wisdom in abundance. 'He was a golden vessel,' Thomas writes, 'on account of the brilliance of [his] wisdom.'[8] He 'taught the mysteries of the most exalted divinity, which belongs to wisdom.'[9] And, among all the writings of the New

---

[4] See I.-M. Vosté, 'Sanctus Thomas Aquinas epistularum s. Pauli interpres', *Angelicum* 19 (1942) p. 276.
[5] M.-D. Chenu, *Toward Understanding Saint Thomas*, trans., A.-M. Landry and D. Hughes (Chicago 1964) p. 248.
[6] Ceslaus Spicq, 'Saint Thomas d'Aquin exégète', *Dictionnaire de théologie catholique*, vol. 14 (Paris 1946) 694–738.
[7] Prologue, *Super epistolam ad Romanos lectura*, in *Super epistolas s. Pauli lectura*, vol. 1, Marietti edition (Turin 1953) p. 1.
[8] Ibid, p. 1:1.
[9] Ibid., p. 1:2.

Testament, his writings are 'the most frequently used' by the Church since, in them, 'is contained almost the whole teaching of theology.'[10]

> It is customary for vessels to be filled with some sort of liquid ... for some are wine vessels, some oil vessels, and are of diverse kinds. In the same way, God fills human beings with diverse graces, as if with diverse liquids: *To some is given through the Spirit the utterance of wisdom and to others the utterance of knowledge according to the same Spirit* (I Cor. 12.8). But the vessel about which we are now speaking was filled with a precious liquid, namely the name of Christ of which it is said: *Your name is oil poured out* (Song of Songs 1.2). Hence our text says *to carry my name*, for he seems to have been completely filled with this name, in accord with Apocalypse 3.12: *I will write my name upon him.* For he possessed this name in the knowledge of his intellect: *For I decided not to know anything among you except Christ* (I Cor. 2.2). He also possessed this name in the love of his affection: *Who will separate us from the love of Christ?* (Rom. 8.35); *If anyone does not love our Lord Jesus Christ, let him be accursed* (I Cor. 16.22). Also, he possessed it in his whole way of life. Hence he said: *I live now not I, but Christ lives in me* (Gal. 2.20).[11]

William of Tocco tells us that Thomas 'had a special devotion (*specialem devotionem*) to the blessed Apostle Paul.'[12] To him, St Paul did not represent merely a wisdom inherited from another age, a theology handed down like a great stone monument from the distant past. No, St Paul's epistles were living wisdom. And Paul himself – a saint belonging to the communion of saints – was a living presence, someone to whom direct appeal could be made in the search for truth and enlightenment.

That fact offers a key which helps, in some way, to explain the remarkable story, reported by William of Tocco and others, concerning a vision Thomas had of St Paul when, on one occasion, he was struggling to understand

---

[10] Ibid., p. 2:6.

[11] Ibid., pp. 1–2:3.

[12] William of Tocco, *Ystoria sancti Thomae de Aquino*, 60, (ed.) Claire le Brun-Gouanvic (Toronto 1996) p. 200.

a particularly difficult text of Isaiah. His secretary, Reginald of Piperno, knowing that something unusual had taken place, begged Thomas to speak of it. But Thomas, in the report according to Tocco, was reluctant to say even a single word. Being asked, however, and insistently by his Dominican confrère, he finally relented, and shared his secret with Reginald:

> Son, you have seen in these days my affliction regarding the doubt I had concerning that text I have been [trying] in some way to interpret. I asked God with many tears to enlighten me. Tonight God had compassion on me. He sent me his blessed Apostles Peter and Paul, whose intercession I had begged, and they taught me everything I needed to know.[13]

As a medieval exegete, Aquinas was accustomed to bringing to the text of Scripture a number of scholastic questions which, if put to St Paul himself, would certainly have surprised the Apostle. It was presumed, for example, by Thomas that the fourteen epistles of Paul represented a kind of doctrinal tract on the grace of Christ. The letters were regarded, therefore, not so much as a series of spontaneous responses, on the part of Paul, to different crises and challenges in the communities he had founded, but rather as a deliberately planned exposition on a single aspect of Christian doctrine. 'And thus the division and order of all the epistles,' Thomas writes, 'is clear.'[14]

That clarity, however, with regard to division and order, was more distinct in the mind of Thomas, the scholastic, than in the text itself – the letters of St Paul being not only made to yield to an Aristotelean logic throughout,

---

[13] William of Tocco, *Ystoria*, 31, p. 159. Tocco reports elsewhere that, when Thomas was in Paris, working on the epistles of Paul, he 'had a vision of the Apostle himself', *Ystoria*, 17, p. 131. And, in an another vision, also reported by Tocco, a Dominican friar, on the day Thomas died, saw the Apostle Paul enter into the classroom where Thomas was lecturing on the Pauline Letters. After a brief exchange between the two men, and after Thomas had been complimented on his understanding of the letters, and been assured that he would have an even greater understanding in the next life, the Apostle took hold of Thomas's cappa and began, to the consternation of the students present, to draw him out of the lecture hall! See Tocco, *Ystoria*, 60, p. 200.

[14] Prologue, 11, *Super epistolam ad Romanos lectura*, in *Super epistolas s. Pauli*, vol. 1, p. 3. In his commentary on Galatians 2: 19–20, Thomas writes: 'It should be noted that the Apostle proceeds by a manner of inquiry, and leaves no doubt un-discussed. Although his words may appear complex, nevertheless, if they are carefully considered, he says nothing without a purpose.' *Super epistolam ad Galatas lectura*, ch. 2, lect 6, 102, in *Super epistolas s. Pauli*, vol. 1, p. 587.

but even scrutinized on occasion for evidence of hidden syllogisms within the text.[15] Decades earlier, with an unembarrassed confidence, the medieval author, Honorius of Autun, had declared: 'Syllogisms lie hidden in Sacred Scripture just like fish in deep water. And just as a fish is drawn from water to be used by us, so a syllogism is said to be extracted from Scripture for its usefulness.'[16]

Needless to say many challenges remain today in coming to terms with the analytic style and rigid procedure of this kind of medieval exegesis. That said, however, Thomas's work more than repays close and devoted attention. There is no theologian more determined to extract from the sacred text its full doctrinal depth and meaning. And, as one commentator has observed, 'He makes many shrewd and penetrating remarks in these pages, and these alone are well worth the trouble of their discovery. The combination of the Apostle to the Gentiles and the Angel of the Schools is not one lightly to be dismissed.'[17]

3. Prayer in St Paul and St Thomas

Prayer, as one would expect, is a subject addressed by Thomas a number of times in his commentaries on the Pauline Epistles. But, unless I'm mistaken, the subject has not so far attracted significant attention from scholars. No single book or article has appeared on the subject. Fortunately, however, what we do have already are a number of helpful studies which treat the general subject of prayer in St Thomas's work.[18] And what emerges from these studies

---

[15] Concerning one text, for example, Romans 8: 5–6, Thomas writes: '[Paul] introduces two syllogisms … First, he posits the minor premise of the first syllogism … Second, he posits the minor premise of the second syllogism … Third, he posits the major premise of the first syllogism', *Super epistolam ad Romanos lectura*, ch. 8, lect. 1, 614–17, in *Super epistolas s. Pauli lectura*, vol. 1, p. 112.

[16] Honorius of Autun, Psalm 1, *Expositio in psalmos selectos*, P. L. 172, col.279 C.

[17] Richard T. A. Murphy, 'Introduction', in *Commentary on Saint Paul's Epistle to the Galatians by St Thomas Aquinas* (New York 1966) p. x.

[18] For Thomas on prayer, see Lydia Maidl, *Desiderii interpres: Genese und Grundstruktur der Gebetstheologie des Thomas von Aquin* (Paderborn 1994); Simon Tugwell, *Albert and Thomas: Selected Writings* (New York 1998) pp. 271–86, 361–523; Tugwell, 'Humpty Dumpty and Thomas Aquinas', in Brian Davies, *Language, Meaning, and God* (London 1987) pp. 24–50; Jean-Pierre Torrell, *Saint*

is that few themes attracted the attention of St Thomas so much as that of prayer. Simon Tugwell writes: 'Thomas returned to the subject of prayer over and over again in the course of his writings; it seems to have been a subject that interested him, and it is certainly a subject on which he achieved a degree of clarity it would be hard to parallel in any other theologian.'[19]

The different words Paul uses, the various ways he speaks about prayer, are not only alluded to by St Thomas in his commentaries, they are also, on occasion, noted down and ordered with an almost exaggerated clarity and precision in the form of numbered lists, a style or method of analysis often favoured by scholastic theologians. In his commentary on Ephesians (6. 18-19), for example, he speaks of no less than seven conditions for authentic prayer. Prayer, he declares, should be 'complete … humble … continual … devout … vigilant … insistent … [and] loving.'[20] And, in his commentary on I Timothy (2.1), echoing Paul, he suggests that all prayer can be divided into four parts: 'entreaties, prayers, pleas and thanksgiving.'[21] In his commentary on Colossians (4.1), Thomas speaks of three distinct characteristics of prayer. It should, he says, be 'assiduous, grateful and vigilant.'[22] Finally, in his commentary on Philippians (4.1), he notes that there are 'four things required in every prayer': first, he says: 'prayer implies the [humble] ascent of the mind to God'; second, 'it should be accompanied by confidence'; third, by 'thanksgiving'; and, fourth, he adds at the end: 'prayer is a petition.'[23]

I will not attempt here to discuss the meaning St Thomas gives to each of these different words when reflecting on St Paul. My intention instead is to

---

Thomas d'Aquin, maître spiritual (Fribourg 1996) vol. 2, pp. 440–7; Servais Pinckaers, *La Prière chretienne* (Fribourg 1989) pp. 121–312; Thomas F. Ryan, *Thomas Aquinas as Reader of the Psalms* (Notre Dame, Indiana, 2000) pp. 61–144; Mary Ann Fatula, *Thomas Aquinas: Preacher and Friend* (Collegeville MN, 1993) pp. 128–53.

[19] Here are a few of the places in his work (apart from the Pauline commentaries) where St Thomas speaks on prayer: *Scriptum super Libros Sententiarum*, dist. 15, question 4; *Contra Gentiles*, Bk 3, chapters 95–6; *De Veritate*, question 6, article 6; *In Orationem Dominum: Commentary on St John's Gospel*, 16:23; *Lectures on Matthew*, 6: 5–15; *Compendium theologiae*, 2: 1–10; *Summa theologiae*, II II q.83.

[20] *Super epistolam ad Ephesios lectura*, ch. 6, lect. 5, 369, in *Super epistolas*, vol. 2, p. 86.

[21] *Super primam epistolam ad Timotheum lectura*, ch. 2, lect. 1, 56, in *Super epistolas*, vol. 2, p. 223.

[22] *Super epistolam ad Colossenses lectura*, ch. 4, lect. 1, 183, in *Super epistolas s. Pauli lectura*, vol. 2, p. 159.

[23] *Super epistolam ad Philippenses lectura*, ch. 4, lect. 1, 157, in *Super epistolas*, vol. 2, p. 119.

explore his general thinking on the subject, and to consider prayer under the rubric of two of the names for prayer which we find repeated in his Pauline commentaries and which are, in some way, inclusive of the others: namely, petition and thanksgiving.

(1) Petition: The Prayer of Asking

At the time St Thomas was writing there was probably no aspect of prayer so undervalued as the prayer of petition. It had somehow come to be regarded by theologians and spiritual authors as almost the poorest cousin within the family of prayer. And it was St Thomas, uniquely in his generation, who took up the challenge of somehow restoring Gospel centrality and importance to this prayer of asking.[24] Thomas's most considered reflection on the subject can be found in the *Summa theologiae,* but also of undoubted interest are a number of the things he says in his commentaries on Paul.

(i) Praying in the Spirit

One point on which Thomas insists again and again is that prayer is nothing other than 'an expression of desire'. He writes: 'When I desire something then I ask for it by praying.'[25] Nothing, it seems, could be more simple, more straightforward. And yet the very simplicity of Christian prayer, as Thomas understands it, hides within it a depth of meaning and mystery for which there are almost no words. When, for example, a prayer of petition or of thanksgiving rises up from the depth of the human heart, that prayer, according to St Thomas, is moved by an impulse, a desire, much greater than our own human desire. He writes: 'The Holy Spirit makes us plead inasmuch as he causes right desires in us. Pleading is a certain unfolding of our desires, and right desires arise from the ardour of love, and this is produced in us by the Holy Spirit.'[26]

Again, commenting on the phrase 'my spirit prays', in 1 Corinthians 14.14,

---

[24] See Tugwell, *Albert and Thomas*, p. 275. The story of Thomas's progress in coming to this conviction is helpfully described by Tugwell in *Albert and Thomas*, pp. 275–8.

[25] *Super priman epistolam ad Thessalonicenses lectura*, ch. 5, lect. 2, 130, vol. 2, p. 189.

[26] *Super epistolam ad Romanos lectura*, ch. 8, lect. 5, 693, in *Super epistolas s. Pauli*, vol. 1, p. 124.

Thomas writes: 'the Holy Spirit who is given to me "prays", inclining me and moving me to prayer. Nevertheless I merit in that prayer, because the very fact that I am moved by the Holy Spirit is a merit for me.'[27] Given the manifest intimacy with God suggested by these bold statements of faith, it comes as no surprise to hear St Thomas make the following confident declaration:

> When we pray to God the very prayer we send forth makes us intimate with him, inasmuch as our soul is raised up to God, converses with him in spiritual affection, and adores him in spirit and truth. This affectionate intimacy, experienced in prayer, prepares a way to return to prayer with even greater confidence.[28]

(ii) Questions about petition

In his commentary on Romans, Thomas speaks of the Spirit pleading and interceding within us 'with unutterable groans'.[29] Paul's text reads: *The Spirit helps us in our weakness, for we do not know what to pray for as we ought, but the Spirit himself pleads for us with unutterable groans* (Rom. 8.26). In general, Thomas says, we know very well, of course, what to pray for but, with regard to specific cases, 'we cannot discern exactly each particular motion of our heart, whether for example we are asking for such and such a thing out of anger or out of zeal for righteousness.'[30]

St Paul, on one occasion, famously pleaded with God to have the 'sting in his flesh' removed. Whether it was temptation or another kind of difficulty, God did not remove it. According to Thomas, 'Someone may desire to be

---

[27] *Super primam epistolam ad Corinthios lectura*, ch. 14, lect. 3, 838, in *Super epistolas s. Pauli*, vol. 1, p. 395. On the subject of the divine indwelling, Daniel A. Keating notes that Aquinas has on occasion been 'faulted for having an instrumental doctrine of grace that minimizes the indwelling of God through the Holy Spirit.' A text like the *Summa* may well be vulnerable to that kind of criticism, but certainly not the biblical commentaries. For, in them, we find 'a rich account of the Christian as temple of the living God and of the indwelling Spirit producing in us all the fruits of faith and love.' See Keating, 'Aquinas on 1 and 2 Corinthians: The Sacraments and Their Ministers,' in *Aquinas on Scripture*, p. 141.
[28] *Compendium theologiae*, 2, [*De spe*] ch. 2, in *Sancti Thomae de Aquino opera Omnia*, Leonine vol. 42, p. 194.
[29] *Super epistolam ad Romanos lectura*, ch. 8, lect. 5, 692, in *Super epistolas s. Pauli*, vol. 1, p. 124.
[30] Ibid., ch. 8, lect. 5, 691, p. 124.

freed from the harassment of some temptation, when in fact that temptation is serving to preserve humility.[31] Such, apparently, was the case with Paul. The quasi-divine knowledge of God he had received, while rapt up into the third heaven in ecstasy, was so great he was given, Thomas tells us, a sting or thorn in his flesh 'to prevent the greatness of his revelations making him conceited, as it says in 2 Corinthians 12.7.'[32]

That particular text from 2 Corinthians about Paul's urgent prayer of petition is discussed by Thomas at much greater length in his commentary on the Letter to the Corinthians. The 'thorn', he declares, was 'a messenger of Satan', and yet God clearly permitted it: 'Satan's intention is to subvert, but God's is to humble and to render approval.'[33] At this point in his reflections Thomas assumes, all of a sudden, the mantle of the preacher, declaring with an unexpected force and alacrity: 'If the Apostle and vessel of election was not secure, let the sinner beware!'[34] Then, continuing further with the question of St Paul's thorn in the flesh, he writes:

A thorn in the flesh, considered in itself, is something to be avoided as troublesome, but inasmuch as it is a means to virtue and the exercise of virtue, it should be desired. But because that secret of divine providence – that it would turn out to his advantage – had not yet been revealed to him, the Apostle considered that, in itself, it was bad for him. But God, who had ordained this to the good of his humility, did not oblige him as to his wish. Once, however, he understood its purpose, the Apostle gloried in it, saying, *I will all the more gladly boast of my weaknesses, that the power of Christ may dwell in me.* And although [God] did not oblige him as to his wish, yet he heard him and does hear his saints to their advantage. Hence, Jerome says in the Letter to Paulinus: 'The good Lord frequently does not grant what we wish, in order to bestow what we should prefer.'[35]

---

[31] Ibid., 690. *See Albert and Thomas*, p. 521.

[32] Ibid.

[33] *Super secundum epistolam ad Corinthios lectura*, ch. 12, lect. 3, 474, in *Super epistolas s. Pauli*, vol. 1, p. 546.

[34] Ibid.

[35] Ibid., 478, p. 547.

The reason for all this, Thomas declares, citing Paul once again, is that God's power is 'made perfect in weakness', a revelation about moral and spiritual development which Thomas clearly finds worthy of note. He writes: 'This is a remarkable way of speaking – *Mirus modus loquendi* – virtue is made perfect in weakness.'[36] And then, as if to underline further the shock of the paradox, he adds, 'fire grows in water' (*ignis in aqua crescit*), an image, a phrase, more obviously revealing of the poet in Thomas than the preacher.

* * *

When Thomas is commenting on St Paul he does not hesitate, on occasion, to bring to the biblical text questions and preoccupations of his own which, though they may have considerable importance in themselves, are not, it would seem, of great or immediate concern to the Apostle. Regarding the subject of petition, for example, when St Paul, in his letter to the Philippians, declares: *let your requests be made known to God* (Phil. 4.6), Thomas responds by asking a rather blunt question: 'Does not the Lord know them?' In other words, if God already knows our requests, why bother to inform him? To this question, Thomas offers the following explanation:

First, *let them be made known,* i.e., approved before God, and be seen as worthy and holy: *Let my prayer* be brought up *as incense in your sight.* (Ps. 141.2)

Or, *let them be made known* to ourselves, that is let us recognize that they [our prayers] are always with God. As if to say: Do not pray to win favour with people. *But when you pray, go into your room and shut the door and pray to your Father who is in secret; and your Father who sees in secret will reward you.* (Mt. 6.6)

Or, *let them be made known* to those who are with God, i.e., the angels, through whose ministry they are brought to God; not because [God] is unaware of them, but because they intercede for us: *The smoke of incense*

---

[36] Ibid., 479.

rose with the prayers of the saints from the hand of the angel before God. (Rev. 8.4)[37]

Another question about the prayer of petition much discussed by Thomas in the *Summa,* and elsewhere, concerns the actual intention of petition. Are we, when making our requests, somehow expecting to change the mind of God? God, by his very nature, is eternal and unchangeable, so what then is the point of petition? In his commentary on I Timothy, St Thomas writes: 'In the case of our speeches to God, we are not aiming to change God's mind, because he is always ready for anything good; our purpose is that our own hearts should be raised to God in prayer.'[38] A similar point is made by Thomas in his commentary on Colossians:

> Praying is the ascent of the mind to God. Asking is requesting things. Praying should come first, so that the one devoutly asking is heard, just as those who are requesting something begin by trying to persuade their listener and bend him to their wishes. But we should begin with devotion and meditation on God and divine things, not in order to bend him, but to lift ourselves up to him.[39]

(iii) Humility and prayer

One of the characteristics of authentic prayer on which both St Paul and St Thomas insist again and again is humility. 'Prayer,' Thomas writes, 'must be

---

[37] *Super epistolam ad Philippenses lectura,* ch. 4, lect. 1, 158, in *Super epistolas,* vol. 2, p. 119.

[38] *Super primam epistolam ad Timotheum lectura,* ch. 2, lect. 1, 56, in *Super epistolas,* vol. 2, p. 223. See 'Lecture on 1 Timothy 2:1,' in *Albert and Thomas,* p. 438. It might appear that petitionary prayer achieves little or nothing in terms of actual effects. But St Thomas, elsewhere in his work, makes it clear that we are, in fact, given the 'dignity of causality'. On this matter Simon Tugwell writes: 'prayer, precisely as petition, can be seen as playing a fully authentic role in the working out of events in the world; it does make a difference to what happens ... God moves our desire, which prompts our prayer, and God carries the whole process through to the fulfilment of our desires.' See Tugwell, 'Humpty Dumpty and Thomas Aquinas', in Brian Davies, *Language, Meaning, and God* (London 1987) p. 46.

[39] *Super epistolam ad Colossenses lectura,* ch. 1, lect. 3, 18, in *Super epistolas s. Pauli lectura,* vol. 2, p. 130. On the question of petitionary prayer, Herbert McCabe writes: 'We must keep this firmly in mind: it is God who prays. Not just God who answers prayer but God who prays in us in the first place. It is when we forget this that we get tangled up about petitionary prayer ... My prayer is not me putting pressure on God, doing something to God, it is God doing something for me, raising me into the divine life or intensifying the divine life in me.' See *God Matters* (London 2000) pp. 221–2.

humble and not presumptuous. *He has had regard to the prayer of the humble, and has not despised their petition* (Ps. 101.18).[40] Prayer is humble when we do not imagine that we will be heard on account of our own merits, but because of the divine mercy.[41] A similar point is made by Thomas when he comments on the following brief statement of Paul to the Philippians: *in everything by prayer and supplication with thanksgiving let your requests be made known to God* (Phil. 4.6). The word 'supplication' here indicates, he notes, 'an appeal to God's grace and holiness; it is the prayer, therefore, of someone humbling himself.'[42] That said, however, although prayer should indeed be humble at all times, it should not be in any way mealy-mouthed. 'It should,' Thomas says, 'be accompanied by confidence of obtaining, and this from God's mercy. *We do not cast our prayers before your face on the basis of our own justification, but on account of your many mercies* (Dan. 9.18).'[43]

Paul, when praying for the Ephesians, employs at one point a rather striking image: *For this cause*, he writes, *I bow my knees to the Father of our Lord Jesus Christ* (Eph. 3.14). Reflecting on this gesture or 'symbol of humility', Thomas writes:

> Physical strength is present in the knees. By bending them a man confesses openly to his lack of strength. Thus external, physical symbols are shown to God for the purpose of renewing and spiritually training the inner soul. This is expressed in the prayer of Manasse: *I bend the knee of my heart.*[44]

(iv) Prayer and charity

Another characteristic of authentic prayer on which both Paul and Thomas insist is that it should be 'charitable',[45] concerned in other words with the needs of others. At root, prayer is, of course, something intimate and personal. But it should not, Thomas insists, be restricted to a concern for one's own good or

---

[40] *Super epistolam ad Ephesios lectura*, ch. 6, lect. 5, 369, in *Super epistolas*, vol. 2, p. 86.
[41] Ibid.
[42] *Super epistolam ad Philippenses lectura*, ch. 4. Lect. 1, 157, in *Super epistolas*, vol. 2, p. 119.
[43] Ibid.
[44] *Super epistolam ad Ephesios lectura*, ch. 3, lect. 4, 166, in *Super epistolas*, vol. 2, p. 42.
[45] Ibid., ch. 6, lect. 5, 369, p. 86.

for one's own salvation.[46] It should be expansive and generous in its concern for other people. And that's why Paul, when writing to Timothy, exclaims: *I desire, first of all, that entreaties, prayers, pleas and thanksgivings be made for everybody* (Tim. 2.1). Thomas, commenting on this passage, remarks:

> When Paul says, 'for everybody', he shows for whom we should pray … And he says that we should pray for everybody. The reason for this is that prayer is the interpreter of our desire since, in praying, we ask for what we desire. And charity requires that we should desire good for all the people to whom our charity extends. *Pray for one another, that you may be saved.* (James 5.16).[47]

Paul has great confidence that when people in the various churches pray for him, he will be aided by their prayers. To the Philippians, on one occasion, he wrote: *I know that, through your prayers and the help of the Spirit of Jesus Christ, this will turn out for my deliverance* (Phil. 1.19). But, while being concerned for his own individual salvation, Paul is also concerned that his work as a preacher be effective in the lives of others. Thomas, commenting on a passage in Ephesians where Paul asks for prayers, writes:

> He asks three things for himself which are necessary for any preacher, namely that his mouth would be opened, that he would prepare himself as much as he can for preaching, and that grace be given him … And for what, Paul? He answers, that I may *with confidence make known the mystery of the gospel, for which I am an ambassador in a chain* … The Apostle does not merely ask that the word or knowledge of preaching be given him. He also prays for the grace of speaking with confidence so that … he might confidently and faithfully fulfill the duty entrusted to him, and begun by him. Third, he asks that suitable time and manner be granted him … Among

---

[46] Preaching, on one occasion, Thomas remarked: 'There are some who want to be dedicated to God, and who pay no heed to the salvation of their neighbours. But the Holy Spirit is not like that. The Apostle Paul was seriously concerned about the salvation of his neighbours, whence he said: *I have been made all things for all people in order to enlighten all*.' Sermon 11: *Emitte Spiritum*. Text by L.-J. Bataillon (Provisional Leonine version). See *Thomas Aquinas: The Academic Sermons* (*The Fathers of the Church: Medieval Continuation*) p. 143.

[47] *Super primam epistolam ad Timotheum lectura*, ch. 2, lect. 1, 57–8, in *Super epistolas*, vol. 2, p. 224.

all people, it is clearly one's manner and quality [of speaking] which make something acceptable. And the Apostle also asked for this in Colossians 4.4: *That I may make manifest what it is I ought to say.* As Proverbs 15.23 expresses it: *A word in due time is best.*[48]

When Paul prays for his brothers and sisters in the faith, he does not pray in a merely ritual or detached manner. No, he prays with great earnestness. In his letter to the Philippians, for example, he speaks openly at one point about the intensity of desire which accompanies and underpins his prayer. On this matter, St Thomas comments: 'Since the desire of the heart is known to God alone, [Paul] calls on God to witness that he prays for them with desire.'[49] Then, as the passage moves forward, St Thomas begins not simply to paraphrase but, at a certain point, actually to extend the message of St Paul. And that is not, I think, without significance. For here, behind the words of the text, we can sense, if I'm not mistaken, something of Thomas's own passion, as a friar preacher, to communicate to others the profound sense of liberation and wonder he experiences in knowing Christ Jesus. Thus, in reflecting on Paul's eloquent phrase, 'How I long for you', Thomas writes:

> *How I long for you,* that is, I, living in the very heart [literally, 'in the entrails'] of Christ Jesus. Or, how I long for you to be in that heart; as if to say: How I long after your salvation and participation in the very core of the charity of Christ. Lk 1.78: 'For out of the innermost depths [literally 'the entrails'] of the mercy of God, He has visited us like the dawn from on high'; as if to say that the power of love reaches down to the most profound and intimate depths of the heart. Or, I long for you to be in the very heart [literally 'in the entrails'] of Christ Jesus, that is, in order that you may love him intimately, and that you may be loved by him; for human life consists in this.[50]

The passage is remarkable. Prompted by a single, brief phrase from Paul's text, the lines bear witness, and with telling force and beauty, to both the apostolic

---

[48] *Super epistolam ad Ephesios lectura,* ch. 6, lect. 5, 370–2, in *Super epistolas,* vol. 2, pp. 86–7.
[49] *Super epistolam ad Philippenses lectura,* ch. 1, lect. 2, 15, in *Super epistolas,* vol. 2, p. 93.
[50] Ibid.

and contemplative energy and passion of St Thomas. The man of Aquino was, of course, a brilliant intellectual, but what tends to be forgotten is his vocation as a preacher. He was a servant of the Gospel, first and last, a servant of the truth *in that sense,* and not a mere speculative genius, not a man living remote from apostolic concerns. If the passion of St Thomas's life was a search for wisdom, it was never that of an imperturbable academic, indifferent to the world around him, but a search rather for the 'saving wisdom' possessed by St Paul.[51] Such wisdom is attentive to the needs of others, concerned to strengthen, for example, those who may be faltering in their faith 'just as a workman will buttress a building against a fall.'[52] To Paul, the preacher, Thomas applies these great words from Job: 'Your words have strengthened those who were staggering' (Job 4.4).[53]

Thomas Aquinas was an academic all his life, but he was also continuously preaching. And a considerable number of his sermons have survived.[54] Bernard Gui, his early biographer, writes: 'In Rome once, in Holy Week, Thomas preached on the Passion of our Lord, moving his hearers to tears; and the next day, preaching on the Resurrection, he roused them wonderfully to joy in the Lord.'[55] From this account, it's obvious that Thomas knew very well how to adapt his preaching to suit his audience, a point emphasized in the *Vita* by Bernard Gui: 'To the ordinary faithful he spoke the word of God with singular grace and power, without indulging in far-fetched reasoning … Subtleties he kept for the Schools.'[56]

A comment included in a sermon delivered in the summer of 1269 makes clear the respect Thomas had for 'ordinary' believers, those men and women who had never received any kind of philosophical or theological education in

---

[51] Prologue, 1, *Super epistolam ad Ephesios lectura,* in *Super epistolas,* vol. 2, p. 1.

[52] Ibid.

[53] Ibid.

[54] See *Thomas Aquinas: The Academic Sermons,* trans., Mark-Robin Hoogland, in *The Fathers of the Church: Medieval Contribution,* vol. 2 (Washington, DC 2010), and *Saint Thomas d'Aquin: Sermons,* trans., Jacques Ménard (Paris 2004).

[55] Bernard Gui, *Vita s. Thomae Aquinatis,* 29, in *Fontes vitae s. Thomae Aquinatis,* (ed.) D. Prümer (Toulouse 1911) p. 195. See also *The Life of St Thomas Aquinas: Biographical Documents,* (ed.) K. Foster (London 1959) p. 48.

[56] Ibid., *Fontes vitae,* 29, p. 195; Foster, p. 47.

the Schools, but whose faith was both strong and deep. With bright, unmistakable conviction, Thomas declares to the assembled scholars: 'A little old
woman (*vetula*) knows more about these matters of faith than all the philosophers of old'![57] In similar vein, he writes in the *Summa*: 'Those who seem
simple, through lack of worldly cunning, can be prudent. Matthew 10:16: *Be
prudent as serpents and simple as doves.*'[58]

Thomas is obviously willing, and more than willing, to acknowledge the
wisdom possessed by many of the non-academic men and women among his
contemporaries. But, while doing that, he never intends to denigrate in any
way the vital task of *thinking* about the faith, the task of learning. He respects
but never romanticizes simple piety. One clear illustration of this attitude is
in the treatise *Contra impugnantes Dei* where Thomas has no hesitation in
declaring: 'the learning of the saints is preferable to the simplicity of the pious'
(*sanctorum scientia praefertur simplicium sanctitati*)![59]

St Thomas, as preacher and academic, devoted his entire life to building-
up, in spirit and truth, the men and women of his generation. 'His goodness
to others,' Gui tell us, 'had a sort of quick spontaneous alacrity which in a
way paralleled the divine outpouring of his doctrine.'[60] How bizarre, then, to
come upon a statement such as the following from the historian F. J. E. Raby:
'[Thomas] lived for philosophy which he prized as a higher occupation than
the care of souls.'[61] Nothing, of course, could be further from the truth. Since
Thomas was, first and last, a friar-preacher, it was the *evangelical* dimension
of his life that gave momentum and direction to his work as an academic. It's
no surprise, therefore, to find Thomas on occasion going deliberately out of
his way to praise the task of preaching. In his Commentary on Ephesians, for
example, he speaks of its 'prominence and grandeur' (*excellentia et altitudine*),
a tribute which springs not so much from the actual message of Paul, at this
point in the letter, but rather from Thomas's very particular enthusiasm for

---

[57] Sermon: *Attendite a falsis*, 083 RSR no. 2, ps2, in Busa vol. 6, p. 35.
[58] *ST*, I II q.58, a.4, ad 2.
[59] *Contra impugnantes Dei cultum et religionem*, ch. 11, 6, in *Opera Omnia*, Leonine vol. 41, A 132.
[60] Ibid., *Fontes vitae*, 33, p. 199; Foster p. 51.
[61] F. J. E. Raby, *A History of Christian-Latin Poetry: From the Beginnings to the Close of the Middle Ages*
(Oxford 1927) p. 403.

the task of preaching. Paul's own immediate preoccupation here, and what he most desires to communicate, is simply his need for confidence so that he might be able to proclaim 'the mystery of the gospel'.[62]

(v) The nearness of God

When in their writings and talks, the subject of prayer comes up for discussion, Dominican preachers, both ancient and modern, are inclined to say that 'prayer is such an easy job'.[63] In large part, this perception is based on the fact that a humble prayer of petition – namely the 'Our Father' – was the prayer given by Christ to his disciples when they asked him how to pray. This prayer, the *Pater Noster*, St Thomas describes as 'the most perfect of all prayers'.[64] And the fact that it is nothing other than a simple prayer of petition was no doubt a key factor in helping Thomas to come to the conviction that the humble prayer of asking is almost the definition of prayer itself. Prayer, in the life of the Christian should, therefore, be as natural as breathing. But if that's in fact the case, why then is prayer experienced so often as an unusually difficult task?

In the opinion of Thomas the problem, at root, is a lack of confidence. As human beings we sometimes find it hard to believe that God really cares for us, or that God wants to come close to us. And our scepticism on the subject is strengthened by the fact that God can appear remote at times, even indifferent. 'But,' Thomas declares, 'the Apostle Paul, preaching to the Athenians, showed the contrary, saying (Acts 17.17-28): *He is not far from each one of us for, in him, we live, move, and exist.*[65] Since we are inclined to lack confidence in God's love, and in God's willingness to hear and answer our prayers, we sometimes approach the task of prayer with a feeling of anxiety. But, Thomas

---

[62] *Super epistolam ad Ephesios lectura*, ch. 6, lect. 5, 371, in *Super epistolas*, vol. 2, p. 86.

[63] See, for example, William Peraldus, *Sermon on Prayer*, in S. Tugwell, *Early Dominicans: Selected Writings* (New York 1982) p. 167. In modern times the Dominican Vincent McNabb declared: 'Prayer is almost the easiest thing in the world'. See *Prayer – How Easy It Is*, in *The Craft of Prayer* (London 1935) p. 64.

[64] *ST*, q.83, a.9. For further information about St Thomas's reflections on the Our Father, see Paul Murray, *Praying with Confidence: Aquinas on the Lord's Prayer* (London 2010).

[65] *Compendium theologiae*, 2, [*De spe*] ch. 6, p. 197.

insists, such anxiety is 'unnecessary' (*superfluam*).[66] Echoing the statement
of St Paul in Philippians, he declares 'the Lord is at hand', and that presence
should be 'a cause of joy', not a cause of anxiety:

> For a man rejoices when his friend is near. But the Lord is near with the
> presence of his majesty. *He is not far from each one of us* (Acts 17.27); He
> is also near in his flesh: *But now in Christ Jesus you who were once far off
> have been brought near in the blood of Christ* (Eph 2.13). Again He is near
> through indwelling grace: *Draw near to God and he will draw near to you*
> (Jas 4.8); and by his kindness in hearing: *The Lord is near to all who call
> upon him* (Ps 145.18) … When [Paul] says, *have no anxiety,* he shows that
> our minds should be at rest … It was fitting to add *have no anxiety* after
> saying that *the Lord is at hand.* As if to say: He will grant everything; hence
> there is no need to be anxious.[67]

We who were once outsiders and 'far off', Thomas notes, have been 'brought
near by the blood of Christ.' Our hope lies in this: that Christ has chosen to
stand between us and the Father. Thomas writes: 'We should also consider
that our hope is through Christ to God, according to Romans 5.1-2: *Justified
by faith, let us have peace with God through our Lord Jesus Christ, by whom
we have access through faith to this grace in which we stand, and in which we
glory in the hope of the glory of the sons of God.*'[68] Accordingly, the prayers
and petitions we make are never made by ourselves alone, on the basis that
is of our own righteousness, but always through him and in him. 'God not
only forgave us our sins, but he gave his own Son to make reparation on our
behalf.'[69]

Aquinas returns to this great theme in his Commentary on Hebrews, a text
which he was confident had been composed by St Paul.[70] Christ, in Thomas's

---

[66] *Super epistolam ad Philippenses lectura,* ch. 4, lect. 1, 155, in *Super epistolas,* vol. 2, p. 119.

[67] Ibid., 154–6, pp. 118–19. The translation here is from *Commentary on Saint Paul's Letter to the
Thessalonians and the Letter to the Philippians,* trans., F. R. Larcher and Michael Duffy (Albany. NY
1969) p. 113.

[68] *Compendium theologiae,* 2, [*De spe*] ch. 5, p. 196.

[69] *Super epistolam ad Ephesios lectura,* ch. 1, lect. 2, 19, in *Super epistolas,* vol. 2, p. 7.

[70] In the 'Prologue' to his *Commentary on Hebrews,* while acknowledging that 'some have doubted that

understanding, in order to fulfil his role as mediator, needed 'by the devotion of prayer to reach God at one extreme and, by mercy and compassion, to reach ourselves at the other extreme.'[71] But how could the One, who is all holy, be the representative of sinners? How could the all-powerful God be the mediator for people weak and infirm? The answer to this question Thomas finds in Chapter 4 of Hebrews: *For we have not a high priest who is unable to sympathize with our weaknesses, but one who in every respect has been tempted as we are, yet without sin* (Heb. 4.15). Christ having taken our flesh 'knows our [human] wretchedness *through experience*,' Thomas explains, 'which, as God, he knew from eternity through simple knowledge.'[72]

The answer to human wretchedness – the *miseria* of those who know themselves to be 'weak and infirm' – is not simply justice (receiving what we deserve) but rather *misericordia*, the kindness and compassion of someone who knows our weakness, and knows what it is to be tempted. 'For if he had been without temptations,' Thomas writes, 'he would not have known them by experience, and then he could not have had compassion.'[73] '*He himself is beset with weakness* … The reason for this is that he may have compassion on the weaknesses of others. This is the reason why the Lord permitted Peter to fall: *Learn from yourself what your neighbour is going through* (Sir 31.18).'[74]

Thomas, at this point in his *Commentary*, makes reference to a phrase which occurs in the Canon of the Mass, *And to us sinners*, noting that both in the Old Law (Lev. 9) and in the New, the priest offers sacrifice 'for his own sins as well as for those of the people.'[75] Christ the new High-priest is, of course, entirely without sin. Nevertheless, because he has assumed our sins as his own, and bears our 'penalties and guilt', he is able to pray to the Father on our behalf as if he himself were the one in need of compassion. And, as mediator,

this was one of Paul's epistles', St Thomas argued on the contrary that it was indeed a genuine work of Paul. See *Prologus* 5, *Super epistolam ad Hebraeos lectura*, in *Super epistolas*, vol. 2, p. 336.

[71] Ibid., ch. 5, lect. 1, 246, in *Super epistolas*, vol. 2, p. 390.

[72] Ibid., ch. 4, lect. 3, 235, in *Super epistolas*, vol. 2, p. 387. My italics.

[73] Ibid., ch. 4, lect. 3, 237, in *Super epistolas*, vol. 2, p. 388.

[74] Ibid., ch. 5, lect. 1, 247, *Super epistolas*, vol. 2, p. 390.

[75] Ibid., ch. 5, lect. 1, 248.

he offers to the Father what St Thomas calls a 'spiritual sacrifice', one that involves 'prayers and supplications'.

> The priesthood of Christ is ordained to that spiritual sacrifice ... *that he might offer* gifts *and sacrifices for sins* ... Two things are necessary in one who prays, namely, fervent love along with pain and groaning. These are mentioned in Ps 37.10: *Lord, all my desire is before you* (as to the first) *and my groaning is not hidden from you* (as to the second). But Christ had these two. Therefore, in regard to the first he says, *with a strong cry*, i.e., with a most determined intention: *And being in an agony he prayed the longer* (Lk 22.43). Again in Luke (23.46): *and crying with a loud voice, he said 'Father, into your hands I commend my spirit'.* Because of the second he says, *and tears,* for by tears the Apostle means the internal groaning of the person praying. But this is not mentioned in the Gospel. It is probable, however, that just as he wept at the resurrection of Lazarus so also during his passion. For, he did many things which are not written down.[76]

The prayer of petition is a prayer said most often in solitude by an individual, but it can also, of course, be a prayer said in common. One last detail regarding this question which I find particularly worthy of note is an observation Thomas makes about petition and the prayer of the Eucharist. His statement is prompted by that passage in I Tim. 2.1 in which the Apostle speaks of prayer as having four different dimensions or 'parts' ('entreaties, prayers, pleas, and thanksgiving'). Thomas notes that this four-part pattern corresponds, in exact detail, to the basic structure of the Catholic Mass. And no small part of that structure, it becomes clear, is *asking*. Thomas writes:

> In the Mass everything up to the consecration of the Body and Blood is 'entreaty', because in them [in the two species] is the memory of sacred things which give us the confidence that we shall obtain our petition. At the mystery of the consecration there is 'prayer', because we meditate on what

---

[76] Ibid., ch. 5, lect. 1, 255–6, pp. 391–2.

Christ did. The rest, up to communion, is 'plea' for the living and dead and for oneself. At the end comes thanksgiving.[77]

We meditate on what Christ did. That tiny phrase draws our attention not only to the sacrifice Christ made on the cross when he became the mediator between ourselves and the Father, but also to the great and saving prayer of Christ that continues in the Mass, a prayer that still to this day pleads on our behalf.

(2) Thanksgiving: The Prayer of Gratitude

St Paul, in the first paragraph of his letter to the Philippians, writes: *I thank my God in all my remembrance of you, always in every prayer of mine for you all, making my prayer with joy* (Phil 1.3). Words such as these occur again and again in the letters of Paul. His prayer of thanksgiving is so spontaneous and insistent, it wonderfully illustrates the sharp, bright comment St Thomas made, on one occasion, when speaking in general on the subject of thanksgiving: 'the obligation of gratitude has no limit.'[78]

(i) Thanksgiving and the virtues

With regard to Paul's wholly positive response to the Philippians, Thomas remarked: 'nothing occurred to the Apostle that was not worthy of thanksgiving; and this is a great thing.'[79] Paul thanks God for the partnership in the Gospel which he is happy to share with the Philippians. They are one with Paul, Thomas explains, by the way they 'share in the doctrine of the gospel teaching, by believing and fulfilling it in work. For this is true partnership.'[80]

Writing in similar vein to the Thessalonians, St Paul exclaims: *We give thanks to God always for you all: making a remembrance of you in our prayers without ceasing, being mindful of the work of your faith and labour and charity,*

---

[77] *Super primam epistolam ad Timotheum lectura*, ch. 2, lect. 1, 56, in *Super epistolas*, vol. 2, p. 224. The same observation about the structure of the Mass is made by Thomas in the *Summa theologiae*, II II q.83 a.17. There he acknowledges that his reflection on the Mass was inspired by 'a gloss on 1 Tim 2'.

[78] *ST*, II II q.106, a.6 ad 2.

[79] *Super epistolam ad Philippenses lectura*, ch. 1, lect. 1, 9, in *Super epistolas*, vol. 2, p. 92.

[80] Ibid., lect. 1, 11, p. 92.

and of the enduring of the hope of our Lord Jesus Christ before God and our Father (1 Thess. 1.2-3). Thomas, when he comes upon this particular passage, remarks: 'Thanksgiving should be unceasing; so Paul says, *always*. It should be universal, so Paul says, *for you all*; and later Paul adds: *give thanks in all circumstances* (5.18).'[81] The actual 'blessings' for which Paul is moved to give thanks are noted and underlined by Thomas, and they are: faith, hope and love.

> First, he mentions faith because it is an essential condition for obtaining the things to be hoped for, a means of revelation not based on appearances: *For whoever would draw near to God must believe that he exists and that he rewards those who seek him* (Heb 11.6). This, however, is not sufficient unless the person practices good works and makes an effort; so Paul says: *your work of faith and labour ...* Paul also gives thanks for the love in which they abounded ... Then he gives thanks for their hope which enables them to endure sufferings patiently ... Finally, Paul gives thanks for *hope in our Lord,* that is, the hope we have in Christ, or the hope Christ gave to us: *We have been born anew to a living hope through the resurrection of Jesus Christ from the dead.* (I Pet. 1.3).[82]

The same three virtues are listed together by St Paul in his letter to the Colossians: *We always thank God, the Father of our Lord Jesus Christ, when we pray for you, because we have heard of your faith in Christ Jesus and of the love which you have for the saints, because of the hope laid up for you in heaven* (Col. 1.3). In his commentary on the letter, Thomas takes the opportunity once again to speak about the virtues of faith, hope and love. What he says about love is sharp and to the point:

> There is a love which springs from charity, and another which is worldly. This worldly love does not include everyone, because we love those with whom there is some communication or sharing, which is the cause of love;

---

[81] *Super priman epistolam ad Thessalonicenses lectura,* ch. 1, lect. 1, 8, in *Super epistolas,* vol. 2, p. 153. Translation taken from *Commentary on Saint Paul's Letter to the Thessalonians and the Letter to the Philippians,* trans., F. R. Larcher and Michael Duffy (Albany, NY 1969) p. 6.
[82] Ibid., 10, p. 166; Larcher and Duffy, p. 6.

but in worldly love this cause is not present in everyone, but is only found in one's relatives or other worldly people. But the love of charity does extend to everyone; and so he says *for all.* For, even though sinners are loved by the love of charity, it is in order that at some time they become holy.[83]

St Paul, in his letter to the Ephesians, doesn't list together, as he did in the other letters, the three theological virtues. The fact, however, that faith, hope and love are at least mentioned at different stages in the letter is enough to attract Thomas's attention. The subject is clearly one of manifest importance for the Dominican. Taking up St Paul's idea of the Christians at Ephesus as 'pillars', he writes: 'They are referred to as pillars since they must be upright, elevated and strong – upright through faith, elevated through hope, and strong because of charity.'[84] What follows, then, is a passage in which Aquinas draws powerfully on images from the Old Testament. And he allows himself to wax eloquent in a way that would never, perhaps, be permitted in an austere text such as the *Summa.*

I say upright through faith because faith reveals the straight way to arrive at the fatherland; it is symbolized by the pillar of cloud in Exodus 13.21: *And the Lord went before them to show the way in a pillar of cloud.* Faith, similar to clouds, is opaque with its mysteries, dissolves when it gives way to vision [literally 'when emptied'], and moistens by arousing devotion. [The faithful are] elevated through hope, for hope points heavenwards; it is symbolized by the column of smoke in Judges 20.40: *And they perceived as it were a pillar of smoke rise up from the city.* Hope, like smoke from fire, comes from charity, ascends upward, and finally vanishes in glory. [The faithful must be] strong through charity, 'for love is strong as death' (Cant 8.6); hence it is symbolized by a pillar of fire which consumes everything, as in Wisdom 18.3: *Therefore they received a burning pillar of fire for a guide of the way which they knew not.* As fire makes the surroundings visible, puts

---

[83] *Super epistolam ad Colossenses lectura*, ch. 1, lect. 2, 11, in *Super epistolas s. Pauli lectura*, vol. 2, p. 128.

[84] Prologue, 1, *Super epistolam ad Ephesios lectura*, in *Super epistolas*, vol. 2, p. 1.

metals to the test, and destroys what can burn, so charity illumines [our] deeds, examines motives, and exterminates all vices.[85]

(ii) The challenge of continual prayer

A point on which Paul insists in his letters is that believers should pray 'at all times' (Eph. 6.18). By his own account, he himself kept faith with the practice of continual prayer, and his prayer was often one of thanksgiving. Aquinas, responding to this theme in Paul's letter to the Ephesians, writes: 'the Apostle gives thanks for the goods and blessings he has heard about, saying, *I never cease to give thanks for you.*'[86] But, then, Thomas raises the common-sense objection about the seeming impossibility of continual prayer, asserting that Paul 'could not have continually offered thanks for them.'[87]

How, then, are we to understand the notion of continual prayer? Thomas puts forward a few suggestions: 'By saying *I never cease*, the Apostle means at the required times; or, *I never cease* because my attitude of thanksgiving for you is without intermission habitually with me.'[88] When, in his letter to the Thessalonians, Paul urges them to 'pray constantly', Thomas in response asks once again: 'How is this possible?' This time Thomas offers a longer and more considered response. Continual prayer, he explains, can take a number of different forms:

> First, that person who does not neglect the appointed hours for prayer, prays always. *You shall eat at my table always* (2 Sam 9.7). Secondly, 'pray constantly' means to pray continuously. But then prayer is considered under the aspect of the effect of the prayer. For prayer is the unfolding or expression of desire; for when I desire something, then I ask for it by praying. So prayer is the petition of suitable things from God; and so desire has the power of prayer. *O Lord, you will hear the desire of the poor* (Ps 10.17). Therefore, whatever we do is the result of a desire; so prayer

---

[85] Ibid. Apart from certain small changes the translation here is from M. L. Lamb, *Commentary on Saint Paul's Epistle to the Ephesians* (New York 1996) pp. 40–1.

[86] Ibid., ch. 1, lect. 6, 47, p. 13; Lamb, 69.

[87] Ibid.

[88] Ibid.

always remains in force in the good things we do; for the good things we do flow from the desire of the good. There is a commentary on this verse pointing out: *He does not cease praying, who does not cease doing good.* A third way by which it is possible to pray without ceasing is through the giving of alms which may be a sort of cause of continual prayer. In the lives of the Fathers we read: *He who gives alms is the one who always prays, for the person who receives alms prays for you even when you are asleep.*[89]

The idea that 'prayer always remains in force in the things we do' finds rather vivid expression in an early work of St Thomas. In his *Commentary on the Sentences,* he writes: 'If you throw a stone, your movement lasts, in itself, only as long as you are actually moving the stone with your hand, but the momentum of your act lasts as long as the stone continues moving as a result of the impetus you gave it at the outset.'[90] Prayer, then, or the effect of prayer, is like the stone which has been thrown. The act itself, like the act of throwing, comes quickly to an end, for 'people cannot pray continuously, or the whole time, because they sometimes have to be engaged in other activities as well.'[91] But the force and momentum of the prayer continues in the different activities and good works that follow.[92] 'For, although we cannot actually pray all the time, nevertheless we ought to pray always out of the habit of charity.'[93]

In this context St Thomas brings up the question of distractions in prayer. Naturally, he wants to encourage us, when we are at prayer, to remain as attentive as possible. But he knows how easy it is to be distracted. So what happens, if we find ourselves hopelessly distracted, does our prayer-time lose all merit? Thomas's reply (in his lectures on 1 Corinthians) shows him to be as sensible and wise as he is compassionate. An individual, he says, who is 'not

---

[89] *Super priman epistolam ad Thessalonicenses lectura,* ch. 5, lect. 2, 130, p. 189; Lamb, pp. 50–1. For all his devotion to prayer, Thomas never exalts contemplation in a way that would in any way diminish the ordinary day-to-day tasks of life. In fact, on one occasion, he remarked: 'the quiet of contemplation is not expedient for the individual who can make progress usefully in some form of activity.' See *Super epistolam ad Romanos lectura,* ch. 8, lect. 5, 690, in *Super epistolas s. Pauli,* vol. 1, p. 124.
[90] *Commentary on the Sentences,* Bk 4, dist. 15, q.4, a.2, (C); Tugwell, *Albert and Thomas,* p. 383.
[91] Ibid.
[92] Ibid. On this question, see the thoughtful reflection in the *Summa theologiae,* II II q.83, a.14.
[93] *Super epistolam ad Colossenses lectura,* ch. 1, lect. 2, 11, in *Super epistolas s. Pauli lectura,* vol. 2, p. 128.

paying attention to his prayer', but who is still somehow praying, will certainly miss out on 'spiritual consolation and devotion' but *not* on merit.[94] Where merit is concerned, 'such a person should not be said to lose that benefit, because in that case a great many prayers would be without merit, since it is hardly possible to say a single Our Father without our minds wandering off to other things.'[95] Thomas then goes on to point out, and with admirable common sense that, in order to be spiritual, we don't have to be thinking holy thoughts all day long. He writes:

> When someone engaged in some meritorious work does not constantly reflect with every move he makes that he is doing this for God, they do not lose the basis for meriting. The reason for this is that in all meritorious activities whose orientation is toward the right goal, it is not required that the intention of the person doing them should be concentrated on that goal in every single action; the initial impetus which inspired the person's purpose remains in effect throughout the entire operation, even if he is sometimes distracted while performing specific parts of it. And this initial impetus makes the whole work meritorious, unless it is intercepted by some contrary feeling which turns the work aside from its original orientation and redirects it in an opposite direction.[96]

*   *   *

St Paul does not simply encourage us to pray at all times, but to pray 'in all circumstances' (1 Thess. 5.18). Thomas, commenting on this phrase in Paul's Letter to the Thessalonians, writes: 'Paul says *in all circumstances,* that is, in good times and in bad times, *give thanks.*'[97] The theme of giving thanks was introduced by St Paul earlier in the letter, but on that occasion, he made no explicit reference to the need to pray 'in all circumstances'. He wrote simply: *what thanksgiving can we render to God for you, for all the joy which we feel*

---

[94] *Super primam epistolam ad Corinthios lectura*, ch. 14, lect. 3, 839, in *Super epistolas s. Pauli*, vol. 1, p. 395.

[95] Ibid. See 'Lecture on 1 Corinthians' in Tugwell, *Albert and Thomas*, p. 434.

[96] Ibid.

[97] *Super priman epistolam ad Thessalonicenses lectura*, ch. 5, lect. 2, 131, p. 189.

for your sake before God, praying earnestly night and day? (1 Thess. 3.9-10). The phrase 'night and day' Thomas takes to refer to 'the frequency' of Paul's prayer, an obvious enough interpretation. But Thomas also understands it to mean giving thanks in good times and bad. He writes: *'night and day,* that is in adversity and prosperity.'[98]

The phrase 'adversity and prosperity', as we have noted already in Chapter 2, is a phrase which occurs not only in the sermons of Aquinas but also in his prayers. When used in these different texts, the phrase represents a willing surrender to the mysterious providence of God, a theme which is obviously of great importance to Thomas. In fact, we find it repeated in another of his commentaries on Paul. The Apostle, in Ephesians, had spoken of 'giving thanks always for all things' (Eph. 5.20). This prayer of thanksgiving, Thomas explains, is possible only when a man 'recognizes that everything he has is from God.'[99] For it is only then, in profound humility, that we are able to give thanks to God for both 'adversity and prosperity', and find strength, even in the most trying of circumstances, to surrender ourselves to the omnipotent and mysterious power of God's providence.

For the more we are affected by our relation to God, and know him, the more we see him as greater and ourselves as lesser, indeed almost nothing, in comparison with God. *Now my eye sees you. And because of that I reproof myself, and do penance in dust and ashes* (Job 42.5-6). So [Paul] says, *giving thanks always for all things,* for all his gifts, whether of prosperity or adversity. *I will bless the Lord at all times; his praise shall be always in my mouth* (Ps 33:1). For adversities are also gifts to us along the way.[100]

The paradox is decidedly Pauline, but it is also, of course, a paradox we find present in all four Gospels. And that's why, we may presume, Thomas is prepared, in the face of both 'prosperity and adversity', to remember and repeat St Paul's extraordinary statement about thanksgiving, declaring in his

---

[98] Ibid., 69, p. 177.

[99] *Super epistolam ad Ephesios lectura,* ch. 5, lect. 7, 314, in *Super epistolas,* vol. 2, p. 73.

[100] Ibid., 314, p. 73. Thomas returns once again to the theme of prosperity and adversity in his commentary on Hebrews. See *Super epistolam ad Hebraeos lectura,* ch. 4, lect. 3, 236, in *Super epistolas,* vol. 2, p. 387.

commentary on Ephesians, and in a number of other commentaries as well: *In all things give thanks.*[101]

Conclusion

One aspect I find particularly impressive about St Thomas's teaching on prayer in the Pauline commentaries is its Gospel simplicity. There is no hint of esotericism in what he says, no daunting list of levels or degrees of prayer from which the ordinary believer will feel excluded. For St Thomas, as for the Apostle Paul, prayer at core comes down to something very simple in practice: asking and thanking. There are different aspects of grace explored by Thomas in his commentaries on Paul and, clearly, of the utmost importance for the Dominican Master is that grace of the Holy Spirit we call prayer. The Pauline commentaries, when read carefully through together, offer a rich and profound theology of grace, but they also offer a theology of prayer: the manifest wisdom of Paul affirmed and wonderfully developed by the wisdom of Thomas; the Apostle to the Gentiles and the Angel of the Schools happily agreeing together that 'of all the things needed for the Christian life the most important is prayer.'[102]

---

[101] Ibid. The actual text being quoted here is 1 Thess. 5.8.
[102] *Super primam epistolam ad Timotheum lectura*, ch. 2, lect. 1, 56, in *Super epistolas*, vol. 2, p. 223.

5

Praying in time of need: Aquinas on the Psalms

The end purpose of this work of Scripture is prayer.
AQUINAS: POSTILLA SUPER PSALMOS

Introduction

St Thomas's *Commentary on the Psalms* was almost certainly 'the last instruction' he gave before he died,[1] a fact which lends to this late commentary a quite unique status. And yet, for some reason, the commentary has generally been overlooked. According to Mark Jordan, 'There is no work of exegesis more unjustly forgotten than Thomas's commentary on the psalms.'[2] But how was it possible that a work of such manifest importance could fail to receive the attention it deserved, and for such a long time?

Here, the first thing to note is that, even in the years immediately following the death of Aquinas, the *Postilla super Psalmos* was for the most part ignored.

---

[1] Louis-Jacques Bataillon, 'La diffusione manoscritta e stampata dei commenti biblici di San Tommaso d'Aquino', *Angelicum* 71 (1994) p. 589.
[2] Mark D. Jordan, 'Préface' in *Thomas d'Aquin: Commentaire sur les psaumes*, (ed.) Jean-Éric Stroobant de Saint-Éloy (Paris 1996) p. 7.

Only four complete examples of the text have survived.[3] I say 'complete' but, in fact, these four manuscripts contain Thomas's reflections on only fifty-one of the psalms. A separate manuscript containing his commentary on three further psalms (Ps. 52–4) was discovered in 1875. Unfortunately, during the bombing of Naples in 1943, this manuscript was destroyed. Happily, however, an edition of the manuscript was made by Pietro Antonio Uccelli who published it in 1875, and so the work survived.[4]

One of the reasons why, in modern times, *Super Psalmos* has been largely ignored is because the text has not been readily accessible. The two modern editions of the work in the *Opera omnia* of Fiaccadori (Parma 1852–73) and of Vivès (Paris 1871–82) are unsatisfactory from a number of points of view. And, what is more, the long-awaited critical edition of the work by the Leonine Commission has still to appear. A translation into French of *Super Psalmos* was published in 1996,[5] but so far there has been no translation of the work into English or German. Fortunately, however, a number of helpful studies on Thomas's *Commentary on the Psalms* have already appeared.[6]

For a long time, scholars had little doubt that *Super Psalmos,* far from being a work of Aquinas's most mature years, belonged in fact to a much earlier

---

[3] See Martin Morard, 'A propos du *Commentaire des Psaumes* de saint Thomas d'Aquin', *Revue Thomiste*, XCVI, 4 (October–December 1996) pp. 655–6, footnote 7.

[4] The work was reprinted five years later in 1880. See Pietro A. Uccelli, *S. Thomae Aquinatis, In Isaiam prophetam, in tres psalmos David ... expositiones* (Rome 1880) 242–53.

[5] *Thomas d'Aquin: Commentaire sur les psaumes,* (ed.) and trans., Jean-Éric Stroobant de Saint-Éloy (Paris 1996). Although helpful in many ways, this translation and the notes accompanying it have been subjected to a severe critique by one of the leading scholars in the field, Martin Morard. See Morard, 'A propos du *Commentaire des Psaumes de saint Thomas d'Aquin',* pp. 653–62.

[6] See Thomas F. Ryan, *Thomas Aquinas as Reader of the Psalms* (Notre Dame, Indiana 2000); Carmelo Pandolfi, *San Tommaso filosofo nel Commento ai Salmi: Interpretazione dell'essere nel modo 'esistenziale' dell'invocazione* (Bologna 1993); James R. Ginther, 'The Scholastic Psalms' Commentary as a Textbook for Theology: The Case of Thomas Aquinas', in *Omnia disce:* Medieval Studies in Memory of Leonard Boyle, (eds), A. J. Duggan, J. Greatrex and B. Bolton (Aldershot 2005) pp. 211–29; Innocenzo Colosio, 'La lode divina nel comment di S. Tommaso ai Salmi', in *Rassenga di Ascetica e Mistica* (April–June 1974) pp. 179–94; Martin Morard, 'Le sacerdoce du Christ et sacerdoce des chrétiens dans le *Commentaire des Psaumes* de saint Thomas d'Aquin', in *Revue Thomiste* XCIX, 1 (January–March 1999) pp. 119–42. Also, it should be noted, there are available on the web translations of a number of Thomas's commentaries on Scripture, including a significant part of his *Commentary on the Psalms.* See Thérèse Bonin, *Thomas Aquinas in English: A Bibliography,* 2012 [online] Available at: http://www.home.duq.edu/~bonin/thomasbibliography.html#dispute (Accessed 23 November 2012).

period in his life. More recently, however, impressive evidence has come to light which points convincingly to a later dating.[7] It now seems almost certain that the commentary was composed at Naples between October 1272 and June 1273 – during the period, in other words, immediately prior to Thomas's death.

It is hard to exaggerate the importance Aquinas gave to the book of Psalms, and to the value, therefore, of a close exegetical reading of the text. '*Materia est universalis*', he declared in the introduction to his commentary: 'The material [in the book of Psalms] is universal, for while the individual books of the Canon of Scripture contain material that is distinctive, this book contains the general material of all theology.'[8] That is no small claim, and Thomas spells out exactly what he means, not hesitating to declare that, in this single text from the Old Testament, the entire work of 'creation', 'governance', 'redemption' and 'glorification', is contained. He writes: 'That's the reason why the Psalter is used most often in Church, because it contains the whole of Scripture.'[9] And again: 'Everything that pertains to faith in the Incarnation is handed down in the Psalter with such clarity we might think we were reading not prophecy but the Gospel itself.'[10]

*   *   *

For Thomas, the psalms contain different levels of meaning but, first and last, what needs to be acknowledged in the text is the hidden presence of Christ. As Thomas explains in his commentary: 'matters are sometimes set forth pertaining to Christ which surpass, as it were, the power of the narrative.'[11] The references to David praying, for example, are quite often, Thomas claims, hidden references to Christ himself at prayer. And, in that perspective, Christ appears as the new David, the composer of a new song, the poet of a new

---

[7] What helped change the thinking of scholars such as Père Bataillon was an allusion in the text (not noticed before 1993) to the sanctity of Louis IX of France.

[8] '*Proemium*', *In Psalmos Davidis expositio, Sancti Thomae Aquinatis Opera Omnia*, Parma vol. 14, p. 148.

[9] Ibid.

[10] Ibid.

[11] Psalm XXI, *In Psalmos*, p. 217.

reality. What, on occasion, appears to refer refer exclusively to David, is by St Thomas understood to refer 'not to the figural but to the true David, namely to Christ.'[12] Commenting, for example, on one particular psalm, he writes: 'here is treated mystically the prayer of Christ to the Father.' That said, however, in the opinion of Thomas F. Ryan, 'claims that entire Psalms refer literally to Christ are the exception (much more often, it is Thomas's exegetical strategy to discover Christ at a mystical level).'[13]

Psalm 21 opens with the terrible cry: *My God, my God, why have you forsaken me*. Aquinas, in his commentary, makes it clear that this wounded cry of anguish, repeated by Christ as he was dying on the cross, is a prayer made to the Father on behalf of all of us, the members of his mystical body. He writes: 'Christ spoke these words in the person of a sinner, or of the Church … for the Church and Christ are as one mystical body; and for this reason, they are spoken of as one person, and Christ transforms himself into the Church and the Church into Christ.'[14] Thomas then goes on to remark that 'when Christ's passion was approaching, he prayed: *Father, if it be possible, let this chalice pass from me.*' Here, Aquinas says, Christ is revealed, as one 'bearing the weight of weakened flesh which naturally fears and flees death.'[15]

Again, speaking in general about Psalm 21 Thomas writes: 'The discussion in this psalm is principally about Christ's Passion. It touches secondarily on the resurrection because … the Passion is ordered to the resurrection.'[16] The reference, at this point, to the resurrection brings to the mind of Thomas an image from an earlier psalm: *He set my feet like that of a stag*. 'By the stag,' Aquinas writes, 'is understood the human nature of Christ, because the stag crosses a thicket of thorns without injury to its foot, just as Christ crossed through this present life without defilement. Again, the stag leaps the best, just as Christ ascended from the pit of death to the glory of his resurrection.'[17]

---

[12] Psalm XXVII, *In Psalmos*, p. 241.
[13] See Ryan, *Thomas Aquinas as Reader of the Psalms* (Notre Dame, Indiana 2000) p. 109.
[14] Psalm XXI, *In Psalmos*, p. 218.
[15] Ibid.
[16] Ibid., p. 217.
[17] Psalm XXI, *In Psalmos*, p. 218. See Augustine, *Ennarationes in Psalmos*, 17:34; *Corpus Christianorum*, ser. Latina 38, Turnhout 1956, p. 99, 1–3.

That last image of the leaping stag, as an image suggestive of Christ's resurrection from the dead is, of course, as wonderful as it is unexpected. But, reading slowly through Thomas's *Commentary on the Psalms*, we quite often come upon such striking images. That does not mean, however, that *Postilla super Psalmos* makes for easy or light reading. No, if anything, the opposite is the case. All medieval commentaries on Scripture present a challenge to the modern reader. And, in this respect, *Super Psalmos* is no exception. But there are, I suggest, particular reasons why, over the centuries, this late commentary of the Doctor Communis has failed to attract the attention it deserves.

For a start the form of the text passed down to us is not that of an *expositio*, which would be something written or dictated by the author himself, but rather that of a *reportatio*, a report of a live lecture taken down by a student or scribe in the form of class notes. What we have, then, in the case of *Super Psalmos*, is a 'report' which was never subsequently looked over or revised or corrected by St Thomas. The text itself does indeed contain all kinds of fascinating information but, to the bewilderment of the modern reader, it also seems hopelessly weighed down by a plethora of academic divisions and sub-divisions. That, of course, is not unusual in a medieval text of this kind. But, here, because the focus of Aquinas's attention is on a series of poems which, in one stanza after another, express states of raw human emotion, the controlled, scholastic commentary can appear, at times, wholly at odds with its immediate subject matter. That said, the more often I return to read the text the more I find that the austere, academic style of St Thomas allows him to cast light on the psalms in all kinds of unexpected ways.

*   *   *

The juxtaposition of urgent statements of human longing and human passion alongside dry scholastic commentary creates an effect not unlike that achieved by St John of the Cross in the placing of his own mystical verse alongside a surprisingly dogged and detailed scholastic commentary.[18] The contrast between the spontaneity and depth of feeling expressed in the poetry, on the

---

[18] Already, of course, in the work of Pseudo-Dionysius, St Thomas would have encountered passages of mystical verse accompanied by prose commentary.

one hand, and the controlled, scholastic nature of the prose, on the other, will inevitably strike some readers as decidedly odd. But, page by page, St John's commentaries contain a depth of wisdom and insight which could not, perhaps, be communicated with the same clarity and brilliance in any other form.

One of the truths about spiritual life which a mystic like St John of the Cross is concerned to communicate is the need – in order for union with God to be attained – for a radical purification of soul and body. And this is achieved, John explains, not only by one's own ascetic effort, but by a special 'initiative' on the part of God. Although, it is true, *God is light in whom is no darkness at all* (1 Jn. 1.5), the effect of his visitation, on these occasions, is a cleansing of spirit that is 'obscure' and 'dark'.[19] For, 'when the divine light of contemplation strikes a soul not yet entirely illumined, it causes spiritual darkness'.[20] And, in this darkness, the individual experiences 'trials, conflicts and temptations'.[21]

The other image John uses to describe this time of purgation is 'fire'. He writes: 'In order to undertake the journey to God the heart must be burned and purified ... with the fire of divine love'.[22] So painful is this purgation, John tells us, the individual is hardly able to bear it.[23] And, in fact, later, when the torment experienced is due to an overwhelming illumination, John says that if God did not to come to the aid of the soul, it would not survive.[24] I have quoted these few texts from the Spanish mystic because, in Thomas's commentary on Psalm 16, there are a number of statements regarding God's visitation to the soul which are remarkably similar.

Commenting, for example, on the phrase 'You have visited by night', Aquinas says that the divine visitation includes a searching examination, and 'this examination is severe and strong, and so much so that no one could withstand it unless helped by [God]; Job 6: *For what is my strength that I can*

---

[19] St John of the Cross, *The Ascent of Mount Carmel*, Bk 1, ch. 1: 3, in *The Collected Works of St John of the Cross*, trans., Kieran Kavanaugh and Otilo Rodriguez (Washington, DC 1973) p. 73.

[20] St John of the Cross, *The Dark Night*, Bk 2, ch. 5, *Collected Works*, p. 335.

[21] Prologue, 4, *The Ascent of Mount Carmel*, p. 71.

[22] *Ascent*, Bk 1, ch. 2: 2, p. 75.

[23] *Dark Night*, Bk 2, ch. 5: 6, p. 337.

[24] *The Spiritual Canticle*, Stanza 13: 4, p. 459.

hold out? Or what is my end that I should keep patience? Neither my strength nor my flesh are [made] of brass.'[25] This testing of the soul, St Thomas makes clear, is not a sign of God's displeasure. On the contrary, it is a sign of his great favour. For only to those who already possess 'rectitude of heart' does God care to visit in this way.

The other image used by Thomas at this point to describe purgation is 'fire'. As it happens, the image does not occur in the Psalm itself, but Aquinas instinctively introduces it. He writes: *'You have visited by night.* This can be understood by night and fire, because [both] disturb the soul; Job 30: *In the night my bone is pierced with sorrows ...* and fire does the same.'[26] And again: *'You have tried me by fire,* that is, by tribulation, because it is apparent by then whether he [the one being tested] is a good friend, and does not withdraw.'[27]

Thomas also notes that the phrase 'by night' can, on occasion, signify 'in quiet and silence', referring, in other words, to a visitation by God that brings 'consolations' to the soul.[28] 'Night', for John of the Cross, can also signify a visitation of this kind – a 'serene' dark night – when God speaks to the soul 'very quietly and secretly'[29] – without the help of words: 'in silence and quietude'.[30] In noting these few striking similarities, I am not suggesting that the 'night' of John of the Cross and the 'night' of Thomas are entirely identical. What, however, the text of Aquinas does indicate clearly is his sharp, contemplative grasp of the inner workings of grace in the life of prayer.[31] St Thomas

---

[25] Psalm XVI, *In Psalmos*, p. 190.

[26] Ibid.

[27] Ibid.

[28] Ibid.

[29] *The Spiritual Canticle*, Stanza 39:12, p. 561.

[30] Ibid., Stanza 39:13.

[31] Another particularly interesting text in St Thomas concerning the life of contemplation, reminiscent of the mystical teaching of St John of the Cross, is the following short passage from Thomas's *Commentary on the Gospel of St John*. He writes: 'the more the soul is free of passions and is purged from affections from earthly things, the higher it rises to the contemplation of truth and tastes how sweet the Lord is ... Therefore, if the human intellect is to see the divine essence it must wholly depart from the body, either by death, as the Apostle says, *We would prefer to be absent from the body and present with the Lord* (2 Cor 5.8); or by being wholly abstracted by rapture from the senses of the body, as is mentioned of Paul in 2 Corinthians (12.3).' See *Commentary on John*, vol. 1, Lecture 11, 213, trans., F. R. Larcher (Albany, NY 1980) p. 103.

is not speaking to us here with mere academic information or knowledge but as a spiritual Master.

One notable aspect of the mystical treatises of John of the Cross, which we don't find in Aquinas's commentary, is a *systematic* presentation of prayer. St Thomas, instead of imposing on the poetic text, in the manner of the Carmelite, an ordered structure of ideas ('active night of the senses', 'passive night of the spirit' etc.) simply takes up and develops whatever ideas or themes are suggested by the individual psalms.[32] But, in terms of likeness, in both Thomas and John we find the same passion to communicate certain basic truths concerning the life of prayer. Thomas F. Ryan, therefore, is undoubtedly correct when he declares that 'Thomas [in *Super Psalmos*] is no indifferent expositor but is deeply concerned about his students. He does not simply teach them about Christ and prayer, for example, but in fact admonishes them to imitate the former and perform the latter.'[33]

* * *

Of the many different themes in St Thomas's commentary worth considering, the one which is the particular focus of attention in this chapter is a theme to which Thomas himself draws our attention in the introduction to *Super Psalmos*. Having already pointed out that the Psalter is read in Church more often than any other book of the Old Testament, because it in some way contains 'the whole of Scripture',[34] he then goes on to propose a second reason why such regular and repeated recitation of the psalms is encouraged by the Church. 'It is,' he writes, 'to give us hope of divine mercy.'[35] To find this theme being underlined by St Thomas at the very beginning of his commentary is

---

[32] St John's 'systematic presentation' is particularly evident in *Ascent* and *Dark Night*. It is not, however, characteristic of his commentaries on *The Spiritual Canticle* and *The Living Flame of Love*.

[33] Thomas F. Ryan, *Thomas Aquinas as Reader of the Psalms*, p. 9. In a fine essay entitled 'The Scholastic Psalms' Commentary as a Textbook for Theology: The Case of Thomas Aquinas', James R. Ginther takes this idea a step further. He writes: '[St Thomas] is keen that his students hear the voice of the praying Christ, and that they understand this orative reality to be inseparable from theological speculation. Prayer, for Thomas, is a fundamental feature of the theological enterprise.' See *Omnia disce: Medieval Studies in Memory of Leonard Boyle*, (eds), A. J. Duggan, J. Greatrex and B. Bolton (Aldershot 2005) pp. 227.

[34] 'Proemium', *In Psalmos*, p. 148.

[35] Ibid.

no accident, for it is a theme to which he will return again and again in *Super Psalmos*.

Aquinas is well aware that the prayers of the Psalter on which he is commenting were composed, almost without exception, in times of grave need. That explains why, in these texts – in the psalms themselves, first of all, and then in St Thomas's commentary – the theme of hope in the mercy of God and in the power of God to save, is regarded as of such critical importance. Two themes, then, or rather two fundamental aspects of this one theme will be explored in the pages which follow: first, prayer as a cry to God for help; and, second, prayer as 'the interpreter of hope'.

(1) *This poor man called:* Prayer as a Cry to God for Help

'The evils that here press upon us compel us to go to God.'[36] This statement which occurs in St Thomas's commentary on Psalm 54 is one which is repeated elsewhere in his work.[37] It is a statement – a stark truth – which is eloquent, we may presume, of the actual experience of Aquinas, but also eloquent of hundreds of years of human and religious experience, both Christian and Jewish. But it is the book of Psalms, I would say, more than any other book in the Bible, which bears the most immediate and most telling witness to this truth.

Over and over again we hear, in these extraordinary texts, the anguished cry of a man rendered naked and vulnerable in the face of bitter and relentless oppression. *My enemies cluster around me, breathing hostility ... they are closing in, they have eyes for nothing but to see me overthrown* (Ps. 17.9-11). Commenting on these words, Aquinas writes: 'This is the first psalm with "prayer" in its title ... It begins with prayer because, in the midst of tribulations, prayer is an unparalleled refuge.'[38] Then he cites the following impressive

---

[36] Psalm LIV: 1, in *S. Thomae Aquinatis opera omnia*, Busa vol. 6, p. 129. St Thomas is here paraphrasing an idea originally formulated by Pope St Gregory the Great. See *Moralia in Iob*, lxxvi, c.13, n.21: CCL 143 B (1985) p. 1280.

[37] See *ST*, I q.21, a.4, ad 3. See also 'Prologue' in St Thomas's *Commentary on St Paul's First Letter to the Thessalonians*, trans., F. R. Larcher and M. Duffy (Albany, NY 1969) p. 3.

[38] Psalm XVI, *In Psalmos*, p. 190.

lines from Psalm 108: '*Instead of making me a return for love, they spoke badly about me, but I gave myself to prayer.*'[39] It is when a man knows 'the wound of his own heart' (*plagam cordis sui*), Thomas tells us, and spreads out his hands in supplication, it is then that God hears.[40] What's more, it is precisely when an individual knows himself to be in grave need that God's mercy is most readily accepted.[41] And that explains why, 'in the time of tribulation, people are converted to God.'[42] Thomas quotes Sir. 35–6: *The mercy of God is beautiful in the time of affliction, as a cloud of rain in the time of drought.* But Thomas, the Dominican, is reaching beyond the beauty of this truth. His thoughts turn to the task of preaching. For since God is indeed 'a helper' in a time of affliction, this fact, he notes, 'ought to be preached' to those who are suffering.[43]

(i) The Prayer of the Inner Heart

According to Aquinas there are three qualities which distinguish genuine prayer. First of all it is *earnest* or *attentive* (*attenta*).[44] This means that prayer, in order to be authentic, must spring from an interior depth of the heart. It should be something genuinely personal. Making this point, Thomas writes: 'When the voice does not go out from the heart, it is not mine.'[45] And he notes further, with a 'silent voice' of this kind (*tacens ore*), rising up from the depth of the heart, 'Moses cried to the Lord', Exodus 14; and, likewise, 'Susanna was also heard crying out with this voice'. Daniel 13: *And she weeping, looked up to heaven, for her heart had confidence in the Lord.*[46]

In the second place, prayer should be well-directed: 'It is pointed straight (*recta*) when it tends to where it should.'[47] Thomas cites a short prayer to God taken from 2 Chron. 20.12: '*Since we don't know what we ought to do, this alone*

---

[39] Ibid.
[40] Psalm XVII, *In Psalmos*, p. 195.
[41] Psalm IX, *In Psalmos*, p. 172.
[42] Ibid.
[43] Ibid.
[44] Psalm III, *In Psalmos*, p. 156.
[45] Ibid.
[46] Ibid.
[47] Ibid.

remains to us, that we turn our eyes to you.[48] In the third place, prayer should be *fervent* (*devota*) just as David's prayer was fervent when he prayed '*I have cried to the Lord with my voice.*'[49]

Commenting on the word '*clamavi*' (I have cried), Thomas notes that 'prayer is called loud (*clamorosa*) according to the magnitude of one's feeling.' And he cites another line from one of the psalms: '*Lord, let my cry come unto you*' (Psalm 101).[50] That 'cry' – that prayer – is of course one which we hear again and again in the psalms attributed to King David. Here, for example, are a few characteristic lines from Psalm 26:

> Lord, hear my voice as I cry!
> Have mercy on me, and hear me!
> My heart has spoken to you,
> My face has searched for you.
> Lord, I will seek your face:
> Do not hide your face from me.[51]

This prayer is said not merely with the lips but from the innermost depth of the heart. It is, therefore, in the understanding of St Thomas, a prayer which is undoubtedly heard by God. 'Sometimes,' he writes, 'a man petitions for something with his mouth, but his heart is engaged with other things … When, however, the petition is from the innermost desire of the heart, then it is accepted by God.'[52] And he notes also: 'Devotion (*devotio*) is the reason why someone is heard by God. Devotion is a cry (*clamor*) of the heart which rouses God to hear. Accordingly [the psalmist] says, *Hear [me]*: because I have cried, not exteriorly but rather interiorly.'[53]

At this point St Thomas notes that there is a second reason why God attends to the anguish of the psalmist. But, here, the divine motive has nothing

---

[48] Ibid.
[49] Ibid.
[50] Ibid.
[51] Psalm XXVI, *In Psalmos*, p. 236.
[52] Ibid., p. 239. For an illuminating reflection on what St Thomas means, in *Super Psalmos*, when he speaks of 'the heart', see Thomas F. Ryan, *Thomas Aquinas as Reader of the Psalms*, pp. 125–34.
[53] Ibid.

whatever to do with a man's merit, and nor is it on account of his eloquent prayer but, purely and simply, 'because of his misery'.[54] By way of explanation, Aquinas adds this brief, telling statement: 'our misery provokes God to hear us.'[55] Echoing the words of the psalmist, *Have mercy on me, and hear me,* the Doctor Communis remarks: 'It is as if he were saying "I am wretched (*miserum*) and I know my wretchedness (*miseriam*). Hence it belongs to you [God] to be merciful (*misereri*)".'[56]

In similar vein, when commenting (in Psalm 30) on the efficacy of the Publican's prayer, Aquinas notes that 'the more a man approaches God the more he becomes aware of his smallness.'[57] But, of course, everything depends here on the nature or character of the actual approach made to God. 'The prayer of the Pharisee was despised because he asked with pride.'[58] In contrast, 'The Publican, because he recognized himself to be a sinner, went down to his house justified. *The prayer of the one who humbles himself penetrates the clouds* (Sir. 35.21).'[59]

Here, in *Super Psalmos* 33, Thomas includes a text or gloss from a commentary on the psalm by St Augustine. 'The cry which attains to God,' Augustine explains, 'is not a cry of the voice but a cry of the heart.'[60] The point, it seems, could hardly be expressed more clearly or more succinctly. But, within the space of a sentence, as if aflame now with a new directness, a new authority, the text ends with this brief, urgent imperative: 'Cry, therefore, from within where God hears!'[61]

(ii) Anxiety and prayer

At the heart of the psalmist's prayer, there is a longing, an aching desire, to see the face of God. Desire, in the opinion of St Thomas, can assume different forms. 'Sometimes it happens that desire is innermost and peaceful, and is not

---

[54] Ibid.
[55] Ibid.
[56] Ibid.
[57] Psalm XXX, *In Psalmos*, p. 255.
[58] Psalm LIV: Busa vol. 6, p. 129.
[59] Psalm XXX, *In Psalmos*, p. 255.
[60] Ibid. See St Augustine, *Ennarationes in Psalmos*, III, 23, CCL 38, 220.
[61] Ibid.

seeking much. But, when it is anxious (*anxium*), then it really seeks. Hence the psalmist says [*My face*] *has sought you,* that is, he has sought frequently and diligently.'[62] Aquinas, commenting on Psalm 41, refers to what he calls 'desire accompanied by anxiety'.[63] He has in mind here that deep, interior thirst which can be a longing for justice, owing to the immediate pressure of external evils (*mala quae hic affligunt*) or to that anxious, interior desire caused by a delay in the coming of the one desired (*ex dilatione rei desideratae*). Here, Thomas is speaking of 'anxiety' in a manner that appears to be wholly approving. How are we to understand this attitude? Elsewhere, when commenting on Rom. 12.8, Thomas gives us the answer. He writes:

> Solicitude sometimes suggests diligence in seeking what is lacking; and this is commendable and opposed to negligence. Sometimes it suggests anxiety of spirit with a lack of hope and with the fear of not obtaining that about which one is anxious. Such anxiety the Lord forbids in Matthew (6.25), and here with the Apostle, because no one should despair, as though the Lord would not grant what is necessary. But in place of anxiety we should have recourse to God: *Cast all your anxieties on him, for he cares about you* (I Pet 5.7). And this is done by praying.[64]

Psalm 41 opens with these words: *Like the deer that yearns for running streams so my soul is yearning for you my God.* Here, Thomas says, the psalmist 'makes manifest his desire' to attain to the living God, the source of all life. The psalmist finds, however, that he is frustrated in his desire. And so he goes on to exclaim with great sadness: *My tears have become my bread, by night, by day, as I hear it said all the day long, where is your God?* 'This sadness,' Thomas explains, 'comes either from sins, which are an obstacle to the attainment of the thing desired, or from troubles coming from outside.'[65] But Thomas

---

[62] Psalm XXVI, *In Psalmos*, p. 239.

[63] Psalm XLI, *In Psalmos*, p. 309.

[64] Although the text referred to is from Romans, Thomas discusses it in his commentary on Phil. 4.6. See *Super Epistolam ad Phillippenses lectura*, 1:156, in *Super Epistolas s. Pauli lectura*, Marietti edition (Turin 1953) p. 119.

[65] Ibid., p. 310.

insists that there is a 'remedy' for this sadness, and it takes the form of 'divine assistance'.[66]

That, of course, occasions no surprise. It is what we expect Thomas to say. But the 'remedy' also takes another, a second form. Aquinas calls it personal or individual meditation. His exact phrase is *remedium ex parte propriae meditationis*.[67] Such 'meditation', he explains, enables us to experience 'delight' and 'consolation' in our inner self (*consolationem mentis* and *mentis delectationem*).[68] In part what occasions Thomas's reflection here is the following mysterious phrase which occurs moments later in the Psalm: *I poured my soul out into myself*:

> These things I remembered
> for I poured my soul out into myself,
> and I will pass through
> to the place of the wonderful tent,
> to the house of God.[69]

'I poured my soul out into myself' (*effudi in me animam meam*) is sometimes understood to mean, 'I poured out my soul *above* myself' (*effudi super me animam meam*).[70] This other meaning (which Augustine also had[71]) prompts Thomas to engage in an extended and truly impressive meditation in which he attempts to give a direct answer to the question, 'Where is your God?', the question which had so troubled the psalmist, and had been the cause of such profound sadness. Thomas writes:

> They say *Where is your God?* And, remembering these things, I have begun to look around at the world of insentient creatures to see if I could find my God. And I discovered in them traces of God: *The invisible things of God have been made visible by the things which have been made, the creatures of the world* (Rom. 1.20). But then I pursued my search further, [this time]

---

[66] Ibid.
[67] Ibid.
[68] Ibid.
[69] Psalm XLI, verse 5, *In Psalmos*, p. 310.
[70] Ibid.
[71] *Ennarationes in psalmos* 41, no. 8 PL 36, CCSL 38.

into the intelligible things in the soul. *And I poured out my soul above myself.* That is to say, I examined them with most attentive care and sought [to find] what is contained in them, as if I placed all these things in front of me, like someone who extracts all that's contained in a vessel so that he can examine what's inside. But my God was not there. There still remained something higher than this. And I attained it.[72] *For I will pass through to the place of the wonderful tent, to the house of God;* as if to say: all the solace I could have is the hope of reaching God.[73]

St Thomas, later in the same text, after repeating the psalmist's question, 'Why are you unhappy, my soul?' imagines the psalmist saying to himself, at this point: 'You ought to rejoice because you are in the tent, and because [you have said] I will go to the house of the Lord. So why, then, are you unhappy? The small evils you are suffering now, compared with the eternal good things to come, are not worthy of attention.'[74] This statement, although obviously voiced for the psalmist, give us access, I think we can say, to something of Thomas's own practice of 'individual meditation'. And meditation is, of course, one of the ways he recommends in order to overcome the hurt and sadness caused by our own and by others' weakness and sin. He calls it a 'remedy'. And it is to this theme he returns with a particular insistence in the very last of his commentaries on the psalms, speaking this time not about meditation as a remedy but about 'contemplation'.

He tells us that the psalmist (in Psalm 54) after having endured great 'affliction of heart', now 'sets down the remedy he has found and put to use, and this remedy consists principally in giving himself to contemplation.'[75] But what constitutes the actual difference, for Thomas, between meditation and contemplation? Nowadays, these words are often used interchangeably.

---

[72] In the Parma edition the Latin for this tiny phrase reads '*et hoc feci*' (literally, *and I did this*). But it's just possible that there may be an error in the text, and the phrase should read '*et hoc fecit*': *and he [God] made this.* St Thomas is following closely, at this point in his commentary, a celebrated passage from St Augustine's *Confessions* 10:6, in which the phrase '*et hoc fecit*' is repeated over and over again. I am grateful to Dr Margaret Atkins for this observation.

[73] Psalm XLI, *in Psalmos*, p. 310.

[74] Ibid., p. 311.

[75] Psalm LIV: 5, Busa vol. 6, p. 129.

St Thomas, however, points to an important difference between them. Citing
the authority of Richard of St Victor, he notes that, whereas 'meditation is the
survey of the mind while searching for truth,' in contrast, 'contemplation is the
soul's free and clear dwelling upon the object of its gaze.'[76]

Needless to say, what is required for contemplation is a certain grace, or
giftedness, a special facility. And 'this facility,' Thomas tells us, 'is designated
by "wings".'[77] He quotes the psalmist's anguished cry of longing: '*Who will give
me wings like a dove that I may fly away and be at rest?*' The psalmist is here
'acknowledging the fact,' Aquinas notes, 'that there is no remedy for avoiding
that affliction except through contemplation, and that he himself has no way
of avoiding it since he does not have wings with which to fly.'[78] So how, then,
to acquire these 'wings'? What must one do to prepare oneself to become a
contemplative? It is worth noting that St Thomas makes no attempt, at this
point, to speak about techniques or methods of meditation. Instead, he draws
attention, very directly and very simply, to the life of virtue. He writes:

> Three things are required for contemplation. First, the ordering of the
> corrupt affections, which ordering is a certain disposition towards contem-
> plation, and this is had through the moral virtues. So the wings are moral
> virtues, such as patience and humility etc. ... Another wing is charity which
> greatly helps one to fly to contemplation ... Another wing is wisdom, and
> by the wings of wisdom, truth is contemplated, for without these wings,
> one is easily taken into errors if divine things are contemplated.[79]

In parenthesis here it's worth noting that, in *Super Psalmos,* the image of
'wings' occurs a number of times and most memorably, perhaps, when
Thomas is referring to the power of Christ's protection. Thus, commenting
on the phrase *Protect me under the shadow of your wings,* he writes: 'The
two wings are the two arms of Christ extended on the cross.'[80] And, in the

---

[76] *ST,* II II q.180, a.3, ad.1. Translation by Benzinger Bros.
[77] Psalm LIV: 5, Busa vol. 6, p. 129.
[78] Ibid.
[79] Ibid.
[80] Psalm XVI, *In Psalmos,* p. 192.

same text, referring to two images used by the psalmist to evoke the 'diligent protection' of Christ (viz. shadow and wings), he writes:

> Now shade protects [literally 'refreshes'] us from heat, just as God's care refreshes us with safety. Likewise a hen protects her chicks in her wings against a bird of prey, just as God defends the just from the rapacity of the demons in his wings, which are charity and mercy. *How often I wanted to gather you just as a hen gathers her chicks under her wings, and you would not. Mt. 23.37*[81]

(iii) Contemplation and action

St Thomas concludes his thoughts on contemplation in his commentary on Psalm 54 by making a distinction between what he calls the wings of 'the raven' in contrast to those of 'the dove'. The 'dove' is that generous contemplative who not only contemplates, but desires also to share with others the fruits of contemplation. The image suggested here is, of course, that of the dove returning speedily back to the ark of Noah in order to bring the good news.[82] In contrast, the 'raven' is an image of the selfish individual whose only real interest in life is his own intellectual fulfilment and satisfaction:

> For the raven did not turn back to the ark. But the dove returned bearing a green olive branch. Those fly like ravens who do not turn back to the ark by the affection of holiness, for they do not think of anything but themselves, namely how they might track down some truth, like the philosophers. But those fly like doves who both contemplate and turn back towards their neighbours, teaching what they have contemplated, those who, with the green olive branch in their mouth, bear as porters the oil of mercy, devoting themselves to their neighbours. The dove, too, is a clean creature, and lovable, a creature that groans [i.e. coos]; and that's how saintly people are affected by their neighbours, and feel compassion for them.[83]

---

[81] Ibid., pp. 192–3.

[82] Psalm LIV: 5, Busa, vol. 6, p. 129. On the image of the dove, see also the extended reflection by Thomas in his *Commentary on the Gospel of St John*, Lecture 14, 270–2, trans., J. A. Weisheipl and F. R. Larcher (Albany, NY 1980), pp. 123–5.

[83] Psalm LIV: 5, Busa, vol. 6, p. 129.

The idea of passing on to others things which we ourselves have contemplated (*contemplata aliis tradere*) is an idea which was most famously expressed by Aquinas in the *Summa theologiae* II II q.188, a.6. There, however, the austere intellectual structure of the work allowed for no more than a brief, straightforward statement. Here, in contrast, St Thomas gives himself more breathing space, as it were, and in order to make his point with greater clarity and vividness, seems to take considerable delight, as an author, in highlighting the contrast between the images of dove and raven. I find that being able to come upon paragraphs of such quiet wit and wisdom marks one of the very real pleasures of reading Aquinas's *Commentary on the Psalms*.

The actual life of contemplation, evoked by the phrase 'contemplata aliis tradere', is a way of life that can hope to survive and flourish only if it is able enjoy a serene, meditative environment. That fact is one which Aquinas, I have no doubt, would be among the first to acknowledge. But those who 'take flight' in contemplation, and in particular those who make great progress in prayer, are not men and women of a complacent and self-satisfied disposition. No, the opposite is the case. Commenting on the text, *This poor man called and the Lord heard him* (Psalm 33), Thomas observes that the individual, in this case, was manifestly 'poor in spirit, or poor in pride, or poor in earthly desires'.[84] And it is men and women who are poor in that way, Thomas insists, whose prayer has real merit in the end, and who, because they cry out 'with the intensity of interior desire' find their prayers answered by God.[85]

> To me, poor wretch,
> come quickly, Lord!
> My helper, my saviour, my God,
> come and do not delay!

These lines of manifest poverty of spirit, and intense longing, comprise the short stanza which concludes Psalm 39. The Dominican Master, instead of simply commenting on the lines, expresses something of their meaning in his own direct and simple prose:

---

[84] Psalm XXX, *In Psalmos*, p. 266.
[85] Ibid.

I am asking for everything because by myself I am not able to do anything since I am a beggar ... A beggar is someone who seeks from another what he needs to live, while a poor man is someone who has not enough for himself ... I must out of necessity, therefore, beg God for the help of his grace. I am also a poor man, and what I possess is not enough for me. Because I recognize this, *the Lord takes care of me.* And, because I am needy, *You, Lord, are my help.* And, because of danger, *Do not delay!* Mt.15: *Lord, come to my aid!*[86]

Reading this passage – the final paragraph of Thomas's commentary on Psalm 39 – one is made aware, if I'm not mistaken, of something more than the intensity of the psalmist's original prayer. For here, in the careful way Aquinas as author has woven together these stark and simple statements, one senses something of his own deep longing and profound poverty of spirit. Thomas is not, of course, primarily concerned to make a *personal* statement of faith. But he is well able, all the same, to communicate his own passionate point of view with regard to prayer. It is no accident, I would say, that in his commentary he seizes every opportunity to make abundantly clear the fact that prayer is not something merely spoken on the lips, but is rather a cry to God for help from the inmost heart – an appeal, a cry, as stark and simple as it is profound. *Cry, therefore, from within where God hears!*

* * *

'The heart of the human being is profound and inscrutable.' St Thomas makes this great statement when commenting on the phrase, *Deep calls to deep in the voice of your waters* (Ps. 41.7).[87] And he goes on to say that the human being

---

[86] Psalm XXXIX, *In Psalmos*, p. 304. The distinction Thomas makes between the 'beggar' and the 'poor man' is not, perhaps, immediately clear. What is clear, however, is that God takes care of both 'beggar' and 'poor man'. Here, I would suggest that the 'poor man' is someone in need who recognizes his need for help, whereas the 'beggar', in the same situation, actually *asks* for help. Thomas, in his commentary on Psalm 26 (as noted earlier on page 18) points out that there are times when God responds to the misery of the poor, not because the individual may be worthy, nor because help was actually asked, but simply because the misery is so great, and is acknowledged. 'It is as if,' Thomas notes, 'he were saying "I am wretched and I know my wretchedness. Hence it belongs to you [God] to be merciful". *In Psalmos*, p. 239.

[87] Psalm XLI, *In Psalmos*, p. 311.

is, in effect, an 'abyss'.[88] From a great depth, he declares, an individual can call another person to Christ 'not on account of his own strength' but because he is acting 'under the inspiration of the Holy Spirit from whom the tongue of the preacher receives its efficacy'.[89] That, I would suggest, is the same profound inspiration under which St Thomas Aquinas delivered his lectures at Naples on the psalms of David. And something of that depth – that *abyss* of inspired wisdom – happily survives in these academic class-notes, these pages from the thirteenth century.

(2) *Out of the pit of misery:* Prayer as 'the interpreter of hope'

The Naples commentary on the book of Psalms, impressive for many reasons, is perhaps most immediately striking for its considerable bulk. It occupies more than 400 columns in the Parma edition. And yet, in all the many pages of reflection which constitute this commentary, no attention whatever is paid by St Thomas to special methods or techniques of meditation or contemplation. Such technical questions would seem to hold little or no interest for him. Instead, what we find in his commentaries are statements, made over and over again, about the wonderful goodness of God's nature, and also about the hope or confidence which that goodness inspires in the one attempting to pray. The psalmist, Aquinas notes, 'has hope in the mercy of God after considering the divine nature, for it is characteristic of the divine nature to be goodness itself.'[90]

---

[88] Ibid.

[89] Ibid. A different but no less interesting reflection on the word 'abyss' can be found in St Thomas's *Commentary on the Gospel of St John*. After noting, first of all, that the name of Doubting Thomas means 'abyss', Thomas writes: 'An abyss has both depth and darkness. And Thomas was an abyss on account of the darkness of his disbelief, of which he was the cause. Again, there is an abyss – the depth of Christ's compassion – which he had for Thomas. We read: "Abyss calls to abyss" [Ps. 42.7]. That is, the depths of Christ's compassion calls to the depths of darkness [of disbelief] in Thomas, and Thomas's abyss of unwillingness [to believe] calls out, when he professes the faith, to the depths of Christ.' See *Commentary on the Gospel of St John*, vol. 2, Lecture 5, 2546, trans., F. R. Larcher (Petersham 1971) p. 614.

[90] Psalm L, *In Psalmos*, p. 345.

(i) The experience of divine mercy

To lend strength to his own conviction concerning the divine nature, Thomas invokes two authorities, first Dionysius, and then Boethius, both of whom make the same claim, namely that 'God is the very substance of goodness.'[91] 'When I consider,' Thomas writes, 'that it is a characteristic of goodness to drive away misery, and that God is goodness itself then, with confidence, I have recourse to mercy.'[92] This 'confidence' is not based simply on an abstract idea regarding the goodness of God, or on a mere theory drawn from the accumulated wisdom of others. No – it is what St Thomas calls 'confidence born from [actual] experience of divine goodness.'[93]

The word 'experience' is a word St Thomas uses again and again in this context. He speaks, for example, of 'the experience of divine help'[94] and of 'the experience of divine mercy'.[95] At one point, reflecting on a particular passage in the psalms which speaks or sings with confidence about God's power to save, Thomas enters into a brief dialogue with the psalmist. 'From where did you get this hope?' he asks. And the reply: 'From God'. And then, significantly, Thomas adds: 'he [the psalmist] demonstrates this by *experience*.'[96]

In his commentary on the closing paragraphs of Psalm 32, St Thomas explores once again the great themes of hope and mercy, focusing all his attention on the last two stanzas of the psalm:

> Behold the eyes of the Lord
> are on those who fear him,
> on those who hope in his mercy
> to rescue their souls from death,
> to keep them alive in famine.
>
> Our soul is waiting on the Lord,
> he is our help and our protector,

---

[91] Ibid.
[92] Ibid.
[93] Psalm XXXIX, *In Psalmos*, p. 303.
[94] Psalm XLIII, *In Psalmos*, p. 315. See also Psalm III, p. 156, and Psalm XXXIX, p. 300.
[95] Psalm IV, *In Psalmos*, p. 157. See also Psalm XLI, p. 312.
[96] Psalm XLIII, *In Psalmos*, p. 316.

> because it is in him our heart rejoices,
> and in his holy name
> we have placed our hope.
> Lord, let your mercy be upon us
> since we have hoped in you.

According to Thomas these words make manifest 'the saving power of divine mercy'.[97] That is the first and most obvious thing to note. But, then, Aquinas goes on to speak of the great impact which the realization or the thought of God's mercy can have on our lives. There are two stages: first of all, he says, we begin to hope; and, then, we begin to pray. Elsewhere, he tells us that God's supreme attribute is mercy.[98] So, if we want to pray, the first thing we need to do is to reflect on the nature of God, and on what our Dominican master calls 'the experience of [past] favours'.[99]

The effect of a reflection of this kind is to strengthen our hope in God's power to save, and that in turn prompts us to pray. So the gift of hope, then, leads directly to the gift of prayer. That, for Thomas, is a fundamental insight. In fact, in the final paragraph of his commentary on Psalm 32, he takes the opportunity to introduce, for the first time in *Super Psalmos*, his brief but illuminating definition of prayer. 'Prayer,' he writes, 'is the interpreter of hope.'[100] Then, by way of clarification, he adds: 'that's why it follows hope.'[101] Since hope is strengthened so powerfully by the memory of 'past favours', Aquinas goes on at once to name the two things in all of human history for which we are most indebted to God's mercy:

> The first is the favour of the Incarnation: *By the entrails of the mercy of our God Lk 1.78-9* ... The other favour is that of salvation; and this favour is beyond us [literally 'above us'] because *it was not because of any works of justice which we ourselves had done that he saved us, but because of his mercy*

---

[97] Psalm XXXII, *In Psalmos*, p. 264.
[98] See *ST*, II II q.30, a.4. See also *ST*, I q.21, a.3 a.4.
[99] Psalm XXXII, *In Psalmos*, p. 264.
[100] Ibid.
[101] Ibid.

Titus 3 ... *For no-one, who has ever hoped in the Lord, has been confounded.* (Sir. 2.11)[102]

On one occasion, we're told, St Thomas found himself in a situation in which there seemed to be little or no hope of physical survival. He was travelling by boat, on his way back to Paris, when all of a sudden an enormous storm arose. The sailors on the boat were convinced they were about to die. In the midst of the storm, however, Thomas remained surprisingly calm. How to explain this phenomenon? How could Thomas remain so apparently serene in the face of great and immediate danger? The incident is described for us by Tocco in his *Life*. There we read: 'In dread of the squalls, the thunder, the tempest, he [Thomas] placed in front of him, like a shield, the sign of the cross, and with that he defended himself, saying: 'God came in the flesh, God died for us' (*Deus in carnem venit, Deus pro nobis mortuus est*).[103] Rather than yielding to panic or despair, Thomas, in a situation of manifest terror, reminded himself of the two greatest 'favours' of God's mercy in all of human history: the Incarnation and the Redemption. And that thought, that memory of grace in itself, was enough to give him confidence and serenity.

(ii) Despair and hope

In Psalm 13, reflecting on other situations of seeming despair when, for example, an individual finds himself continually oppressed by evil, the psalmist makes bold to declare, *The Lord is his hope.* Thomas, echoing this declaration, remarks: 'In this world those who are oppressed have nowhere to place their hope except in God who is the hope of the saints.'[104] Obviously, the psalmist has learnt *by experience* that there are certain times in life when one is simply unable to defend oneself, unable to rely on one's own resources. Trusting no longer, therefore, in his own power to save, the psalmist waits, according to Aquinas, for 'help from God'. In fact, the saint pictures him exclaiming at one point: 'Only [God] can set me free, for he alone is higher

---

[102] Ibid.

[103] William of Tocco, *Ystoria sancti Thomae de Aquino*, 38, (ed.) Claire le Brun-Gouanvic (Toronto 1996) p. 167.

[104] Psalm XIII, *In Psalmos*, p. 185.

than all truth, he who is truth itself.'[105] St Thomas then puts into the mouth of the psalmist a quite unforgettable prayer: 'Although I am nothing of myself, nevertheless all that I hope to be, and all that I am, is in you.'[106]

*　*　*

The theme of hope is taken up again in the commentary on Psalm 39. But, this time, all the attention is focused on Christ as Saviour, on Christ as the one who alone can lift us out of our misery. The psalm itself announces, *Blessed is the man whose hope is in the name of the Lord*. And Thomas, the Christian disciple and theologian, unhesitatingly declares: 'This name, Jesus, is the true hope, because salvation is in him.'[107] Commenting on the line, *He has pulled me out of the pit of misery*, Aquinas notes that this could refer to the misery of sin itself, or to 'the Hell from which the saints where brought/led out by Christ.'[108] In any case, it is because of Christ, Thomas explains, that an entirely new kind of prayer has been made possible. The praise we are now able to offer to God is something which, in itself, is beyond all human capacity, all human strength. And so, being 'greater than all praise', it is fitting, Thomas notes, that in our worship, 'God is praised by God.'[109]

This striking reflection was prompted by Thomas's reading of the line, *He has put into my mouth a new song*. The song is new because of the remarkable 'new benefits' we have received in Christ and because of 'the new mode of liberation' which has now been realized. 'The new song,' Thomas declares, 'is the New Testament.' And he goes on at once to cite Isa. 53.3: *'I will make with you an eternal covenant [which will demonstrate] as true the mercies promised*

---

[105] Psalm XXXVIII, *In Psalmos,* p. 298.

[106] Ibid.

[107] Psalm XXXIX, *In Psalmos,* p. 301. In his commentary on an earlier psalm Thomas declares that the holy name of God is 'the name of his mercy'. By placing our hope in that name, while still here on earth, we will be able in the future, Thomas says, to rejoice with perfect joy. For, as he goes on to explain, placing our hope in God's name means hoping 'in his goodness, or in his mercy, and not in our own merits.' See Psalm XXXII, *In Psalmos,* p. 264.

[108] Ibid., p. 300.

[109] Ibid.

to David.[110] But now, Thomas makes clear, there is a 'new king', and a 'new law', and there are 'new joys'.[111] He writes:

> All the people of the new law sing a new song which the New Man, Christ, has brought [to them]. *Behold I will make all things new* (Apoc 21). A new people, therefore, sing about new things, namely about the Lord's Incarnation, about his Resurrection, about his Ascension, about his Birth, and about his other mysteries. That's why, on the occasion of these principal solemnities, the ministers of the Church sing and read, dressed in white or silken vestments, for no-one can presume to sing a new song who has not been renewed [in Christ].[112]

Thomas ends his commentary on the psalm speaking directly once more about the unique joy which comes from the experience of being liberated from great misery by God. The psalm itself reads: *May they exult and rejoice, all those who seek you! May they say continually 'Great is the Lord!' who love your salvation.* The Doctor Communis comments: 'He [the psalmist] is asking that good people might rejoice in God's help and liberation, and might praise God.'[113] According to Aquinas, such people 'love the salvation of God which is Christ' and 'they rejoice at finding the Beloved.' They literally 'exult' in God.

Thomas refers, at this point, to a phenomenon which often accompanies spiritual joy. He calls it 'expansion of the heart'. It's an aspect of spiritual life, and of the life of prayer, to which he refers many times in his work. In *Super Psalmos*, 34, he calls it 'the joy of the saints': 'a gladness proper to the just'.[114]

---

[110] Ibid.

[111] Ibid.

[112] Ibid. The *newness* of the Christ event is something to which St Thomas often refers. In one of his sermons, for example, he declared: 'Christ is called the "new man" for his conception is new ... Also his birth is new, since his mother remained a virgin after birth. It is a new suffering, since it is without guilt. It is a new resurrection, since it is quick and renewing: quick, because he also rose in glory. It is a new ascension since he went up by his own strength, not by someone else's ... And because through Christ all things are renewed, we use new vestments on solemn feast days in the Church, so that we *sing a new song to the Lord.*' Sermon 11: *Emitte Spiritum*; text by L.-J. Bataillon (Provisional Leonine text). See *Thomas Aquinas: The Academic Sermons* (*The Fathers of the Church: Medieval Continuation*) p. 155.

[113] Ibid., p. 304.

[114] Psalm XXXIV, *In Psalmos*, p. 276.

But those who, in the past, have fallen into grave sin, they too, it appears, can experience this great blessing. David, the author of the psalms, points out that he is by no means excluded from such joy. 'It is,' Thomas says, 'as if he were saying, "Not only are those others able to rejoice, I too am able to partake in the joy of the saints"!'[115]

One of the common effects of sin is a deep feeling of sadness. Aquinas in one place quotes Prov. 14.34: *'Sin has made the people unhappy.'*[116] And sadness can also, of course, be provoked by certain hurts experienced in the immediate present or in the past. But Thomas insists in his commentary on Psalm 41 that, with regard to sadness, prayer is an agent for change like almost no other. Citing the line, *Why are you cast down my soul, why groan within me?* Thomas speaks of 'the double effect' of prayer: 'One effect is the banishment of sadness, the other is an increase in hope.'[117] He writes: 'Through prayer the human spirit ascends to God; and because God is supremely good, when the soul clings to him, it experiences very great delight (*delectationem maximam*), and such delight either expels sadness or diminishes it.'[118]

(iii) 'O taste and see!'

One thing worth noting about Thomas's commentary is that he speaks not only about the wondrous, necessary knowledge of God and of God's nature, as preparation for prayer, but also about the actual experience of God's nature *within* prayer itself. The psalmist, Aquinas writes, 'urges' us to have this experience when he declares in Psalm 33, *O taste and see that the Lord is sweet!* Earlier, in Chapter 1, I referred to a remark Thomas made about this experience, how it has the wonderful effect of creating in us 'certitude of understanding' and 'security of love'. But why make use of a vivid word such as 'taste' to describe this experience? By way of explanation, Thomas, in his commentary on Psalm 33, speaks first about the nature of experience in general, and then about the experience of divine goodness itself. He writes:

---

[115] Ibid.
[116] Psalm XL, *In Psalmos*, p. 306.
[117] Psalm XLI, *In Psalmos*, p. 312.
[118] Ibid.

The experience of anything comes through the senses but in different ways, depending on whether the object is close or at some distance. If it is removed at a distance, then the experience of it comes through sight, smell or hearing; if it is close, then through touch and taste, but each in its own way. For, touch senses the outside of the object, whereas taste senses the inside. Now God is not far from us, nor outside us, but rather he is in us, as Jeremiah 14 says: *You are in us, O Lord.* Thus the experience of the divine goodness is called tasting.[119]

The particular verse from Psalm 33 we have been considering, reads: *O taste and see that the Lord is sweet! Happy is the man who hopes in him!* (33.9). It is, beyond question, one of the most encouraging verses in all of Scripture. But the verse, which immediately follows, would appear to make a completely different statement. We hear no more talk about the sweetness of God's nature. Instead, we read: *Fear the Lord, all you his saints; they lack nothing those who fear him.* How are we to make sense of the seeming contradiction between these two verses? Those who live in fear of God, are they really able to experience also the kindness and goodness of God's nature? If 'the very essence of God is sweetness,'[120] why should we fear him? Will such fear of God not somehow undermine our hope and our joy? And why should the saints, in particular, be invited to fear God?

By way of explanation, Thomas begins with the bold statement: 'no-one can be holy unless he is fearful (*nisi sit timens*).'[121] But why? The answer: 'because not only is fear necessary for those growing in holiness but even for those already established in it ... Nothing eliminates holiness more than pride, but fear binds pride.'[122] In *Super Psalmos* 32, Aquinas addresses a related question, speaking this time about the relationship between fear and hope. He writes: 'One without the other is not sufficient; for fear without hope despairs, and hope without fear presumes. For fear is roused from a consideration of divine

---

[119] Psalm XXXIII, *In Psalmos*, p. 266.
[120] Psalm XXIV, *In Psalmos*, p. 231.
[121] Psalm XXXIII, *In Psalmos*, p. 266.
[122] Ibid.

power ... hope from divine mercy. From the first, flight from sin; from the second, hope for pardon.'[123]

Again, commenting on the clear imperative in Psalm 2, *Serve the Lord with fear, and exalt him with trembling,* Thomas notes that the psalmist does not hesitate to say 'with fear'. This is not, however, an invitation to live one's life in a continual state of nervousness or unhappiness. On the contrary, – Thomas writes: 'lest this service be understood as misery, he [the psalmist] adds: *And exalt him with trembling.* Because the fear of the Lord is not a misery but a joy, as was said in Leviticus 10: *And Aaron answered Moses, How can they please God with a lugubrious mind?'*[124]

Worth noting here, in passing, is an entry Gerard Manley Hopkins made in his journal when, for the first time he saw the Northern Lights. The experience was so truly awe-inspiring, it quickened in him a sense of fear before the infinite mystery of God. But, in order to describe this fear, he made use of an unexpected adjective of which Aquinas would, I have no doubt, have approved. Hopkins wrote:

> First saw the Northern Lights. My eye was caught by beams of light and dark ... I saw soft pulses of light one after another rise and pass upwards arched in shape but waveringly and with the arch broken ... This busy working of nature wholly independent of the earth and seeming to go on in a strain of time not reckoned by our reckoning of days and years but ... dated to the day of judgment was like a new witness to God and filled me with *delightful* fear.[125]

Fear of the Lord, as Thomas understands it, far from preventing us from experiencing the sweetness of God, is actually an important help to that end. In commenting on verse 16 from Psalm 30: *How great, Lord, is the abundance*

---

[123] Psalm XXXII, *In Psalmos,* p. 264. For a comparable reflection on fear and hope, see Psalm XXXIX, p. 301.

[124] Psalm II, *In Psalmos,* p. 155. Thomas distinguishes between what he calls a 'servile fear' and a 'filial fear'. The former is happily cast out by love, but the latter is a manifestation of something so fundamental to the Christian experience it in some way survives into the next life. See Psalm XVIII, *In Psalmos,* p. 210.

[125] Journal, 24 September 1870. See *The Journals and Papers of Gerard Manley Hopkins,* (eds), H. House and G. Storey (London 1959) p. 200. My italics.

of your sweetness which you have reserved in secret for those who fear you, Thomas once more cites the text *O taste and see the sweetness of the Lord!*[126]

Unfortunately, the word 'sweetness' in English has lost much of its strength and beauty, being linked since Victorian times with a decidedly mawkish and sentimental piety. But the Latin word *'dulcedo'* is free of all such associations. When used by Aquinas, for example, to refer to the serene and wholly delightful character of God's nature, it possesses always a quiet, straightforward candour, a fine simplicity of thought and expression. Thomas writes:

> In whatever way sweetness (*'dulcedo'*) is talked about, it contains delight; for, though it is in itself one and simple, it is the root and source of all good. That's why all that is the object of delight in this world, is found completely in God: namely wisdom, truth, honour, excellence, pleasure – all these things are found in God in superabundance. Accordingly, the psalmist says *How great [Lord] is the abundance [of your sweetness],* unsurpassable according to greatness, and infinitely incomprehensible for us.[127]

That St Thomas, the Master of the Sacred Page, should describe God's nature as 'infinitely incomprehensible' is of no small significance. He has, after all, by this stage composed countless pages of detailed theological reflection and analysis and, with a dogged scholastic genius, has invoked the wisdom of centuries concerning the nature of God and the nature of prayer as revealed in the book of Psalms. And yet here, in his commentary on Psalm 30, he is prepared openly to admit that, for him, God is, in the end, 'incomprehensible'. Master Thomas, the greatest teacher of his age, is it would appear quite simply disarmed – *mastered* – by the overwhelming mystery of the God whom he is seeking to understand. Commenting on verse 10 from Psalm 34, *All my bones will exclaim, Lord, who can compare with you ...?* Thomas writes: '*All my bones,* that is to say, regarding whatever is virtuous in me, or whatever knowledge of truth [I possess] or fervour, charity, and other such things, the psalmist says, *O Lord, who is like you,* since, it is asserted, nothing is comparable to God

---

[126] See Psalm XXX, *In Psalmos,* p. 254.
[127] Psalm XXX, *In Psalmos,* p. 254.

(*nihil est Deo comparabile*).[128] Thomas, in a Pauline turn of phrase, declares, 'All of man's strength is weakness when compared to God, and thus the more knowledge someone has of God, the less he estimates his own ability to be.'[129]

That said, the theologian, whether man or woman, who is wholly dedicated to the pursuit of truth and to the love of God, may well appear on occasion to seize hold of some central part of the mystery. Urged on by the desire to know God intimately, and emboldened by the strength of a graced wisdom, the strenuous effort to understand is at last rewarded, it would seem, with the 'victory' of living knowledge. At the core of that 'victory', however, there is, Thomas tells us, an experience of God, an experience of the divine sweetness, so overwhelming it leaves the contemplative – the prayerful theologian – 'limping' like Jacob who had spent an entire night wrestling with the angel of God's presence.[130]

St Thomas quotes Pope St Gregory the Great: 'when the soul strives to contemplate God, it is in a state of struggle which, at one point, it almost overcomes because by understanding and feeling it tastes something of the incomprehensible light, but then it succumbs, because even while tasting, it fails.'[131] This failure, this defeat, does not mean the death of hope. On the contrary, it marks the beginning of a truly wondrous blessing, the fulfilment of a desire beyond anything that could ever have been foreseen or imagined.

Marie-Dominique Chenu, in his book on the nature of theology, paraphrases wonderfully well, at one point, the teaching of St Thomas with regard to the mysterious agony and ecstasy involved in the contemplative search for God. I can think of no better way to end this chapter than by quoting now in full the vivid picture painted for us by Chenu:

The whole night they wrestled, muscles straining, neither yielding; but at daybreak the angel disappeared, apparently leaving the field clear to his adversary. But Jacob then felt a violent pain in his thigh. He was left wounded and limping. It is thus that the theologian grapples with the

---

[128] Psalm XXXIV, *In Psalmos*, p. 272.
[129] Ibid.
[130] See Gen. 32.23-32.
[131] *ST*, II II q.180, a.7, obj.2

mystery when God brings him face to face with it. He is taut, like a bent bow, grappling with human language; he struggles like a wrestler; he even seems to win the mastery. But then he feels a weakness, a weakness at once painful and delicious, for to be thus defeated is in fact the proof that his combat was divine.[132]

---

[132] M.-D. Chenu, *La theologie est-elle une science?* (Paris 1943) pp. 47–8. Most probably the Aquinas texts Chenu has in mind are the following: *ST*, II II q.180, a.7 and a.8.

Part Three

Poet of the Eucharist: the hymns and canticles of Aquinas

Introduction

Is Thomas Aquinas a poet? Can we say, without hesitation, that he belongs not only to the history of theology and philosophy but also to the history of imaginative literature? If asked a question of this kind today, most people would probably be inclined to answer at once in the negative. Bryan Magee, in his book, *Talking Philosophy: Dialogues with Fifteen Leading Philosophers*, remarks:

> Some of the great philosophers have been also great writers in the sense of great literary artists – I suppose the outstanding examples are Plato, St Augustine, Schopenhauer, and Nietzsche ... Yet there have been great philosophers who were bad writers, two of the very greatest – Kant and Aristotle – being two of the worst. Others were just pedestrian – one thinks of Aquinas.[1]

What Magee has in mind here, we may presume, are the prose writings of Aquinas, not the poetry. For, whether it is accurate or not to apply the adjective 'pedestrian' to the scholastic prose of Aquinas, the term can certainly not be applied with justice to St Thomas's achievement in verse.[2] Regarding the hymns composed for the Eucharist, no poet after him ever achieved the same miracle of sound and sense, the same harmony of music and meaning.

---

[1] Bryan Magee, *Talking Philosophy: Dialogues with Fifteen Leading Philosophers* (Oxford 2001) p. 230.

[2] Olivier-Thomas Venard, in a three-volume work entitled *Thomas d'Aquin, poète théologien*, suggests that Aquinas was not only a poet in the composition of his eucharistic hymns, he was also a fine rhetorician in the composition of his theological works. See vol. 1: *Littérature et théologie, une saison en enfer* (2003). In this original study, very much in the French tradition, Venard is concerned to make lively the links which he perceives between the language and rhetoric of St Thomas and that of certain modern French poets. For further discussion on related topics, see Catherine Pickstock, *After Writing* (Oxford 1998) pp. 253–66, and John Milbank, 'Postface' in Venard's vol. 3: *Pagina sacra: Le passage de l'Écriture sainte à l'écriture théologie* (Paris 2009) pp. 911–15.

Generally speaking, the words of hymns, when detached from the music that accompanies them, are not particularly impressive. But, happily, there are exceptions: texts composed for hymns which, in terms of beauty and meaning, of imagery and lyric power, are poems in their own right, and can stand on their own feet. The eucharistic hymns and canticles of Aquinas are in that category.

It's not surprising, therefore, that Frederick Brittain, in his Introduction to *The Penguin Book of Latin Verse*, could describe the eucharistic hymns of Aquinas as 'beautiful poems, dignified, majestic, and of perfect technique.'[3] And, writing a century earlier, Gerard Manley Hopkins could go even further, declaring in a letter to Robert Bridges that the canticles of St Thomas are 'remarkable works of genius.'[4]

In this third and final section, my aim is to test the validity of Hopkins' confident assertion, a task which will require not only a close reading of the poems themselves, but also an examination of the question of authorship. Can we say for certain that Aquinas really is the author of these impressive lyrics? And, if we can, what are the factors in his biography which help explain his apparently sudden, unexpected emergence as a gifted poet?

---

[3] Frederick Brittain (ed.), *The Penguin Book of Latin Verse* (Harmondsworth 1962) p.xxxv.
[4] Letter, 10 June 1882, in *The Letters of Gerard Manley Hopkins to Robert Bridges*, (ed.) C. C. Abbott (Oxford 1955) p. 148.

6

A poet in the making

Now
the bread of angels
feeds the sons of men.
Figures and types
are fled
never to come again.
O what a wondrous thing!
The poor,
the humble, the lowly,
consume the Master and King.

These lines are justly famous. Here St Thomas is not speaking in the dogged, abstract idiom of a scholastic philosopher or theologian. The mood, on the contrary, is one of calm amazement, an ecstasy of quiet thought and feeling. And the words, though plain and simple, are words transformed, quickened into rhythm, into song, by a sense of manifest wonder. Not surprisingly, the stanza has become one of the most admired and celebrated, being set to music on more than one occasion and, countless times, performed by artists and singers across the world.

Panis angelicus
fit panis hominum,
dat panis caelicus
figuris terminum.
O res mirablis!

Manducat Dominum
pauper, servus et humilis.

What impresses at once is the concentrated rhythm of the stanza, and the graced insistence and persuasive authority of its rhymes. Yes, the work undoubtedly bears the weight of a striking revelation, a truly profound theological message. But no less impressive is the way, with quiet, purposeful intensity, the lines *sing*. Here we are, without question, in the presence of a master craftsman. Aquinas, in the making of this particular stanza, must have experienced – and in no small measure – something of that deep sense of satisfaction and delight known to every creative artist and craftsman. Once, when he was commenting on a passage directly concerned with the close connection poets have with their own work, Aquinas remarked:

> Every artisan loves his own work ... And this is especially true in the case of poets who love their own poems superabundantly as parents love their children ... To all humans their own being is an object of preference and love. For everything, to the extent that it exists, is good. And the good is lovable and an object of preference. Now our own being consists in some activity ... There can be no life without vital activity of some kind. Hence the performance of vital actions is desirable to everyone.[1]

Aquinas then goes on to add that, in the act of composing, in the actual making of a work of art, something of the poet or craftsman enters into the work itself. 'And it is for that reason,' he concludes, 'both artisans and poets ... love their own works, because they love their own being. And this is in the nature of things, namely, that everything loves its own being.'[2]

1. An apprentice poet?

The fact that Aquinas, without any clear or obvious preparation, was capable in

---

[1] See *Sententia libri ethicorum*, Bk 9, lect. 7, 1167 b 33–1168 a 5, in *Opera omnia*, Leonine vol. 47/2 (Rome 1969) p. 525.
[2] Ibid., lect. 7, 1168 a 5, p. 525.

mid-career of writing poems and canticles of undisputed quality is something which has been a source of puzzlement to students of Aquinas's work for generations. Did the contemporaries of Aquinas not regard him, first and last, as the author of rigorously technical scholastic texts on philosophy and theology? Why, then, should Aquinas be considered capable, all of a sudden, of turning his hand to the composition of verse? Are we to understand that he was somehow a 'poet by decree', a talent prompted *ex nihilo* by the command of Pope Urban IV? Or is it possible that, apart from his long apprenticeship as theologian and philosopher, Aquinas had also been initiated, at some earlier stage in his life, into the craft or art of literary composition?

As it happens, we have information available to us which is of no small interest with regard to this question. In an article entitled 'Il Dottore Angelico a Montecassino' (The Angelic Doctor at Montecassino), the Benedictine scholar, Tommaso Leccisotti, offers an illuminating picture of the kind of education young Thomas d'Aquino would have received at the Monastery after he had been sent there by his parents at the age of five.[3] Apart from learning to recite the psalms by heart, Aquinas, we're told, would have been expected to give time also to the study of music and to the art of composition. It is almost certain, therefore, that Thomas's eventual mastery of the craft of verse-making was a skill acquired, at least in some initial form, as a direct result of his literary schooling at Monte Cassino.[4] Another scholar, the Dominican Angelus Walz, writes: 'The art of writing … was still cultivated [in the Monastery at that time]. The rules of language and style were taught together with grammar. Thus the way was open to the great treasures of literature and to the whole output of the world of letters.'[5]

---

[3] D. Tommaso Leccisotti, 'Il Dottore Angelico a Montecassino,' *Rivista di filosofia neo-scholastica,* XXXII, fasc. vi (November 1940) p. 530 and p. 539.

[4] Ibid. At Monte Cassino, although attention was paid most especially to Latin prose and poetry, attention was also given to the literature of the '*vulgare*'. See Leccisotti, pp. 530–1.

[5] Angelus Walz, *St Thomas Aquinas: A Biographical Study,* trans., S. Bullough (Westminster, Maryland: The Newman Press, 1951) p. 14. Monte Cassino was one of the most celebrated places of learning in the Middle Ages. In the monastery's *scriptorium* many texts of Greek and Roman poetry, grammar and geometry, were carefully transcribed by the monks. And an impressive number of the monks themselves were gifted poets, among them Alfanus (d. 1085), Alberic (d. 1105), and Abbot Bertharius (c. 810–83).

Immediately after he left Monte Cassino, young Thomas was sent to the University of Naples. There he inscribed in the Faculty of Arts, and was able to continue his study of composition and literature. According to Walz 'the literary studies in the Faculty of Arts ... were principally concerned with instruction and exercise in the art of *cursus,* or skill in correct speech and writing. The *cursus* was a rhythmic prose whose words were disposed according to certain rules of a special kind of harmony.'[6] In time the young Aquinas would move forward in his studies to devote himself almost exclusively to the disciplines of philosophy and theology. But the earlier link he had with the arts was never lost. Many years later, when the news of Aquinas's death reached Paris, it was significantly the Faculty of Arts not the Faculty of Theology which took the initiative in writing to express their profound condolences to the Dominican friars gathered in Lyons for a General Chapter of the Order:

> With a clamour of grief and tears we lament the loss that has befallen the whole Church and this University of Paris in particular ... For news has come to us which floods us with grief and amazement, bewilders our understanding, transfixes our very vitals, and wellnigh breaks our hearts ... that the venerated Master, brother Thomas of Aquino, has been called forever out of this world. Who could have expected that divine Providence would permit it – that this morning star which shone on the world, that the light and glory of our time ... should already be withdrawn from us?[7]

The letter, unrestrained in its feeling and rhetoric, demonstrates the depth of regard and affection which the members of the Arts Faculty felt for their deceased academic colleague, a man who was a true Master not only of the science of theology but also of philosophy, a Master of the Sacred Page, a biblical theologian, who was at the same time the revered author of the Corpus Christi canticles.

---

[6] Ibid., p. 21.

[7] A Letter to the Faculty of Arts in the University of Paris to the General Chapter of the Order of Preachers at Lyons in 1274; cited in Foster, *Biographical Documents,* p. 153.

2. A sonnet by Aquinas?

All the poems and hymns which have been attributed to Aquinas are in Latin, with one curious exception. In a manuscript, dating from the middle of the fourteenth century, a short poem has been discovered attributed to the saint, a work composed not in Latin but in Italian. Scholars such as Scandone[8] and Mandonnet[9] have not hesitated to declare it to be a genuine work of St Thomas, but the majority of scholars are a lot more sceptical. Nevertheless, the fact that these few lines, written in the '*vulgare*', might just possibly have been composed by the young Aquinas when he was an arts student at Naples, lends the work an undoubted fascination. On this point, Kenelm Foster has remarked: 'so long as the question of authenticity is not finally decided, the poem gains in interest by this "perhaps".'[10]

Concerning the poem itself, Foster writes: 'It is the work of a thinker, and one who is much more thinker than artist: abstractedly conceived, stiff in its syntax, with the logical joints all showing and hardly a touch of imagery, but vigorous, elevated and intense.'[11] Mandonnet dates the poem or sonnet to the years 1244–5, and puts forward the theory that, in this work, Thomas, the young scholar, was responding to his brother Reginaldo's accusation that, by becoming a humble Dominican – a friar preacher – he was betraying the honour of his family.[12]

Here is the text of the poem together with a prose translation into English:

Tanto ha virtù ciascun, quanto ha intelletto;

(Each man has virtue to the extent that he has understanding;)

E a valor quanto in virtù si stende;

(and he has worth in proportion to his virtue;)

---

[8] See Francsico Scandone, 'La vita, la famiglia e la patria di S. Tommaso', in *Miscellanea Storico-Artistica* (Rome 1924).

[9] See P. Mandonnet, 'Thomas d'Aquin, novice prêcheur, 1244–1246', *Revue thomiste*, vol. 8 (May–June 1925) p. 241.

[10] *The Life of St Thomas Aquinas: Biographical Documents*, 13, (ed.) Kenelm Foster (London 1959) p. 165.

[11] Ibid.

[12] Reginaldo, while in attendance at the court of Frederick II, was regarded as one of the court's finest poets. See L.-H. Petitot, *The Life and Spirit of Thomas Aquinas*, trans., C. Burke (Chicago 1966) p. 137.

E tanto ha 'llhor di ben, quanto l'intende,

(and he possesses goodness to the extent that he aims for it,)

E quanto ha d'honor gentil diletto.

(and to the extent that he takes a noble delight in honour.)

E il diletto gentil, quanto ha l'effetto,

(And this noble delight, in so far as it has its effect,)

Adorna il bel piacer, che nel chor scende;

(adorns the fine joy which surges in the heart;)

Il quale adorna tanto, quanto splende

(for such joy adorns to the extent that it shines forth)

Per somiglianza del proprio subietto.

(through likeness with its proper subject.)

Dunque chi vol veder, quanto d'honore

(Whoever, then, wishes to see how much honour)

Altrui è degno e di laude perfecta

(and perfect praise another person merits)

Miri in qual disio amante ha il core.

(let him consider to what desire the lover turns his heart.)

Però ch'esser felice ogni uomo affecta,

(For, though everyone desires to be happy,)

Massimamente quell, che per l'onore

(this is especially true of the man who, for honour,)

Verace adopra, tal corona aspetta,

(works faithfully, his gaze fixed on that crown.)[13]

There are, in this unusual work, a number of striking resemblances to certain key ideas in the mature work of Aquinas. Most notably, perhaps, the idea expressed on the third last line which echoes or repeats one of the most dominant Thomisic themes, namely that every human being craves happiness. V. J. Bourke draws our attention also to the lines concerning the '*bel piacer che … splende*' which are, he notes, 'reminiscent of St Thomas's famous description

---

[13] See Foster, *Biographical Documents*, p. 166. The English translation is by the present author.

of the beautiful as that which gives pleasure when seen (*quod visum placet*), and as having the quality of shining forth (*claritas*).'[14]

That this poem was composed by the young Thomas Aquinas is by no means certain. Only a very few scholars seem persuaded by the Aquinas attribution. But what, we need to ask, of the eucharistic canticles? These great works have often been attributed to St Thomas. The enthusiasm of attribution, however, has not always been matched with outright or convincing proof. So what, if anything, is different today with regard to evidence? In light of the most recent academic research on the subject, can we be certain at last that Aquinas really is the author?

---

[14] Vernon J. Bourke, *Aquinas: Search for Wisdom* (Milwaukee 1965) p. 24.

7

'Corpus Christi': authorship and history of composition

1. The question of authorship

Since the fourteenth century until modern times it has generally been accepted that Thomas Aquinas composed the whole liturgy for the feast of Corpus Christi. The most authoritative source for this attribution comes from one of his contemporaries, a Dominican who had been his confessor and confidant, Tolomeo of Lucca (c. 1236–c. 1336). In a work of history, written sometime between 1312 and 1317, Tolomeo addressed directly the question of authorship: 'By order of the same pope, Friar Thomas also composed the Office for Corpus Christi …The Corpus Christi Office Thomas composed in full, including the lessons and all the parts to be recited by day or night; the Mass, too, and whatever has to be sung on that day.'[1]

That Thomas was the author of the Corpus Christi liturgy was also indicated, sometime later, in the work of two other confrères and disciples, William of Tocco and Bernard Gui. Their work was probably influenced by that of Tolomeo.[2] In 1323, the year of Thomas's canonization, the Corpus

---

[1] Tolomeo of Lucca, *Hist. Eccl.*, lib. 22, c.24, col. 1154; cited in Weisheipl, p. 177.
[2] See Pierre-Marie Gy, 'L'Office du Corpus Christi oeuvre de s. Thomas d'Aquin', Chapter XI in *La liturgie dans l'histoire* (Paris 1990) pp. 224–5.

Christi Office which had been linked with his name was formally adopted by the Dominican Order. The relevant passage in the Acts of the General Chapter reads:

> Since our Order ought to conform in the Divine Office to the Holy Roman Church, in so far as possible, and particularly in an office which is a product of our Order by apostolic command, we now wish that the Office of Corpus Christi, composed, as it is said, by the venerable doctor Thomas d'Aquino, be observed throughout the entire Order on the Thursday after the feast of Trinity and throughout its octave inclusive.[3]

Although Aquinas's authorship of the Office of Corpus Christi was something taken for granted by the vast majority of people for hundreds of years, a change occured in the middle of the twentieth century when serious doubts began to be expressed by a number of eminent scholars.[4] It was noted, first of all, that support for the attribution to Aquinas came decidedly late in the day. In the biography of the saint, by Peter of Calo, no mention whatever was made of the Corpus Christi Office, and nor was it listed in the material presented at the canonization enquiry. Furthermore, Dominicans were notably slow in accepting the new liturgy, a fact which would seem to argue strongly against Aquinas's authorship. For, if the Dominicans had been persuaded the work was that of their illustrious confrère, they would surely have had no hesitation whatever about adopting it, and as quickly as possible.

Needless to say, these doubts and queries presented no small challenge to the earlier claim that Aquinas had been the principal author of the new liturgy. But, in more recent years, the various objections to the Aquinas attribution have themselves been challenged by the scholarly work of two scholars in particular, Pierre-Marie Gy and R. J. Zawilla.[5] Given the quality of their research, J.-P. Torrell, in his acclaimed study of the life and work of Aquinas,

---

[3] *Monumenta Ordinis Praedicatorum Historica* [MOPH] 4, 138; cited in Weisheipl, pp. 183–4.
[4] See Cyrille Lambot, 'L'Office de la Fête-Dieu. Aperçus nouveaux sur ses origins', *Revue Bénédictine* 54 (1942) p. 67. See also L. M. J. Delaissé, 'A la recherché des origins de l'office du Corpus Christi dans les manuscrits liturgiques', *Scriptorium* 4 (1950) p. 221.
[5] See R. J. Zawilla, *The Biblical Sources of the Historia Corporis Christi attributed to Thomas Aquinas*, Unpublished Doctorate, Toronto 1985. See also P.-M. Gy, 'L'Office du Corpus Christi' (1990).

felt able to conclude that the 'attribution to Saint Thomas can no longer reasonably be placed in doubt.'[6]

The absence of any reference to the Corpus Christi liturgy in the catalogue of St Thomas's works, prepared for his canonization enquiry, can be explained first of all by the fact that this particular catalogue contains only scholarly and scientific works. And there is another reason, and a far more telling one, which will help explain the omission. The liturgy attributed to St Thomas had, by order of the Pope, been adopted for use by the Church world-wide. It ceased, therefore, to be the private property of its author, and could not reasonably be included among the private writings of the Dominican.

But how to explain the tardy reception by the Dominican Order of this new liturgy? When the Office of Corpus Christi was first introduced into the liturgy of the Friars Preachers in 1319, the form used was not the one attributed to Aquinas. It was only after four years, in 1323, that the Aquinas form was finally adopted. Why the delay? In answer to this question Miri Rubin writes: 'one must bear in mind that the feast had fallen into oblivion, even in the very *curia* within which it was founded ... we should not be surprised that it took four years for it to be re-established in the Dominican Order.'[7]

There are, I believe, clear indications, both external and internal, which point to St Thomas as the author of the Corpus Christi liturgy. In the first place, he was resident at Orvieto when, at the request of Pope Urban, the work was undertaken. At that time, St Thomas, we know, was one of the people closest to Urban, and one of the most respected. A year previously, in 1263, he had already completed, at Urban's request, the first book of the *Catena aurea*. And it by no means unlikely, therefore, that he would also have been asked by Urban to compose the liturgy for the new feast.

With regard to the internal indications that point to Aquinas's authorship, a number of important things can be said. But, first of all, it will be necessary to explain what is meant by composing or creating a liturgy. It does not mean making something entirely new. It means rather drawing together into a new whole individual elements from past tradition, texts for example from

---

[6] Torrell, vol. 1, p. 130.
[7] Miri Rubin, *Corpus Christi: The Eucharist in Late Medieval Culture* (Cambridge 1991) pp. 186–7.

the Scriptures and the Fathers, and prayers and hymns belonging to already existing liturgies, and then forming out of these disparate sources something at once manifestly ancient and manifestly new. The particular elements lying behind the making by St Thomas of the Corpus Christi liturgy include not only an already existing liturgy, but also the truly absorbing story of that liturgy's unusual genesis and development.

2. 'Corpus Christi': The feast and its founder

The story of the making of 'Corpus Christi' begins not with a planned text or an idea but with a mysterious vision. The year was 1210, and the name of the visionary was Juliana, a young and devout religious woman living and working at the *leprosarium* of Mont Cornillon, situated near Liège in Belgium. In her vision Juliana beheld a radiant full moon, but a moon mysteriously blemished as if some small part of it was missing. In her *Vita* we read: 'A moon appeared to her in its splendor, with a little break in part of its sphere. She watched this for a long while, wondered a lot, and did not know what this might portend.'[8] Some years later the meaning of the vision was made wonderfully clear: 'Christ revealed to her that the Church was in the moon, and that the missing part of the moon stood for the absence of one feast in the Church, which he would want his faithful to celebrate on earth.'[9]

That feast was, of course, the feast of Corpus Christi. Juliana's confessor passed on the news of the vision to the local bishop of Liège, Robert of Turotte. And when certain authorities were consulted, including a few Dominican scholars, and the vision was judged to be genuine, Bishop Robert set about establishing the feast in his diocese. It was to be celebrated, he decreed, on the first Thursday after Trinity Sunday. A member of the community of Mont Cornillon, a certain Brother John, was selected by Juliana to compose the Office and Mass for the new feast. John was thought to be 'inexperienced in

---

[8] *Vita Juliana*, II, 2. C. 2, no. 6; cited in Rubin, p. 170.
[9] Ibid.

literary matters',[10] but his work found acceptance, at least initially, within the diocese of Liège. Of his liturgy we read in the *Vita* of Juliana: 'the texts and melodies are of such beauty and sweetness that they should be able to wring devotion even from hearts of stone.'[11]

One man who was in no way impressed by this novel liturgical innovation was the new bishop of Liège, Henry of Guelder. From the start Henry was opposed to Juliana, and for a while it seemed as if the fledging liturgy might not survive. But then, by a happy providence, the celebrated Dominican scholar and preacher, Hugh of St Cher, came on a visit to Liège. He was at once interested in the new liturgy, and it was he who saw to it that the feast spread far and wide beyond the diocese of Liège.[12]

Hugh's support for Juliana was typical of the quality of support he gave everywhere to women religious at that time. When, as Cardinal-Legate, for example, he visited Germany, we are told that he 'passionately defended the women's religious movement, supporting women's houses and communities to the best of his strength.'[13] Hugh, it would appear, 'had come to understand the importance of and needs of the women's religious movement as had few others.'[14] On 19 March 1263, Hugh of St Cher died at Orvieto, the place where, as it happened, his Dominican confrère, Thomas Aquinas, was living and working at the time. One year later, in 1264, we find Thomas working on a new version of the Corpus Christi liturgy.

Mention has been made already of the vision received by St Juliana, an event which marked the beginning of the history of 'Corpus Christi'. But another miraculous event has long been linked with this history, an event known as the Miracle of Bolsena. A German priest, we are told (in the *Chronica* of St Antoninus of Florence), while making a pilgrimage to Rome, found himself deeply troubled by doubts regarding the doctrine of transubstantiation. His

---

[10] *Vie de Sainte Julienne de Cornillon*; cited in Barbara R. Walters, *The Feast of Corpus Christi* (Pennsylvania 2006) p. 7.

[11] Ibid., Walters, p. 8.

[12] Ibid., pp. 11–12.

[13] See Herbert Grundmann, *Religious Movements in the Middle Ages*, trans., S. Rowan (Notre Dame, Indiana 1995) p. 126.

[14] Ibid.

doubts were, however, completely overcome by an event which occurred when he was celebrating Mass in the town of Bolsena (in Lazio, but close to the border with Umbria). To his astonishment, he saw blood issuing from the consecrated elements, and drenching the corporal. News of the miracle spread at once throughout the village. And, after some time, when the miracle had been pronounced genuine, a procession was formed, and the blood-stained corporal carried to Pope Urban IV at Orvieto, a short distance away. The corporal was then enshrined in a reliquary, and placed in the Church of Santa Christina where it remains to this day.

The miracle was subsequently depicted by Raphael in a famous painting now hanging in the Vatican. Pope Urban IV, it has often been claimed, failed to promote the new feast until the reported miracle at Bolsena caught the imagination of the Italian people. This may possibly be true, but the veracity of the link between the miracle and the establishment of the feast has not, in fact, been accepted by most contemporary scholars.[15]

3. 'Corpus Christi': The contribution of Aquinas

The Corpus Christi Office composed at Orvieto, at Pope Urban's request, came to be known as the 'Roman Office' in order to distinguish it from the earlier Office inspired by St Juliana at Mont Cornillon. Up to the middle of the twentieth century only one version of the Roman Office was known to scholars, the *Sacerdos in aeternum*. In 1942, however, Cyrille Lambot discovered the manuscript of another Office, an earlier and less perfect work known as the *Sapientia aedificavit*.[16] This discovery raised all kinds of questions: Why were there two Roman Offices for the feast of Corpus Christi

---

[15] R. J. Zawilla, *The Biblical Sources of the Historia Corporis Christi attributed to Thomas Aquinas*, Unpublished Doctorate, Toronto 1985, pp. 47–9. According to St Thomas, the blood which appears during a eucharistic miracle, and which remains visible afterwards for the eye to see, may indeed represent an important truth, making manifest the fact that 'Christ's body and blood are truly in this Sacrament.' This does not mean, however, that the blood which remains is a relic of Christ, a part of Christ. Whatever else it may be, it is not the blood of Saviour. See *ST*, III, q.76, a.8.

[16] See C. Lambot, 'L'Office de la Fête-Dieu. Aperçus nouveaux sur ses origins', *Revue Bénédictine* 54 (1942) pp. 61–123.

and not simply one? Was Aquinas the author of both of them? And how did they differ from each other and from the earlier Office at Mont Cornillon?

As a result of his research, Lambot concluded that Aquinas was indeed the author of both Roman Offices. The first Office (*Sapientia*), he noted, showed signs of being hastily composed. And the reason, Lambot suggested, was that the Pope at the time, Urban IV, sensing he had not long to live, brought forward the date originally fixed for the celebration.[17] Only afterwards, according to this hypothesis, was Aquinas able to revise his work, and create (along with the Mass *Cibavit eos*) a final version of the Roman Office. This second version (*Sacerdos*) and the Mass (*Cibavit*) were promulgated by Urban IV on 11 August 1264, and thus the feast of Corpus *Christi* was transmitted to future generations.[18]

Already, in this chapter, what might be called the external evidence indicating St Thomas as the author of the Corpus Christi liturgy has been noted. But there exists also, as it happens, impressive *internal* evidence to support the claim. A number of scholars have drawn attention, for example, to the close link that exists between the use of biblical material in the Office for the feast and the use of similar material in Thomas's own eucharistic writings. Let it suffice here if I offer a few brief examples of their exhaustive research.

During that period in the Middle Ages it was common practice among authors, when writing about the presence of Christ in the Eucharist, to cite from St Matthew's Gospel the phrase, *Behold I am with you until the end of time* (Mt. 28.20). But, over the years, the phrase had come to be associated, in theological discourse, with a decidedly exaggerated idea of Christ's 'corporeal' presence in the Eucharist.[19] Thomas, being opposed to that idea, and to the

---

[17] Ibid., p. 93.

[18] It should be noted, however, that the text of the Office *Sacerdos* does not correspond exactly to the versions we find today in contemporary breviaries and missals. To begin with, there were changes made in the fifteenth century. And then, according to Weisheipl, 'The revised text of the fifteenth century was reformed by Pope Pius V in the sixteenth century, and again by Pius X in the twentieth.' See Weisheipl, pp. 177–8.

[19] Aquinas accepts, of course, that the body of Christ is truly present in the Eucharist. Nevertheless, he writes: 'Christ's body is not in this sacrament in the same way as a body is in place which by its dimension corresponds with the place, but rather in a special way appropriate to this sacrament.' *Summa theologiae*, III, q.75, a.1, ad 3.

kind of excessive realism it represented, had always avoided citing the Matthew passage in his theological writings on the Eucharist. Its omission, therefore, from both the *Sapientia* and the *Sacerdos* Offices is taken by scholars of St Thomas to be a likely indication of his authorship.[20]

An even 'clearer argument', in the view of J.-P. Torrell, is the surprising presence, in one of the readings for Matins, of an extended scholastic discourse on the Eucharist. Although 'not a point of view that is exclusively Thomas's own,' nevertheless, Torrell notes, Thomas's 'rigorous Aristotelian perspective makes him probably the only one of his contemporaries who would think to use it in such a context, for it was he alone who gave it such great importance.'[21] So, once again, we can say, the passage is 'the equivalent of a signature'.[22]

Aquinas's identity as a scholastic is evident here, as it is evident throughout all his work. But what most distinguishes the liturgy he composed for the feast of Corpus Christi is its *biblical* character. In this regard, his work stands apart from all the other Offices composed during this period. The liturgy of Mont Cornillon, for example, in spite of its undoubted charm, is almost entirely bereft of a solid biblical character, relying for the most part on inherited hymns and poems. In contrast, all the antiphons and responses in both Offices composed by St Thomas, the *Sapientia* and the *Sacerdos*, are (with one exception) biblical throughout.[23]

This fact, and others like it, should not come as a surprise. Around the time when Thomas was working on the Corpus Christi liturgy, he made the following brief but powerful declaration to Pope Urban IV. It is a statement which evokes something of the essential character and genius of the Mass and Office he composed. Thomas wrote: 'it is principally in the Gospel that

---

[20] See Pierre-Marie Gy, 'Office liègeois et office romain de la Fête-Dieu' in *Actes du colloque 'Fêtes-Dieu'* (Liège 1996) p. 124.

[21] Torrell, vol. 1, pp. 131–2.

[22] Ibid., p. 131. With regard to other internal evidence which helps confirm St Thomas's authorship of the Corpus Christi liturgy, see important research done by Pierre-Marie Gy in 'L'Office du Corpus Christi' (1990) and 'Office liègeois et office romain' (1996), and also by Zawilla, *Biblical Sources of the Historia Corporis Christi* (1985) pp. 88–120.

[23] See Gy (1996) p. 121.

the "form" of the Catholic faith is handed on, for that is the rule of the entire Christian life'.[24]

*   *   *

In order to present, in this chapter, even the briefest outline of the story regarding the authorship and history of composition of Corpus Christi, it has been necessary to draw together a considerable number of historical and theological facts and details, some minor, some major. But now, as the chapter ends, what might prove helpful for the reader, I would suggest, is to step back from a consideration of the details and contemplate instead, for a few moments, the phenomenon that is this great Feast of Corpus Christi – a liturgy of the Church prompted by a dream-vision of a young girl, and given final literary shape and form by the greatest theologian of the period. Familiarity with its hymns and lessons, its antiphons and canticles, should never be allowed to dull our perception of the truly astonishing claim which the Corpus Christi liturgy announces and celebrates: a humble piece of bread is changed into living flesh, 'a fragile, small, wheatern disc into God'.[25]

---

[24] *Epistola dedicatoria ad Urbanum PP. IV* in *Catena super Matthaei Evangelio editam.* See *Catena aurea,* Marietti edition (Rome 1953) p. 4.
[25] See Mari Rubin, *Corpus Christi: The Eucharist in Late Medieval Culture* (Oxford 1997) p. 1.

8

Aquinas on poetry and theology

The hiding of truth in figures is useful for the exercise of thoughtful minds.
ST, I, Q.1, A.9, AD 2.

What best uncovers the truth of things? For most people, I suspect, the obvious answer to this question is our capacity to *think*, the ordinary yet extraordinary gift of human reason. But, if that's the case, what are we to say about poetry in relation to truth? Does the genius of poetry serve to reveal truth or does it obscure it? This question is almost as old as imaginative literature itself. As one commentator puts it:

> Plato raised it early, and answered it negatively. He denied poetry any claim to truth, in both the logical and the moral senses of the word: – the logical, because poetry, according to him, imitates an imitation of reality and is thus thrice removed from the truth of the Ideas; the moral, because poetry is a lie, a fiction that 'feeds and waters the passions instead of drying them up.' Aristotle was the better philosopher here. He saw that poetry grew out of man's mimetic and harmonic instincts, and that, though dealing in fictions, it was akin to philosophy in its adumbrations of the universal: 'Poetry, therefore, is more philosophical than history, for poetry tends to express the universal, while history describes the particular.'[1]

---

[1] Victor M. Hamm, *Language, Truth and Poetry* (Milwaukee 1980) pp. 53–4.

Aquinas, as we know, is often inclined to take the side of Aristotle and, in this matter, he has no hesitation in emphasizing the mimetic genius of the art. He writes for example: 'Poetry makes use of metaphors for the sake of representation since as human beings we naturally take delight in representation.'[2] And he says further: 'the poet's task is to lead us to something virtuous by some excellent description.'[3] But elsewhere Aquinas speaks of poetry or 'poetic knowledge' as being 'deficient in truth' (*defectum veritatis*).[4] What can he possibly mean by such a declaration? At first hearing, it sounds like a rather unlikely statement for a Christian artist and theologian to make. Is Aquinas not aware that divine revelation itself, in its final and definitive expression, makes use again and again of the language of poetry?

Aquinas, as it happens, has no hesitation whatever in asserting that in Holy Scripture 'spiritual truths are fittingly conveyed with bodily metaphors.'[5] He cites a passage from the Old Testament in which, through one of the prophets, the God of Israel declares: *I have multiplied visions, and I have used likenesses by ministry of the prophets* (Hos. 2.10).[6] And, then, in a further, clear affirmation of the language of metaphor, Aquinas notes: 'God provides for everything according to the capacity of its nature. It is natural for human beings to come to intellectual truths through sense perception, since all our knowledge takes its origin from the senses.'[7]

But one question still remains to be answered. St Thomas, when addressing the subject of poetry in these texts, is clearly affirmative in his judgment. Why, then, does he find it necessary elsewhere to speak about poetry as 'deficient in truth'? To answer this question it will be helpful to understand the context in which the phrase *defectum veritatis* occurs. In the *Summa*, for example, when Aquinas employs the phrase, his concern is to compare poetic

---

[2] *ST*, I q.1, a.9, ad 1.
[3] *In Primum librum posteriorum analyticorum Aristotelis expositio*, ch. 1, lect. 1, 6, Leonine vol. 1, p. 140.
[4] See *Scriptum super sententiis*, Bk 1, q.1, a.5, ad 3. See also *ST*, I II q.101, a.2, ad 2.
[5] *ST*, I q.1, a.9.
[6] *ST*, I q.1, a.9, *sed contra*. The same text from Hosea is quoted by Aquinas later in the *Summa* (II II q.173) when reflecting on the nature of prophecy. There he explains the special role that 'pictures in the imagination' can play in prophetic revelation.
[7] *ST*, I q.1, a.9.

knowledge and expression with sacred knowledge and expression.[8] And he is impressed by the fact that poetry, unlike theology, tends by its very nature to resist abstraction. In that sense, it remains inaccessible to speculative thinking. Thomas writes: 'Poetic knowledge is about things which because of their deficiency of truth (*propter defectum veritatis*) cannot be laid hold off by reason.'[9] Walter Ong, commenting on this statement, remarks:

> [Aquinas] is aware of the unsatisfactory and inconclusive nature of discussion about any poem. Because of its peculiar insistence on remaining concreted within the act of apprehension itself, a poem resists the very abstraction by which we would understand it. Abstraction, in one way or another, destroys it, dissolves it away. So we must content ourselves largely with simply apprehending the poem by reading or hearing it read, and as for any strict understanding of a poem, we must content ourselves with thinking and talking *around* it. Thomas does not put it in exactly the same words, but when he speaks of its 'deficiency of truth', he is concerned with the same thing about a poem which prompts Archibald MacLeish to observe that 'A poem should not mean / But be.'[10]

That last suggestion of Ong is immediately striking but it represents, at best, I would say, only a part of the truth. It does not represent Aquinas's entire thinking on the question of meaning in a work of art. Nowadays, in certain schools of literary criticism, it's common for a stark distinction to be made between the truth of logic and the truth of poetry, as if the latter were entirely outside the realm of logical discourse and reason. But Thomas, in his *Commentary on the Posterior Analytics of Aristotle,* speaks of what he calls 'poetic logic'.[11] It's true, he thinks of it as occupying a place below that of the logic of scientific demonstration, and below even that of dialectic and rhetoric. Nevertheless, the art of poetry, he maintains, is still somehow within the domain of reason and logic.[12]

---

[8] *ST,* I II q.101, a.2 ad 2.

[9] Prologue, *In Primum librum Sententiarum Petri Lombardi,* q.1, a.5 ad 3, Parma vol. 6, p. 9.

[10] Walter Ong, 'Wit and Mystery: A Revaluation', *Speculum* 22 (July 1947) p. 326.

[11] See *In Primum librum postoriorum analyticorum,* Bk. 1, lect.1, 6, p. 128.

[12] Ibid. Occasional comments Thomas makes about art and poetry might seem to suggest that his view

Meaning, therefore, for Aquinas, is certainly not absent from the special discourse which constitutes a poem. He writes: 'poems partake of reason – by which man is man – to a greater degree than other mechanical works.'[13] These statements of Aquinas clearly imply a much more positive view of reason, in its relation to art, than the view which has become dominant since the Romantic period. During that time the majority of artists and poets reacted with understandable but, at times, exaggerated passion against Rationalism. St Thomas, in contrast, writing prior to the development of these somewhat extreme, modern dichotomies, does not hesitate, in his work, to speak of 'right reason' in relation to the making of works of art.[14] That confidence in reason – that *thomistic* confidence – inspired Flannery O'Connor to make the following memorable remark:

> When I write, I am a maker. I think about what I am making. St Thomas called art reason in the making. When I write I feel I am engaged in the reasonable use of the unreasonable. In art the reason goes wherever the imagination goes. We have reduced the use of reason terribly. You say a thing is reasonable and people think you mean it's safe. What's reasonable is seldom safe and always exciting.[15]

* * *

St Thomas, in his *Commentary on the Metaphysics*, speaks of 'theological poets'. He writes: 'among the Greeks, the first who were famous for their learning were certain theological poets, so called because of the songs they wrote about

---

corresponds with modern and contemporary opinions on the autonomy of art. He writes, for example, 'The value of things produced by art does not consist in their being good for human appetite, but in the good of the works of art themselves.' See *ST*, I II q. 57, a.4. To read this statement, and conclude that Thomas is an advocate of art for art's sake would, of course, be a huge misunderstanding. The entire system of Aquinas is based upon *finality*. He has no scruple, therefore, in declaring that art 'seems to be nothing more than a particular procedure established by reason whereby human acts, in prescribed ways, attain their appropriate end.' See *In primum librum posteriorum analyticorum*, Bk 1, lect. 1, 1.

[13] See *Sententia libri ethicorum*, Bk 9, lect. 7, 1167 b 33, in *Opera omnia*, Leonine edition, vol. 47/2 (Rome 1969) p. 525.

[14] *ST*, I II q.57, a.3.

[15] *Conversations with Flannery O'Connor* (1959), (ed.) Betsy Lochridge (London 1987) p. 39.

the gods.'[16] Thomas mentions Orpheus, Museus, and Linus: 'These poets deal to some extent with the nature of things by means of figurative representations and myths' (*Isti autem poetae quibusdam aenigmatibus fabularum aliquid de rerum natura tractaverunt*).[17] So Thomas allows that the 'fabulous stories' told by the poets do tell us *something* about 'the nature of things'. But he is clearly not greatly persuaded about the value of 'representations and myths'. It's no accident, I would say, that in the same text he goes on to refer to 'a story' which, far from communicating truth, revealed something totally false. Meister Eckhart, the Dominican preacher and mystic of the fourteenth century, although well aware of Aquinas's teaching, is much more positive about the usefulness of the poet's parables and stories. He writes:

> All the ancient theologians and poets generally used to teach about God, nature and ethics by means of parables. The poets did not speak in an empty and fabulous way, but they intentionally and very attractively and properly taught about the natures of things divine, natural and ethical by metaphors and allegories. This is quite clear to anyone who takes a good look at the poet's stories.[18]

The fact that poetry, and indeed all the creative arts, by the imaginative use of 'metaphors and allegories', can reveal critically important truths about human life, is something happily taken for granted in the modern period. The Irish poet, Seamus Heaney, writes: 'It is precisely this masquerade of fictions and ironies and fantastic scenarios that can draw us out and bring us close to ourselves. The paradox of the arts is that they are all made up and yet allow us to get at truths about who and what we are or might be.'[19]

Aquinas was living in an age which tended to exalt philosophy over poetry. The scholastic theologians were not unaware, of course, of the great classics of Graeco-Roman civilization, but they were living in an age which, in certain

---

[16] *In Libros metaphysicorum Aristotelis expositio*, Bk 1, lect. 4, no. 83, Marietti edition (Rome 1950) p. 25.
[17] Ibid.
[18] Meister Eckhart, *Essential Sermons*, trans., E. Colledge and B. McGinn (London 1981) p. 93.
[19] Seamus Heaney, *Finders-Keepers: Selected Prose 1971–2001* (London 2003), pp. 68–9.

ways, 'had turned its back on the Classics.'[20] According to E. K. Rand, 'In the battles between philosophy and poetry, which Plato calls an ancient battle and which crops us in various periods of human history ... the thirteenth century witnessed the triumph of philosophy over letters.'[21]

Painting, poetry, music, all the different creative arts possess integrity and significance within their own order. That goes without saying. But, if judged by the medieval classification of values to which Aquinas adhered, poetry, viewed as a creative art of fantasy, when compared with speculative thinking, or with the science of theology, must be content to yield ground, and accept a relatively minor position. As soon as it is viewed under the strict, academic gaze of medieval scholasticism, poetry will appear, in spite of its undoubted capacity to charm and delight, as an *infirma doctrina*. Accordingly, in the scholastic world of St Thomas, poetry occupies a place at the opposite end of human knowledge from that of theology. It tends to dip, in his opinion, below the range of human reason whereas theology soars above it.

That said, however, St Thomas was clearly struck by the fact that these two very different forms of human knowledge both rely, and to a significant degree, on *metaphor*. Reflecting on this phenomenon, in his *Commentary on the Sentences,* Thomas gives space to an objection which appears to be directly opposed to his own thesis. It reads: 'Widely differing sciences ought not to share the same method. But poetry, which contains the least truth, differs to the greatest degree from this science [theology] which is most true. Therefore, since poetry proceeds by metaphorical sayings, the method of the science of theology should be different.'[22] In his answer, Aquinas makes clear at once that theology has manifest need of metaphor. Nevertheless, he seems both to agree and to disagree with the objection raised. He writes:

Poetic knowledge is of things which cannot be grasped by reason because of a deficiency of truth. Hence reason must be drawn off to the side by

---

[20] See E. K. Rand, 'A Friend of the Classics in the times of Saint Thomas Aquinas' in *Melanges Mandonnet: Études d'histoire littéraire et doctrinale du moyen age,* vol. 2 (Paris 1930) p. 261.

[21] Ibid. And see also pp. 274–5. This claim is only partly accurate. As well as an undoubted distrust in the medieval monasteries, there was also a manifest admiration for pagan literature. See Jean Leclercq, *The Love of Learning and the Desire for God,* trans., C. Misrahi (New York 1961).

[22] Prologue, *In Primum librum Sententiarum,* q.I a.5, obj 3, Parma vol. 6, p. 8.

certain likenesses (*quod quasi quibusdam similitudinibus ratio seducatur*). Theology, however, is about things that are above our reason, and so the symbolic mode is common to both since neither is proportioned to our reason.[23]

Nowadays it tends to be taken for granted that poetry or 'poetic knowledge' is something which cannot be grasped by reason. But what is less often acknowledged and what is, for that reason, worthy of note here, is St Thomas's insistence that theology likewise operates on what has been called by Walter Ong 'the periphery of human intellection'.[24] In the practice of theology a point is reached where the abstract, rational approach to God, or to thinking about God, simply doesn't seem to work or, at least, not as well as we might have hoped. We have no choice but to come to terms with a certain 'unmanageableness'. And that's why we find both spiritual authors and theologians drawing again and again, as if by instinct, on the life-blood of metaphor.[25] Poetry and theology, although manifestly different from each other, appear again and again to make similarly impossible demands on human reason. Walter Ong writes:

> Poetry really demands too much of the reason in its insistence both that it be understood and that it be understood somehow without resort to abstraction. From this fact arises the strain … the state of tension in which poetry leaves reason …Thomas's explanation of the use of metaphor in theology moves along quite another, but a similar line. In the science of theology based on Christian revelation, as well as in the science of poetry, the intellect must come upon its objective by a kind of flank movement. It grasps it only by the periphery.[26]

Clearly Thomas is *not* thinking here of the truths of the faith 'to which even

---

[23] Ibid., q.I, a.5, ad 3, p. 9. In the *Summa* Thomas writes: 'Just as human reason fails to grasp poetical expressions on account of their being lacking in truth, so does it fail to grasp divine things perfectly, on account of the sublimity of the truth they contain: and therefore in both cases there is need of signs by means of sensible figures.' See *ST*, I II q.101, a.2, ad 2.

[24] Ong, p. 325.

[25] Ibid., p. 327.

[26] Ibid.

natural reason can attain, such as the truth that God exists.'[27] No – what Thomas has in mind are those 'truths concerning God which completely exceed the power of human reason',[28] the mystery of the Incarnation, for example, and the mystery of the Holy Trinity, truths to which unaided human reason simply cannot hope to attain. Nevertheless, for all the bewilderment provoked, there is no inherent contradiction in these great and saving truths. In the end, believers are able to accept with strong faith and conviction the paradox of a God who is One and yet Three, and the paradox of an infinite, unseen God who has, in the Incarnate Word, become finite and visible.

When, however, in Christian revelation or in Christian theology, these mysteries are given expression in finite, human language, an almost intolerable pressure is placed on the limited, finite capacity of mere words. This pressure, in the opinion of the English poet, W. H. Auden, is altogether too great for the art of poetry to bear. Human imagination, he declares, simply cannot comprehend the paradox of a God who assumes flesh, and becomes a human being. So there is 'something a bit questionable,' Auden writes, 'about all works of art which make overt Christian references.'[29]

> The Incarnation, the coming of Christ in the form of a servant who cannot be recognized by the eye of flesh and blood, but only by the eye of faith, puts an end to all claims of the imagination to be the faculty which decides what is truly sacred and what is profane ... Christ appears looking just like any other man, yet claims that He is the Way, the Truth, and the Life, and that no man can come to God the Father except through Him. The contradiction between the profane appearance and the sacred assertion is impassible to the imagination.[30]

The message is clear. Poetry, as Auden sees it, is struck dumb before the mystery of the Word incarnate. In his opinion, the unspeakable paradox of the

---

[27] *Summa contra gentiles*, Bk 1, ch. 3, Leonine vol. 13, p. 7.
[28] Ibid.
[29] W. H. Auden, 'Postscript: Christianity and Art', in *Selected Essays* (New York 1956) p. 218. Auden's statement here betrays the unmistakable influence of the Danish Christian philosopher, Sören Kierkegaard.
[30] Ibid., p. 217.

revelation of the Son of God simply cannot be contained within the aesthetic realm. And so, he is forced to the conclusion – astonishing though it sounds – that 'poetry is small beer.'[31] This unexpected down-grading by the English poet of the role and power of poetry with respect to 'paradox-religion' might seem to indicate agreement between his way of thinking and that of St Thomas. But the paradox inherent in Christian religion which, in Auden's opinion, clearly stifles the voice of the poet is the very thing which, in the case of Aquinas, actually makes possible his finest verse, a point wonderfully illustrated in the following short stanza cited earlier from *Sacris solemniis*:

Panis angelicus	Now the bread of angels
fit panis hominum,	feeds the sons of men.
dat panis caelicus	Figures and types are fled,
figuris terminum;	never to come again.
O res mirabilis!	O what a wondrous thing!
Manducat Dominum	The poor, the humble, the lowly
pauper, servus, et humilis.	consume the Master and King.

Here, mere words are being asked to express the impossible/possible paradox of a God who not only takes on human flesh but actually offers his flesh and blood to be consumed by the least among his followers. It is no small achievement for Aquinas, as an imaginative author, that in the original Latin, the words and lines of this stanza actually *sing*. In other words, the very paradox which, in Auden's opinion, places too much strain on the poet's gift of imagination, acts in the case of Aquinas as nothing less than a spur to creativity, a kind of sharp, artistic challenge. Thomas Aquinas, known for centuries as a thinker of outstanding clarity, a true master of logic and reason, is also, it now begins to appear, a quite remarkable poet of paradox.

---

[31] Ibid., p. 216.

9

The individual hymns and canticles

Introduction

When theologians take time to reflect on the hymns composed for Corpus Christi – something that happens rarely[1] – they tend to direct their attention almost exclusively to what Chenu calls the 'conceptual' aspect of the verse, ignoring not only the liturgical setting of the hymns, but also their character as poetry.[2] The likely explanation for this omission is the almost insuperable difficulty confronting anyone who is concerned to provide a commentary on the verse for readers or students who possess little or no knowledge of Latin. But, by ignoring the 'poetry' in this case, we risk ignoring the near miracle of Aquinas's achievement.

How can this difficulty be overcome? Is there a way? Or will it be necessary, in the end, when speaking about the individual hymns, to settle for a reflection on 'the conceptual aspect' only, ignoring the form, the shaping spirit of the work, the actual rhythm of the verse, the music?

---

[1] Alain Michel notes how even authors such as Jacques Maritain will 'analyse in depth the aesthetic thought of [Aquinas]' while, at the same time, 'neglecting to approach the poems.' See *In hymnis et canticis:* culture et beauté dans l'hymnique chrétienne latine (Paris 1976) p. 223.
[2] M.-D. Chenu, *Toward Understanding Saint Thomas,* trans., A.-M. Landry and D. Hughes (Chicago 1965) p. 344.

With regard to ***Adoro te devote***, we have the good fortune of having available to us the superb translation made by Gerard Manley Hopkins. As much if not more than any theological commentary, this translation gives us privileged access to both the meaning and music of the work. *Adoro te* does not, however, form part of the Corpus Christi cycle. Although familiar to us now as a hymn, the work was originally composed by St Thomas as a private prayer to assist his meditation when attending Mass.[3]

Pange lingua gloriosi, the hymn composed by St Thomas for First Vespers of Corpus Christi, is generally regarded as the most pleasing of all the eucharistic hymns. Apart from its use on the Feast of Corpus Christi, it is also sung on Holy Thursday during the procession to the Altar of Repose. Its final two stanzas, beginning with the phrase '*Tantum ergo sacramentum*' have been sung at Benediction of the Blessed Sacrament since the fifteenth century. The rhythmic structure of the work, and its intricate rhyme scheme, present an enormous challenge to translators. Those who have taken up the challenge, over the years, although clearly gifted in many respects, have not possessed the genius of Hopkins. Nevertheless, something of notable worth has been achieved. The translation I will present later represents a composite work based on the best translations with which I am familiar.[4] On occasion I have not hesitated to change a number of lines and phrases where a change, however small, appeared to make the meaning more clear or the music of the verse more felicitous.

Sacris solemniis, the hymn for Matins, has presented an even greater challenge for translators. Of the many attempts made so far to re-create, in an English version, the precise rhyme-scheme and musical pattern of the original while, at the same time, keeping faith with the meaning of the hymn, none has been entirely successful.[5] For that reason, when *Sacris solemniis* is being

---

[3] Information regarding this subject will be discussed in Chapter 10, '*Adoro te devote:* The Finest Prayer of Aquinas', [exact pages to be given after type-setting.]

[4] Among the names of those who have worked at translating *Pange lingua*, two names stand out: Edward Caswall (1814–78) and John Mason Neale (1818–86). See *The English Hymnal with Tunes*, (eds), W. J. R. Birbeck et al. (Oxford 1933) p. 459. See also *Medieval Hymns and Sequences*, (ed.) John Mason Neale (1951) pp. 127–8.

[5] Of them all the most satisfactory, I find, is a version by John David Chambers (1805–93). See *Lyra eucharistica: Hymns and Verses on Holy Communion, Ancient and Modern*, (ed.) O. Shipley (London 1864) pp. 70–1.

quoted later in the chapter, rather than attempt an exact lyrical translation, repeating as it were the precise musical structure of the Latin, I will offer instead a modest prose version of the work – a prose-poem in fact – hoping that this might give at least some impression of the hymn's original pattern and core meaning. On the subject of translation, Thomas has this to say:

> It belongs to the task of the good translator … to preserve the meaning (*sententia*), while changing the manner of expression (*modus loquendi*) according to the particularity (*proprietatem*) of the language into which the work is being translated … When things expressed in one language are translated merely word for word into another, it will be no surprise if, in the end, there is doubt [about the meaning].[6]

St Thomas speaks here of the 'particularity' of a given language (*proprietatem linguae*) and that, of course, includes the idea of a language's distinctive idiom. But when, nowadays, we attempt to read medieval Latin, the impression we receive quite often is of almost an *absence* of idiom – an absence, that is, of many of the small human nuances we tend to associate with a living language. Writing on the subject of Aquinas's hymns, Hopkins, remarked in a letter to Robert Bridges that, like 'all medieval verse … [they] show want of feeling for or command of *any* idiom.' Significantly, however, that awareness did not prevent Hopkins, in the same letter, from using the word 'genius' when speaking of Aquinas's verse.[7]

The third hymn in the Corpus Christi cycle, ***Verbum supernum prodiens,*** the canticle for Lauds, presents, in its own turn, a not inconsiderable challenge for translators. The version I will cite later is based on translations done mostly

---

[6] *Contra errores Graecorum ad Urbanum IV Pontificem Maximum,* 1030, in *Opuscula theologica,* Marietti vol. 1, pp. 315–16.

[7] Letter, 10 June 1882, in *The Letters of Gerard Manley Hopkins to Robert Bridges,* p. 148. Walter Ong, reflecting on the medieval command of idiom, writes: 'Large areas of fact and feeling were to some extent isolated from [medieval] Latin: people usually did not cook in it or manage labor in it or swear in it either.' Nevertheless, Latin possessed an 'immediacy' of expression comparable to that of the vernacular languages, and there flowed through the language itself, Ong suggests, 'the life of a whole continent in however distilled a form.' In the end 'the very lack of idiom becomes an idiom of itself.' See Walter Ong, 'Wit and Mystery: A Revaluation', *Speculum* 22 (July 1947) pp. 340–1.

by John Mason Neale (1818–66) and Edward Caswall (1814–78).[8] The translation is not satisfactory throughout, but it has the merit of staying close to the
rhyme scheme of the original, and its fifth stanza, beginning with the words 'O
saving Victim' is, in itself, an impressive lyric.[9] Here, once again, I presume to
introduce a number of small changes. And my plan, when commenting on the
poem, is also to offer, on occasion, a prose alternative to the lyrical versions of
Neale and Caswall.

The last canticle of the Eucharist to be considered is ***Lauda Sion salvatorem***. This work, unlike the hymns composed for the Divine Office of Corpus
Christi, is not a hymn, strictly speaking, but rather a 'sequence', a special
canticle composed to be sung during the Mass of the Feast. The work has
always been highly regarded and, of the hundreds of sequences which have
come down to us from the Middle Ages, it is one of only four still retained
in the Roman Missal.[10] Many authors, over the centuries, have attempted to
translate *Lauda Sion*, among them celebrated poets such as Robert Southwell
and Richard Crashaw.[11] The particular version I will cite later represents a
composite translation, a work of many hands. And here, once again, I have not
hesitated to make small changes, even adding a few small phrases. But, if the
translated work actually *sings* with authority and grace – and I think it does
on occasion– that is due entirely to the work of earlier translators.

When an individual canticle or hymn becomes the focus of attention in
the pages which follow, the work will be cited, first, in the original Latin and,
second, in a *free* translation into English, the aim being to present, for those
readers who possess little or no knowledge of Latin, something of the lyrical

---

[8] See *The English Hymnal with Tunes*, pp. 464–5.

[9] This particular stanza was translated by Caswall. The nineteenth century translations of Aquinas's
eucharistic hymns, it should be noted, are a lot more satisfactory than the twentieth century
versions. The best known of the twentieth century versions is a work composed jointly by Robert
Anderson and Johann Moser: *The Aquinas Prayer Book: The Prayers and Hymns of St Thomas Aquinas*
(Manchester, New Hampshire 1993). Unfortunately, with regard to the hymns, the brave attempt to
echo, in a modern English translation, the impressive rhyme scheme of the Latin original has not been
successful. More helpful and illuminating are the versions of the prayers attributed to Aquinas.

[10] One of the four, *Stabat Mater*, the sequence for Our Lady of Sorrows on 15 September, is an optional
text. The three other sequences, *Lauda Sion Salvatorem*, *Victimae Pascali Laudes* and *Veni Sancte
Spiritus*, are obligatory on the solemnities on which they occur.

[11] The names of other translators include E. Caswell, J. D. Aylward, E. B. Pusey and H. T. Henry.

form and content of the original. That said, however, in order to assist the fullest possible understanding of the *meaning* of the texts, a literal translation will be included in an Appendix at the end of the book.

(1) *Pange lingua* The hymn at Vespers

Pange, lingua, gloriosi	Sing, my tongue, the Saviour's glory,
corporis mysterium,	of his flesh the mystery sing,
sanguinisque pretiosi,	of the blood, all price exceeding,
quem in mundi pretium,	shed by our immortal king,
fructus ventris generosi	destined for the world's redemption,
rex effudit gentium.	from a noble womb to spring.
Nobis datus, nobis natus	Given for us, and condescending,
ex intacta virgine,	to be born for us below,
et in mundo conversatus,	high with lowly converse blending
sparso verbi semine,	far the seed of truth to sow,
sui moras incolatus	till he died with wondrous ending,
miro claudit ordine.	bearing all our weight of woe.
In supremae nocte coenae	At that last great supper lying,
recumbens cum fratribus,	circled by his chosen band,
observata lege plene	humbly with the law complying,
cibis in legalibus,	first he finished its command,
cibum turbae duodenae	then immortal food supplying,
se dat suis manibus.	gave himself with his own hand.
Verbum caro panen verum,	Word-made-flesh, the bread of nature,
Verbo carnem efficit;	by his Word to flesh he turns;
fitque sanguis Christi merum:	wine into his blood he changes
et si sensus deficit,	though our sense no change discerns.
ad firmandum cor sincerum	But, if inmost heart be earnest,
sola fides sufficit.	faith her lesson quickly learns.
Tantum ergo sacramentum	Therefore, we, before him bending,
veneremur cernui,	this great Sacrament revere;

et antiquum documentum	types and shadows have their ending,
novo cedat ritui,	for the newer rite is here;
praestet fides supplementum	faith, our outward sense befriending,
sensuum defectui.	makes our inward vision clear.
Genitori genitoque	Glory, let us give, and blessing
laus et jubilatio,	to the Father and the Son,
salus, honor, virtus quoque	honour, might, and praise addressing
sit et benedictio,	while eternal ages run;
procendentis ab utroque	ever, too, his love confessing,
compar sit laudatio.	who, from both, with both is one.

Pange lingua
A commentary

'Sing, O tongue, the Saviour's glory.' The first word chosen by Aquinas to open the *Pange lingua*, should alert us at once to the nature of the work before us.[12] Here, Aquinas is no longer engaged in composing one of his philosophical or theological treatises. He is not attempting to write prose. Instead, we find him engaged in writing words for a sacred song. In effect, he is writing a poem. And, as readers of Aquinas's work, instead of being, as it were, together in a classroom with a teacher, we find ourselves in a place of worship, in a liturgical context. For in 'this place' we are invited not merely to *think* about the mystery of the Eucharist, and not merely to pray, but instead, raising our voices in prayer, to *sing* together, as it were, First Vespers of the Feast of Corpus Christi.

1. Meaning and music

How well can we say Aquinas has succeeded in his task as author, as poet? In a remarkable play by the Baroque dramatist, Pedro Calderón de la Barca (1600–81), we witness a singing competition being enacted between some of

---

[12] The word '*Pange*', in the ecclesiatical world of the Middle Ages, is the imperative form of the verb '*pangere*' meaning to sing. Originally the verb meant to make or fix or to compose.

the greatest teachers within the Christian tradition, St Augustine, St Ambrose and St Gregory among them. *Pange lingua* is the particular hymn presented by Aquinas and, for this one canticle, he is named as victor, and is awarded the prize of 'a golden sun'.[13] Calderón's play represents a judgment made about *Pange lingua* in the seventeenth century, a decidedly positive judgment. In the twentienth-century we find the work praised no less highly, described for example by the scholar, F. J. E. Raby, as 'one of the most sublime productions of sacred poetry'.[14] It is, he remarks, a hymn 'beyond all praise', a work distinguished not only by a fine 'precision of thought', but also by 'a severe and rigid beauty'.[15]

Pange lingua is indeed astonishing in the way it links together profound dogmatic reflection with a carefully wrought musical and rhythmic structure. The work is divided into six stanzas of six lines each. And, with respect to metre, it is composed in the 'rolling' rhythm that is called the trochaic metre. Originally developed by poets such as Euripides, Seneca, Catullus, and Sophocles, this metre consists of a stressed syllable followed by an unstressed syllable. Thus:

> Pánge, língua, glóriósi
> Córporís mystériúm

One other feature of the hymn, and it is something entirely original in medieval hymnody, adding greatly to the strength and beauty of the work, is the alternating triple rhymes in every stanza. For example, in the first stanza, the rhymes, glori*osi*, preti*osi* and gener*osi*, alternate with myster*ium*, pret*ium* and gent*ium*. The artistic delight Aquinas must have had in inventing the challenge of this new stanza form, and then his genius in answering the challenge with such manifest success, attests not only to an undeniable sophistication in the Dominican, as a maker of verses, but also to an instinctive

---

[13] The 'play' was one of a number of one-act allegorical plays composed in honour of the Eucharist by Calderón for performance during the feast of Corpus Christi. See Calderón de la Barca, *El sacro pernaso*, (ed.) A. R. Rípodas (Kassel 2006) pp. 133–260. See also Jan-Heiner Tück, *Gabe der Gegenwart: Theologie und Dichtung der Eucharistie bei Thomas von Aquin* (Freiburg 2009) p. 188.

[14] Ibid.

[15] Raby, *A History of Christian-Latin Poetry: From the Beginnings to the Close of the Middle Ages*, p. 409.

love of play where words are concerned, a marked awareness of the taste and shimmer of words which, in the end, separates the genuine poet from the mere versifyer. 'Poets,' writes Dylan Thomas, 'have got to enjoy themselves sometimes, and the twistings and convolutions of words, the inventions and contrivances, are all part of the joy that is part of the painful, voluntary work.'[16]

*   *   *

At the level of ideas, *Pange lingua*'s first four stanzas articulate the actual foundation of eucharistic devotion, and in particular its history with regard to the work of Christ Jesus: the mystery of a God who, first of all, assumes our human flesh, and then chooses to die on our behalf, offering his life's blood for our redemption (stanzas one and two). After that we have the story of the institution of the Eucharist at the Last Supper (stanzas three and four). The intended impact of these first four stanzas is not that we should simply reflect intellectually on the history of eucharistic devotion, and nothing else. But rather, contemplating these things, we should be led to bow with reverence before the great mystery itself.

The one crucial word, which makes this point clear, and which serves to link the first four stanzas with the last two, can be found on the very first line of stanza five. It is the word 'therefore' (*ergo*). Because of all that Christ has done for us, and because of the mystery of divine love evoked in the first four stanzas, *therefore* we find ourselves instinctively drawn to bow low in adoration and, with a new and illumined faith, to acknowledge the real presence of Christ Jesus in the Eucharist:

Tantum ergo sacramentum	*Therefore*, we, before him bending,
veneremur cernui,	this great Sacrament revere;
et antiquum documentum	types and shadows have their ending,
novo cedat ritui,	for the newer rite is here;
praestet fides supplementum	faith, our outward sense befriending,
sensuum defectui.	makes our inward vision clear.

---

[16] Dylan Thomas, 'Poetic Manifesto' in *The Poet's Work: 29 Masters of 20th Century Poetry on the Origins and Practice of Their Art*, (ed.) Reginald Gibbons, Boston 1979, Houghton Mifflin Company, pp. 188–9.

2. The sources of *Pange lingua*

Pange, lingua, gloriosi, the first words with which Aquinas's hymn opens have been much admired, and for good reason. But the entire phrase belongs, as it happens, to the first line of a hymn composed by Venantius Fortunatus (c. 530–?609): '*Pange, lingua, glorisi lauream certaminis.*' What's more, Aquinas's work follows faithfully the metre of the earlier hymn, and the resulting rhythm, like the stroke of an oar in water, or like the step of a man striding forward, constitutes no small part of its achievement.

The hymn of Fortunatus is not the only source on which Aquinas drew for inspiration when composing the *Pange lingua*. In the final stanza of the hymn, for example, the phrases '*genitori genitoque*' (to the Begetter and the Begotten) and '*procendentis ab utroque*' (proceeding from both) are a clear echo of a stanza originally composed by Adam of St Victor for the Solemnity of Pentecost: '*qui procedit ab utroque, genitori genitoque*'.[17] And the vivid phrase '*Nobis natus, nobis datus*' (born for us, given for us) is also taken over from a work by the same Adam.[18]

Hearing of these 'borrowings', for the first time, some readers today may well feel somewhat dismayed. For how exactly is this phenomenon to be understood? Can it be that the apparently original work of Aquinas is little more, in fact, than a mosaic of quotations? Has Aquinas simply plagiarized at will the work of other poets and authors? Regarding this question, the first thing to note is that, far from being guilty of any kind of plagiarism, Aquinas was simply following one of the accepted literary conventions of his time. It was taken for granted, in the Middle Ages, that the best poets and artists were quite often the best borrowers. It was no shame, therefore, as a medieval author, to find oneself, on occasion, speaking in the acquired cadence and voice of some earlier poet or theologian. Originality was simply a form of inspired development. The borrowing, to call it that, far from being

---

[17] Sisto Terán, *Santo Tomás, Poeta del Santísimo Sacramento* (Tucumán 1979) p. 76.

[18] One stanza from Adam's 'Hymn to the Nativity' reads: '*Nato nobis Salvatore/Celebremus cum honore/ Diem natalitium:/Nobis datus, nobis natus/Et nobiscum conversatus/Lux et salus gentium.*' See L. Gautier, *The Liturgical Poetry of Adam of St Victor* (London 1881) p. 34.

a crime, represented nothing less, in fact, than a compliment to the author whose words or work had apparently been 'stolen'. It was a convention which enabled authors to place themselves in relation to the work of their forebears, announcing themselves as new arrivals while, at the same time, making manifest their presence within the living tradition.

That's why, without the least hesitation, we find the medieval author, Bernard of Morlaix, openly and happily admitting to significant 'borrowings' from the work of earlier medieval poets: 'I am not jealous of my forbears. The metre I am using is theirs. It is not mine only, but also the metre of the Fathers.'[19]

In modern times the question of 'borrowings' from the work of other artists has come to be regarded in an altogether different light. At least, in popular understanding, the modern artist or poet is expected to produce work which betrays little or no trace of dependence on the work of predecessors. But this idea of 'originality' is not one which has been generally promoted by artists and poets over the centuries. An outstanding modern poet such as T. S. Eliot, for example, refuses to accept that the encounter between tradition and the individual talent is anything other than a necessary and irreplaceable aid to artistic creativity. Referring, on one occasion, to 'our [modern] tendency to insist, when we praise a poet, upon those aspects of his work in which he least resembles anyone else,' Eliot writes:

> We dwell with satisfaction upon the poet's difference from his predecessors, especially his immediate predecessors; we endeavour to find something that can be isolated in order to be enjoyed. Whereas if we approach without this prejudice we shall often find that not only the best, but the most individual parts of his work may be those in which the dead poets, his ancestors, assert their immortality most vigorously.[20]

---

[19] See *Carmina de Trinitate et de fide catholica*, 1012–13. Cited in John Balnaves, *Bernard of Morlaix: The Literature of Complaint, The Latin Tradition and the Twelfth Century 'Renaissance'*. Unpublished Thesis, Australian National University, March 1997; Chapter 6, *Metre and Rhyme*, pp. 2–3. Bernard of Morlaix is also known as Bernard of Cluny. He was a Benedictine monk of the first half of the twelfth century.

[20] 'Tradition and the Individual Talent,' *Selected Prose*, (ed.) J. Hayward (London 1963) p. 22. For

This strong and telling statement from Eliot regarding originality and tradition applies, I am inclined to think, in a most particular way, to the creative process at work in the composition of the hymns of Aquinas.

3. A poetry of parodox

Two mysteries of Christian revelation are sung and celebrated by Aquinas in the first two stanzas of *Pange lingua*: the Incarnation and the Redemption. And what we find highlighted from the very beginning is the striking paradox of both of these events. The majestic 'king' referred to in the first stanza, 'the king of the nations', is born from the womb of a girl, who, in giving birth to him, loses nothing of her virginity: 'Given for us, born for us, from a pure Virgin' (*ex intacta virgine*). And this king, we are told later, at the close of the second stanza, ends his life in 'a wondrous manner' (*miro ... ordine*).[21] But, here, the paradox becomes even more startling, even more strange. For the 'end', in this case, the cause of wonder, is not an event of manifest triumph, nor is it one of unparalleled human success, but rather the utter and complete destruction of a human life: 'precious blood ... poured out for the ransom of the world.'

The next stanzas which follow (stanzas three and four) describe the institution of the Eucharist, stanza three, opening with an unusually relaxed and beautiful image of Christ (*In supremae nocte cenae/Recumbens cum fratribus*): Christ 'reclining with his brothers on the night of the last supper.' The stanza comes to a close with a statement as stark and uncompromising as it is mysterious. For here Aquinas is describing Christ's gift of himself to his friends as actual food: '*Cibum turbae duodenae/Se dat suis manibus*', literally: 'He gives himself with his own hands, as food, to the twelve.' I have no doubt that, at the back of Aquinas's mind when he was composing these few lines, was a short stanza from a poem on the Eucharist written, some years earlier, by an anonymous medieval author. When, in the *Summa,* Thomas comes to

---

further reflection on the question of literary influence, see Paul Murray, *T. S. Eliot and Mysticism: The Secret History of Four Quartets* (London 1991).

[21] The phrase '*miro ordine*' recurs in one of the prayers attributed to St Thomas, the Prayer for Study. See *Piae preces* in *Opuscula theologica*, vol. 2, Marietti edition (Turin 1954) pp. 285–6.

reflect on the event of the Last Supper, he takes care to include this particular fragment of verse:

Rex sedet in Cena,	The King at supper sits,
Turba cintus duodena;	The Twelve as guests he greets;
Se tenet in manibus,	Clasping himself in his hands,
Se cibat ipse cibus.	The food himself now eats.[22]

The one notable difference between this stanza and that of St Thomas is the emphasis, given in the Aquinas hymn, to the food of the Eucharist as a gift for *others*. Christ gives himself, not to *himself*, as in the earlier stanza,[23] but rather to 'the twelve', the Latin for 'gives' (*dat*) echoing the phrase '*given* for us' (*nobis datus*) of the preceding stanza, and echoing also the idea (expressed in the same stanza) of Christ's entire life, from birth to death, being poured out *for us* as a sheer gift: '*nobis* datus, *nobis* natus'. One enormously important aspect of this outpouring was, of course, the initial proclamation of the Word. Thomas gives it pride of place in stanza two between the event of Christ's birth and the event of his death: Christ, 'in the world, sowing the seed of the Word' (*in mundo conversatus/Sparso verbi semine*). Thomas's canticle is, first and last, a hymn in praise of the Sacrament of the Eucharist. But he was a friar of the Order of Preachers. It should come as no surprise, therefore, to find space being given by Aquinas to the preaching of the Word of God by Christ the living Word.

*   *   *

The fourth stanza, highlighting aspects of the mystery of Christ's presence in the Eucharist, might very easily, under the weight of theological reflection, have begun to sound rather stiff and abstract. But, happily, the music of the stanza more than matches the dogmatic element. The intellect of Aquinas

---

[22] See *ST*, III q.81, a.1, ad 1. This free version of the stanza is taken from the 1948 Benzinger Bros. translation. A more literal version, in the Blackfriars translation, reads: 'The King sat at supper/Girdled by the twelve/In his hands he held himself/And gave himself that food.'

[23] In the *Summa*, III q.81, a.1, Thomas asks the question 'Whether Christ received his own body and blood?', and he replies: 'Someone has said that Christ ... did not partake of it himself. But this seems improbable, because Christ was the first to fulfil what he required others to observe.'

is here as alive as ever, but also in evidence are two of the necessary gifts or qualities of the poet: craft and imagination. And so, by the grace and alchemy of art, discourse combines with image, and thought with phrase, to achieve an impressive harmony of sense and sound, a 'dance of the intellect among words'.[24]

Verbum caro panem verum,	Word made flesh, the bread of nature,
Verbo carnem efficit;	by his Word to flesh he turns;
Fit sanguis Christi merum:	Wine into his blood he changes
Et si sensus deficit,	though our sense no change discerns.
Ad firmandum cor sincerum	But, if inmost heart be earnest,
Sola fides sufficit.	faith her lesson quickly learns.

It's impossible, in English translation, to capture the full play of sound and sense in this fourth stanza. The many-layered paradox of the first two lines is particularly striking. Here, as elsewhere in his work, it can be said that 'the distinctively Christian element creates a tension in linguistic expression' and 'this tension establishes a point of *similarity* with poetry'.[25] Thomas is, in fact, developing a conceit reminiscent of the writings of some of the great metaphysical poets of the seventeenth century. The 'Word' who takes flesh is the eternal Word of God, and when, at the Last Supper, he is on the point of converting bread into flesh, he uses *words* as his sole instrument.

This rather fine detail – the coincidence of words and the Word being brought together, and the dual providence of bread and Word being both changed into flesh – clearly caught the attention of both the poet and theologian in Aquinas. For not only was this coincidence noteworthy in itself, it was also eloquent of what lies at the core of the eucharistic mystery. And, for that reason, it must have seemed to St Thomas, when engaged in writing his hymn, a paradox demanding to be expressed. As a result, the fourth stanza opens with the following celebrated conceit: '*Verbum caro panem verum/ Verbo carnem efficit*'; literally, 'The Word in flesh makes/True bread flesh

---

[24] The phrase belongs to Ezra Pound. See Pound, *Literary Essays* (New York 1968), p. 25.
[25] Ong, p. 324.

by a word.' The next line in the stanza reads: '*Fitque sanguis Christi merum*'; literally, 'And the pure wine becomes the blood of Christ.'

It might seem obvious that what is being sung and celebrated here is the mystery of bread becoming Christ's body, and wine becoming Christ's blood. But the Italian scholar, Costante Marabelli, has come forward with a different interpretation.[26] He argues that the translations of Aquinas's stanza, up to this point, have been mistaken. Instead of bread becoming flesh and wine becoming blood, the actual form in which the mystery is described by Aquinas is in terms of flesh becoming 'true bread' and of blood becoming 'true wine'. The text, in other words, has as its source that passage in St John's Gospel (Jn. 6.32) where Jesus reveals himself as 'the true bread': *I tell you most solemnly, it was not Moses who gave you bread from heaven, it is my Father who gives you the bread from heaven, the true bread* (in the Vulgate: '*panem verum*').[27] According to this interpretation the phrase, 'true bread', does not refer to ordinary bread, but rather to that Bread of Life which is Christ himself, and which takes away our hunger.[28]

Likewise the word '*merum*', which translates as 'pure wine', should not be made to refer to a common drink, but rather to the wine – the saving blood – which Christ has given us to drink. Accordingly, the translation should read, Marabelli argues: 'The Word incarnate makes flesh true bread by a word / And the blood of Christ becomes true wine.'[29] Is Marabelli's interpretation accurate? After some initial hesitations, I find I am as much convinced by the Marabelli reading as I am by the more familiar, more traditional interpretation. Both readings have their own strong persuasiveness, their own authority. Perhaps, therefore, both should be allowed to resonate as possible alternatives for those readers anxious to interpret the meaning of this particular stanza.

*   *   *

---

[26] Costante Marabelli, 'Tommaso d'Aquino: poeta eucaristico', in *L'Intelletto cristiano: Studi in onore di mons. Giuseppe Colombo* (Milan 2004) pp. 479–80.

[27] Ibid., p. 479.

[28] Ibid., p. 480. Something not noted by Marabelli but which, I think, supports his reading is the fact that when, in a later canticle (*Lauda Sion*), the phrase '*panis* vere' occurs, it refers not to ordinary bread, but rather to Christ, the Bread of Life: '*Bone pastor, panis vere/Jesu nostri miserere*'.

[29] Ibid., p. 479.

So manifestly profound is the mystery enacted in the Eucharist, and so truly ineffable, it completely exceeds the grasp of our senses. Accordingly, as believers, we have to rely for evidence not on what our senses tell us but rather on faith alone. '*Et, si sensus deficit,/Ad firmandum cor sincerum/Sola fides sufficit*'; literally, 'if sense is deficient to confirm the sincere heart, faith alone suffices.'[30] Aquinas, we know, was an outstanding intellectual. But, on this occasion, the gift of faith is presented not so much as a confirmation for the *mind* in its search for truth, but rather as an encouragement for the inmost *heart*: *Ad firmandum **cor sincerum***. In stanza five, the stanza which follows, the need for faith is once again clearly underlined: '*Praestet fides supplementum/Sensuum defectui*'; literally, 'Let faith stand forward to make good the defect of the senses.'

Faith is crucial when contemplating the mystery and institution of the Eucharist. For what we are invited to enact is a completely new rite, one which altogether surpasses the Old Law: '*Et antiquum documentum/Novo cedat ritui*'; literally, 'Let the old teaching/Yield to the new rite.'

A rather fine summary of a number of the themes contained in the stanzas we have been considering can be found in the first *Lesson* St Thomas composed for the feast of Corpus Christi. This *Lesson*, with its unaffected simplicity of expression, and its quiet rapture of belief in the eucharistic mystery, can serve now as a final, brief commentary or gloss on the six stanzas of the *Pange lingua*. Thomas writes:

In order that the memory of such a perpetual kindness might remain with us [Christ] left to be consumed by the faithful, under the appearance [*species*] of bread and wine, his body for food and his blood for drink. O precious and wonderful banquet, health-giving and full of all delight! For what can be more precious than this banquet, in which not the flesh of calves and goats (cf. Heb 9.12), as in the old law, but Christ true God is set before us to be consumed? What is more wonderful than this Sacrament? For, in it, the substance of bread and wine is changed into the body and

---

[30] The phrase '*sola fides sufficit*' is included by William Langland in his late fourteenthth century poem, *Piers Plowman*.

blood of Christ, and therefore Christ, perfect God and man, is contained under the appearance of a little bread and wine.[31]

(2) *Sacris solemniis* The hymn at Matins

Sacris solemniis	To these our solemn sacred rites
iuncta sint gaudia	let all our joys be joined,
et ex praecordiis	and from our inmost heart and mind
sonent praeconia,	let songs of praise resound.
recedant vetera,	Let ancient forms depart
nova sint omnia,	and everything be new: new in word,
corda, voces, et opera.	new in deed, and new in heart.
Noctis recolitur	That night we now recall, that
cena novissima,	final meal, at which
qua Christus creditur	it is believed, obedient to all
agnum et azyma	the rites and precepts
dedisse fratribus	of the law, Christ
Iuxta legitima	with his brothers shared
priscis indulta patribus.	unleavened bread and lamb.
Post agnum typicum	The lamb consumed,
expletis epulis,	the feast complete,
corpus dominicum	then, to the chosen twelve,
datum discipulis	in form of bread,
sic totum omnibus	he gave, whole and entire
quod totum singulis,	to each,
eius fatemur manibus.	his flesh to eat.
Dedit fragilibus	To those who were weak
corporis ferculum,	he offered the support

---

[31] *First Lesson* [for the Feast of Corpus Christi]. I am grateful to Adriano Olivo OP of the Leonine Commission for making available to me the provisional Latin text of this *First Lesson* and the text also of five other *Lessons* composed for Corpus Christi. These *Lessons* of Aquinas, it should be noted, are different in a number of ways from the *Lessons* we find in today's breviary. The original texts of Corpus Christi were significantly revised at the time of Pope Pius V.

dedit et tristibus	of his body, as living food,
sanguinis poculum,	and to those who were sad
dicens: accipite	the chalice of his blood,
quod trado, vasculum,	and said: Take the cup I hand
omnes ex eo bibite.	to you, and drink from it.
Sic sacrificium	The sacrifice, once given
istud instituit,	shape and form,
cuius officium	he willed the care of it, the task
committi voluit	of sharing it with others,
solis presbyteris,	be assigned to priests,
quibus sic congruit,	but they should first partake
ut sumant et dent ceteris.	of it themselves.
Panis angelicus	Now the bread of angels
fit panis hominum,	feeds the sons of men.
dat panis caelicus	Figures and types are fled,
figuris terminum;	never to come again.
O res mirabilis!	O what a wondrous thing!
Manducat Dominum	The poor, the humble, the lowly
pauper, servus, et humilis.	consume the Master and King.
Te, trina deitas	O Triune Deity
unaque, poscimus,	as we offer you our worship,
sicut nos visitas,	visit us, we pray, and towards
sicut te colimus:	the goal of our desire,
per tuas semitas	guide us along your paths:
duc nos, quo tendimus	lead us to the radiance
ad lucem, quam inhabitas.	in which you dwell.

Sacris solemniis
A commentary

Of all the Corpus Christi hymns composed by St Thomas, *Sacris solemniis* is probably the least celebrated. And that's surprising. For apart, maybe, from one of its stanzas, it seems to possess all the characteristics for which the other eucharistic hymns are justly famous. There is evidence, for example, from start to finish, of the same superb craftsmanship (in this case the use of the difficult asclepiad rhythm with cross rhymes) and the same austere beauty of thought and theological expression, and the same deliberate joining together of thought and music – the happy consonance of sound and metre with the meaning of the words.

1. Solemnity and joy

What, taken as a whole, the hymn proclaims most memorably is that 'angelic bread' has become the food of mere mortals, and that this holy 'bread' is nothing less than the body of Christ Jesus the Lord. Towards the end of the hymn, when this statement is made, Aquinas exclaims '*O res mirabilis*'! (O wondrous thing). He is clearly convinced that the eucharistic event deserves to be recalled and celebrated with full and fitting solemnity. He writes:

> It is fitting, for the devotion of the faithful, solemnly to recall the institution of such a saving and wonderful sacrament, so that we may venerate the ineffable mode of the divine presence in a visible sacrament, and praise God's power which works so many wonders in the same sacrament, and so that we may pay our debts to God for the workings of grace and for such a salutary and gracious favour.[32]

This passage is taken from the *Third Lesson* composed by Aquinas for the Office of Matins. It underlines the importance of a *solemn* celebration. But, of course, solemnity is by no means the only thing of importance in this context. According to Aquinas, in order fully to celebrate the feast, there must be *joy* as well as solemnity. And that's why, from the beginning of *Sacris solemniis,* we are invited to bring to the solemn rites and rubrics of the feast – to the *external* form of the celebration – an inner exuberant joy.[33]

---

[32] *Third Lesson* of the Feast of Corpus Christi. Translation based on the provisional text of the Leonine Commission.

[33] On the need for a joyous celebration, Gerard Manley Hopkins was in clear agreement with St Thomas. Reflecting on a eucharistic event attended by his friend, Robert Bridges, Hopkins wrote: 'I

Sacris solemniis	To these our solemn sacred rites
iuncta sint gaudia	let all our joys be joined,
et ex praecordiis	and from our inmost heart and mind
sonent praeconia,	let songs of praise resound.
recedant vetera,	let ancient forms depart
nova sint omnia,	and everything be new: new in word,
corda, voces, et opera.	new in deed, and new in heart.

For St Thomas true religion is never a matter of mere external observance. What is required, therefore, if a celebration such as Corpus Christi is to be fully authentic, is some spontaneous movement of the *inner* self, a welling up from 'the inmost heart' (*ex praecordiis*) of gratitude and praise. And something else as well. Mere religious feeling by itself, no matter how intense or seemingly profound, will mean little or nothing if not accompanied by practical charity. It is no accident, therefore, that Aquinas also speaks here of actual deeds or good works. In fact, at the close of the hymn's first stanza, he lists all three of these fundamental dimensions of the Christian experience: '*corda*' is mentioned first, the praise of the inner heart, then '*voces*', the shared, external act of worship, and then finally '*opera*', the putting into practice of the Christian faith in the form of good deeds: '*Nova sint omnia,/Corda, voces, et opera*' (Let all things be new:/hearts, voices and works).

* * *

After the conclusion of the first stanza, we are led by St Thomas into the Upper Room where we are allowed to witness, as it were, the different stages of the hallowed meal: first, the eating of the prescribed foods according to Jewish custom, then the breaking of bread and, finally, the words of blessing said over the bread and wine. It is significant that lamb and unleavened bread were eaten first by the disciples immediately before they received the Body of the Lord: the customary Jewish meal, and its ancient ritual, immediately preceding the enormous surprise of the second rite and celebration, the unheard-off, wholly

---

wish our procession ... had been better ... it was heavy and dead. Now a Corpus Christi procession should be stately indeed, but it should be brisk and joyous.' Letter, 10 June 1882, in *The Letters of Gerard Manley Hopkins to Robert Bridges*, p. 148.

unexpected Paschal meal and sacrifice prepared by Christ for his friends: the final passage from the Old Law to the New. St Thomas, in his commentary on Colossians, writes: 'Under the Old Law there were constantly repeated ceremonies.'[34] Some of these, of course, such as the Passover, came only 'once a year'.[35] But all these rites and ceremonies, Thomas notes, were 'merely a shadow' of what was to come, namely Christ. And he adds: 'When we see a shadow, we expect a body to follow.'[36]

Sacris solemnis differs from *Pange lingua* in one notable aspect: the doctrinal element is very nearly absent. According to F. J. E. Raby 'the picture is more human, Christ appears almost like the Jesus of Leonardo as one taking leave of his friends'[37] – a telling image of the grace and meaning of the Last Supper as understood by St Thomas, and one made even more vivid when we read the *Second Lesson* composed for the Office of *Matins*. Here is an extract:

> No-one can adequately express the truly delightful nature of this sacrament in which spiritual sweetness is tasted in its source, and the memory is recalled of the most excellent love that Christ showed in his Passion. Therefore, in order to imprint the immensity of this love more deeply on the hearts of the faithful, at the Last Supper, after celebrating the Passover with the faithful, and about to leave this world and go to the Father, he instituted the sacrament as a lasting memorial of his Passion. It fulfilled the foreshadowing of ancient rites, being the greatest of the miracles he worked, and he left it as a unique comfort to his disciples saddened by his absence.[38]

---

[34] *Super epistolam ad Colossenses lectura*, ch. 2, lect. 4, 120, in *Super epistolas s. Pauli lectura*, vol. 2, p. 148.

[35] Ibid.

[36] Ibid, 121. Elsewhere St Thomas writes: 'The end of the Old Law was the justification of human beings. The Law, however, could not accomplish this, but forshadowed it by certain ceremonial actions, and promised it in words. And, in this respect, the New Law fulfils the Old by justifying us through the power of Christ's Passion ... Wherefore the New Law is called the law of reality; whereas the Old Law is called the law of shadow or figure.' *ST*, I II q.107, a.2.

[37] F. J. E. Raby, *A History of Christian-Latin Poetry: From the Beginnings to the Close of the Middle Ages* (Oxford 1927) p. 410.

[38] *Second Lesson* of the Feast of Corpus Christi. Translation based on the provisional, as yet unpublished text of the Leonine Commission.

In *Sacris solemniis* the institution of the Eucharist is presented by Aquinas as a response to the most immediate needs of the disciples of Jesus: their need, because of weakness, to be strengthened, and their need, because of sorrow, to be comforted.

Dedit fragilibus	To those who were weak
corporis ferculum,	he offered the support
dedit et tristibus	of his body, as living food,
sanguinis poculum,	and to those who were sad
dicens: accipite	the chalice of his blood,
quod trado, vasculum,	and said: Take the cup I hand
omnes ex eo bibite.	to you, and drink from it.

These 'last words' of Jesus seem to have impressed themselves deeply on the mind of Aquinas. In the *Summa* he writes: 'Last words, especially those spoken by friends when parting, are committed most deeply to memory; since, then especially, affection for friends is more enkindled, and the more our affections are involved, the more deeply things are impressed upon our soul.'[39] And again:

> Our Lord instituted this sacrament at his last parting with his disciples, so that it might be held in the greater veneration. And this is what Augustine says: 'Our Saviour, so as to impress on us the more strongly the depth of this mystery, willed this last act to be fixed in the hearts and memories of the disciples when leaving them to go to his Passion.'[40]

2. The priest and sacrifice

The institution of the Eucharist is an event that clearly belongs to the past. Nevertheless, the grace of the event survives into the present in an ecclesial, sacramental form. And, in this form, the priest, the acting minister of the sacrament, is given a significant role.

---

[39] *ST*, III q.73, a.5.
[40] Ibid.

Sic sacrificium	The sacrifice, once given
istud instituit,	shape and form,
cuius officium	he willed the care of it, the task
committi voluit	of sharing it with others,
solis presbyteris,	be assigned to priests,
quibus sic congruit,	but they should first partake
ut sumant et dent ceteris.	of it themselves.

The information provided here is wholly accurate. And yet the stanza carries, perhaps, too much explanatory detail to be able to maintain the lyric grace and power of the other stanzas. The poetry has, in effect, come down at least a tone or two, and has become, as a result, less poetry-as-poetry and more poetry-as-information. The rhyme scheme is maintained throughout, of course, but the combinations of word and rhythm, the interweaving of rhyme and assonance, which so distinguish the rest of the hymn, are here far less convincing, far less natural.

Almost the first word of stanza five is '*sacrificium*'. St Thomas calls this new sacrament instituted by Christ a 'sacrifice'. And naming it thus should, of course, come as no surprise. Again and again, in his prose writings, St Thomas refers to the Eucharist as a '*sacrificium*'. In the *Summa,* for example, he writes: 'the celebration of this sacrament is an image representing Christ's Passion, which is his true sacrifice.'[41] For Thomas, the sacrificial element does not end with Calvary but forms part of the sacramental celebration. 'This sacrament,' he writes, 'is called a sacrifice inasmuch as it represents the very Passion of Christ. Moreover it is a victim (*hostia*) because it contains Christ himself who is, as Ephesians 5.2 tells us, a "fragrant offering" [literally, fragrant *victim*].'[42]

The Holy Sacrifice of the Mass, because it actually contains Christ, the innocent Victim, who offered his life on behalf of humanity, is not a mere symbolic sacrifice, and nor is it simply a commemoration. Under the signs of bread and wine Christ the Victim, we can say, is present but no longer

---

[41] *ST,* III q.83, a.1.
[42] *ST,* III q.73, a.4, ad 3.

suffering, of course, as he did on Calvary.[43] But the *form* of that passion is different from that of Calvary. The body of Christ, though clearly present in the reserved Sacrament (whether in a pyx or tabernacle) is no longer vulnerable to external torture, 'such as to be mocked, spat upon, crucified, scourged, and the rest.'[44] St Thomas, in the *Summa,* to underline this point, cites the following few lines of verse:

Pyxide servato poteris	Our Lord can grieve beneath
sociare dolorem	the sacramental veils
innatum, sed non illatus	but cannot feel the piercing
convenit illi.	of the thorns and nails.[45]

The grace of Christ's sacrifice is available to every person within the Church. But the actual task of distributing the Sacrament is a task given 'to priests alone'. Why this should be the case St Thomas explains in Question 82 of Part III of the *Summa*:

The dispensing of Christ's body belongs to the office of the priest for three reasons. First, because the priest consecrates in the person of Christ who consecrated his body at the Supper, and gave it to others also to be received. Accordingly, as the consecration of Christ's body belongs to the priest, so likewise does the dispensing belong to the priest. Second, because the priest is constituted an intermediary between God and the people, it is his task to offer the gifts of the people to God, and his task also to hand over the hallowed gifts to the people. Third, because out of reverence for the sacrament, nothing touches it but what is consecrated, the corporal, the chalice, and likewise the priest's hands, are consecrated for the touching of this sacrament. Hence, nobody else can lawfully touch it except out of

---

[43] See Stepan Martin Filip, '*Imago repraesentativa passionis Christi*: St Thomas on the Essence of the Sacrifice of the Mass,' *Nova et Vetera,* English Edition, vol 7, no. 2 (2009) pp. 405–38.

[44] *ST*, III q.81, a.4.

[45] Ibid. I have taken this translation from the 1948 Bennzinger Bros. translation of the *Summa*. A more literal translation of the stanza can be found in the Blackfriars edition of the *Summa*. It reads: 'When reserved in the pyx he can grieve from within, yet cannot be hurt from without.'

necessity, for instance if it were to fall upon the ground, or else in some other case of necessity.[46]

Although as minister of the sacrament of the Eucharist, the role given to the priest is of undoubted importance, St Thomas is at pains in his work to demonstrate that the living source of the Eucharist – the *principal* agent – is not the priest, but rather Christ himself. It is true, at Mass, the priest does pronounce the words of consecration but, in spite of that enormous privilege, he remains what Thomas calls an *extrinsic* instrument.[47] At the eucharistic celebration everything depends on the grace of Christ and on the power of Christ. Accordingly, the priest does not use his own words but the words of Christ.

Stanza Five comes to a close with the observation that before priests distribute the Sacrament to others they must first partake of it themselves. This point, which might seem, at first hearing, rather obvious, is taken up and explained later by St Thomas in the *Summa*.

> The Eucharist is not only a sacrament, but also a sacrifice. Now whoever offers a sacrifice must also be a sharer in the sacrifice. For the outward sacrifice the priest offers is a sign of the inward sacrifice whereby he offers himself to God … And so, by participating in the sacrifice, he shows that inwardly it is also his. Likewise, by dispensing the sacrifice to the people he shows himself to be a dispenser of divine things, of which he himself ought to be the first to participate.[48]

3. The bread of angels

The penultimate stanza of *Sacris solemniis*, which begins with the words '*Panis angelicus*' is universally regarded as one of Aquinas's finest achievements in

---

[46] *ST*, III q.82, a.3.
[47] *ST*, III q.64, a.3. See also *ST*, III q.78, a.1. 'In this sacrament the consecration of the matter consists in the miraculous change of the substance which can only be done by God. Thus the minister, in performing this sacrament, has no other act save the pronouncing of the words.'
[48] *ST*, III q.82, a.4.

verse. Not only is there a felicitous inevitability about the lines from the point of view of rhyme, assonance and alliteration, the actual message which the stanza contains is itself truly impressive, namely the statement that even the least among us is invited to the banquet of the new Pasch.

Panis angelicus	Now the bread of angels
fit panis hominum,	feeds the sons of men.
dat panis caelicus	Figures and types are fled,
figuris terminum;	never to come again.
O res mirabilis!	O what a wondrous thing!
Manducat Dominum	The poor, the humble, the lowly
pauper, servus, et humilis.	consume the Master and King.

Aquinas has no doubt whatever that the phrase 'the bread of angels' is a fitting term for the Eucharist. Here on earth, it is true, we are able to eat the Bread of Life, but 'it belongs to the angels to do so firstly and principally.'[49] Angels stand in the presence of the Lord. They see him 'in his proper species'.[50] 'Both angels and human beings,' Thomas explains, 'belong to the fellowship of Christ's mystical body; human beings by faith and angels by manifest vision.'[51] This means that 'receiving Christ under this sacrament is ordained to the enjoyment of heaven, as to its end, in the same way as angels enjoy it.'[52] That 'end' is, as it happens, the focus of the final words of the final stanza of *Sacris solemniis*. At this point, the hymn turns into a prayer. We are addressing the Holy Trinity, asking for grace in the present, but asking, as we long for the fulfilment of our desires, that we also might be led into the radiance of God's presence.

Te, trina deitas	O Triune Deity
unaque, poscimus,	as we offer you our worship,
sicut nos visitas,	visit us, we pray, and towards
sicut te colimus:	the goal of our desire,
per tuas semitas	guide us along your paths:

---

[49] *ST*, III q.80 a.2, ad.1.
[50] *ST*, III q.80, a.2, ad.1.
[51] *ST*, III q.80, a.2, ad.2.
[52] *ST*, III q.80, a.2, ad.1.

| *duc nos, quo tendimus* | lead us to the radiance |
| *ad lucem, quam inhabitas.* | in which you dwell. |

The phrase, 'bread of angels', is repeated twice by Aquinas in the *Fourth Lesson* for the Feast of Corpus Christi. There the phrase is referred back to its original context in the Old Testament, to that moment in the lives of the people of Israel when, starving for food in the desert, they were fed by God with 'manna' from heaven. I can think of no better way of ending this brief commentary on *Sacris solemniis* than by citing now in full St Thomas's own reflection on the 'bread of angels'. The text, it should be noted, is not that of an uninvolved spectator. The voice we hear is that of a preacher-theologian, a disciple of the Word, a man anxious to alert us to the full wonder and meaning of the sacrament under consideration.

This sacrament was prefigured when God rained down manna for the fathers in the desert and they then ate food from heaven every day. Thus it is said, 'Human beings ate the bread of angels.' But, although they ate that bread, all of them died in the desert. The bread which you receive, however, that living bread which comes down from heaven, ministers to you the substance of eternal life. Anyone who eats this bread will never die, because it is the body of Christ. Now consider which is to be preferred, the bread of angels or the flesh of Christ – the very body of life? That manna came down from heaven, but this from above heaven. That was of heaven, this of the Lord of the heavens. That was subject to corruption if kept for more than a day, this free from all corruption; whoever tastes it with devotion cannot experience corruption. For them, water flowed from a rock, for you, blood from Christ. Water satisfied them for an hour, but blood soaks you forever. The Jews drank and were thirsty; when you drink, you cannot thirst. That happened in shadow, this in reality. If you are amazed at what is a shadow, how much more are you amazed at what that is a shadow of? ... You have come to know the better things. Light is better than shadow, reality than a figure, the body of the Author himself than manna from heaven.[53]

---

[53] *Fourth Lesson* of the Feast of Corpus Christi. Translation based on the provisional text of the Leonine Commission.

(3) *Verbum supernum prodiens* The hymn at Lauds

Verbum supernum prodiens	The Word of God proceeding forth
Nec Patris linquens dexteram,	yet leaving not the Father's side
Ad opus suum exiens,	and going to his work on earth,
Venit ad vitae vesperam.	had reached at last life's eventide.
In mortem a discipulo	Then, sadly, to a death accursed,
Suis tradendum aemulis,	by a disciple he was given,
Prius in vitae ferculo	but, to his twelve disciples first,
Se tradidit discipulis.	he gave himself, the bread from heaven.
Quibus sub bina specie	To them, beneath a two-fold sign,
Carnem dedit et sanguinem,	he gave his flesh, he gave his blood,
Ut duplicis substantiae	that man, of two-fold substance blent,
Totum cibaret hominem.	might know the fullness of the good.
Se nascens dedit socium,	By birth, our fellow man was he,
Convescens in edulium;	our meat, while sitting at the board,
Se moriens in pretium,	he died our ransomer to be;
Se regnans dat in praemium.	and ever reigns, our great reward.
O salutaris hostia,	O saving Victim, opening wide
Quae caeli pandis ostium,	the gate of heaven to all below,
Bella premunt hostilia,	our foes press hard on every side,
Da robur, fer auxilium.	your aid supply, your strength bestow.
Uni trinoque Domino	To your great name be endless praise,
Sit sempiterna gloria,	Immortal Godhead, One in Three,
Qui vitam sine termino	O grant us endless length of days
Nobis donet in patria.	in our true fatherland with thee.

Verbum supernum prodiens
A commentary

Verbum supernum prodiens is not a lengthy work – a mere six short stanzas – and yet it is able to include reference to all of the following: the abiding union of Christ with his Father, the mystery of the descent of the Word, the institution of the Eucharist, the two-fold species comprising the Eucharist, the betrayal of Christ by his enemies, the death of Christ on the cross, and a prayer addressed to Christ for protection when suffering oppression. Needless to say, these great themes taken together are a particularly heavy weight for a short poem or hymn to carry. The fact, therefore, that the author has been able to maintain a fine, lyric intensity throughout is no small achievement.

1. The gift, the miracle

By far, I would say, the most impressive part of the hymn is its last three stanzas, and in particular stanza 4. Although consisting of a mere sixteen words, what impresses at once is the structural beauty of the stanza, the harmony of its multiple *internal* and *end* rhymes, and the way it is able, with a few quick strokes, to sketch for us the key moments in the life of Christ, and to indicate also the nature of the gift achieved for us, the undeserved, unimaginable grace of actual fellowship with God, a grace offered not only in the past, but also in the present, and in the future to come.

> *Se nascens dedit socium,*   By his birth he gave himself as our
> *Convescens in edulium;*   companion, at the Supper as our
> *Se moriens in pretium,*   food, dying as our ransom; reigning
> *Se regnans dat in praemium.*   he gives himself as our reward.

Included here, among the four forms of Christ's self-giving, is the gift of his own body and blood at the Last Supper. This sacred event, this 'handing over' of himself to his disciples, was already described for us earlier in the hymn: the entire third stanza of *Verbum supernum prodiens* being devoted to the subject. But the manner in which the Last Supper is presented here in *Verbum supernum* is quite different from its appearance earlier in the hymn for Matins, *Sacris solemniis*. There Aquinas painted for us a warm and moving image of Christ taking leave of his friends. Here, in contrast, the language of the hymn is noticeably more detached and abstract. The great gift and treasure of the Eucharist is described in the plain, academic language of scholasticism:

Quibus sub bina specie	To them, under a twofold species
Carnem dedit et sanguinem,	he gave his flesh and blood
Ut duplicis substantiae	that he might feed the whole man
Totum cibaret hominem.	made up of twofold substance.

If, in the Corpus Christi Office, there was one place where we might have expected to find the scholastic imprint visible, it was not in the poetry – not in the hymns – but in the prose Readings or *Lessons* composed for the hour of Matins. For the most part, however, that is not the case. Scholastic words, generally familiar in the academic world of the Middle Ages, such as 'species' and 'accidents', occur in only a few of the *Lessons*. For the rest, the language and images employed throughout are exclusively biblical. That said, however, one indication that the author of the *Lessons* is a determined teacher, and not simply a disciple of the Word, is the *teacherly* manner with which two of the readings are introduced. *Lesson V*, for example, opens with words which give the impression Aquinas is engaging in earnest dialogue with one of his students, a 'student' not afraid to strike a note of scepticism regarding the Real Presence: 'Maybe you object,' the *Lesson* begins, 'I see something else. How can you tell me that I am receiving the Body of Christ?'

St Thomas, when he sets his mind to answer this question, speaks at once of the power of God manifest in the symbols and stories of the Old Testament, a power which can completely transform the world of nature, and so, with the same miraculous strength, can also transform bread and wine into the body and blood of Christ.[54]

Thus Moses held a staff, threw it, and it became a serpent. Then he took the tail of the serpent and it returned to the nature of a staff. Thus you see that by prophetic grace nature was changed twice, that of a serpent and that of a staff. The rivers of Egypt ran with pure streams of water, suddenly blood erupted from the springs and the rivers were undrinkable. Then, at the prayers of the prophet, the blood of the rivers stopped, and the natural water flowed back. The Hebrew people were surrounded on every side, on

---

[54] St Thomas's answer to the question does not come to an end with *Lesson V*, but continues on into *Lesson VI*. These two *Lessons*, in effect, comprise a single text.

one side by the Egyptians, on the other by the sea. Moses lifted his staff, and the water divided and froze in the form of walls, leaving a walkway in between. The Jordan river turned back, against its nature returning to its source. Is it not clear that nature, whether of the sea or of a river, was changed? The people of the fathers were thirsty; Moses touched the rock, and water flowed out. Did grace not operate apart from nature, so that a rock could discharge water which, by nature, it does not have?[55]

Marah was a most bitter river, where the people could not drink. Moses put a piece of wood in the water and the bitterness which it had by nature was tempered by grace suddenly flowing in. At the time of Elisha the prophet, one of the sons of the prophets lost his axehead and it sunk in the water. He complained to Elisha the prophet, who put a piece of wood in the water, and the axehead floated. This too we recognize to have happened apart from nature. For the nature of iron is heavier than water. So we see that grace is greater than nature, and we admire the grace of the prophet's blessing. If a human blessing could be so powerful as to change a nature, what do we say about the divine consecration where the very words of the Lord Saviour are at work? For that sacrament which you receive is effected by the pronouncement of Christ. If the pronouncement of Elijah was so powerful as to bring fire from heaven, is not the pronouncement of Christ strong enough to change the nature of the elements?[56]

The strong reliance here on the symbols and stories of the Old Testament, caught the attention of a number of St Thomas's own contemporaries. As I have already noted, Tolomeo of Lucca, in a history which he published sometime between 1312 and 1317, remarked: 'An attentive reader will see

---

[55] *Fifth Lesson* of the Feast of Corpus Christi. Apart from the addition of numerous and illuminating footnotes, the provisional Leonine text of *Lesson V* is almost indistinguishable from the text established by C. Lambot in 'L'Office de la Fête-Dieu: Aperçus nouveaux sur ses origines', *Revue Bénédictine*, vol. 54 (1942) p. 78. Since a particularly fine English version of the Lambot text already exists (translated by Joseph Kenny OP) that translation of *Lesson V* is the one given here. See http://www.josephkenny. joyeurs.com/CDtexts/Corpus Christi.htm (accessed 2 May 2012).

[56] *Sixth Lesson* of the Feast of Corpus Christi. Again, apart from additional footnotes, the text established by Lambot of *Lesson VI* is almost indistinguishable from the provisional Latin text of the Leonine Commission. See Lambot, pp. 78–9. Translation by Joseph Kenny OP. See http://www. josephkenny.joyeurs.com/CDtexts/Corpus Christi.htm

that it [the Corpus Christi Office] comprises nearly all the symbolic figures of the Old Testament, clearly and appropriately relating them to the Sacrament of the Eucharist.'[57] *Lesson V* opens in a manner which clearly indicates that the author was someone well used to academic discourse. But that is not the main reason I have cited this particular *Lesson* at such great length. The text is, of course, written in prose but it is a *miracle* of prose. The concentration in a single passage of so many powerful images, the unusual force of the text's central argument, and the carefully structured form and grace of its composition, all join together to make an impact not at all unlike, I am persuaded, that of the greatest poetry.

2. The handing-over

One theme not mentioned in the other hymns composed by Aquinas is touched on briefly in the second stanza of *Verbum supernum*: the theme of betrayal.

In mortem a discipulo	Before having to be handed over to
Suis tradendum aemulis,	his enemies by a disciple, and be put
Prius in vitae ferculo	to death, he first handed himself over
Se tradidit discipulis.	to his disciples on the plate of life.

Christ is seen here as a victim, a man betrayed by his close friend and disciple, Judas. But that is not the final message of the stanza. Yes, Christ is indeed a victim of betrayal, but he is not a mere *passive* victim. Although *handed over* by Judas into the hands of his enemies, Christ, we are told, first *handed himself over* to his friends. And, by that gesture of utter self-giving, he changed everything. From then on, what seemed like a necessary fate, imposed on him from without, was in fact completely transformed from *within*, and became the free act of a free man. The author of the hymn, in order to draw attention to the grace of this event, uses the same or almost the same word to describe the two different kinds of *handing over* – a play on words intended to help us

---

[57] Tolomeo, *Hist. Eccl.* Lib. 22, c.24, col.1154; cited in Weishipl, p. 177.

see how the terrible gesture of the betrayal, the '*tradendum*' of Judas, is now matched and overcome by the utter kindness and love of the '*tradidit*' of Christ Jesus.

The grace of that surrender, although a blessing like no other, was also, in itself, a sacrifice like no other. And that no doubt explains the decidedly strong phrase used in the second stanza to describe the self-offering of Christ at the Last Supper: '*in vitae ferculo se tradidit discipulis*': 'on the plate of life / he handed himself over to his disciples.' The word '*ferculum*', which I have translated here as 'plate', means literally 'that on which anything is carried or borne', from the verb *fero* to carry or support. Since the word occurs here in the context of a meal, 'plate' strikes me as the most obvious and most fitting translation. But 'plate' is not, as it happens, the only possible translation of *ferculum*. Another meaning, found in both Classical and Medieval Latin, is 'bier' or 'litter'.[58]

Apparently, in ancient Rome, *ferculum* was the word used to describe the frame for carrying things such as the spoils of one's enemies or the images of the gods in public processions. If the author of the hymn intended this particular echo, I consider it a touch of genius. In the opinion of the critic R. P. Blackmur (writing in another context) 'when a word is used in a poem it should be the sum of all its appropriate history made concrete and particular in the individual context.'[59] Part of the 'history' of the word *ferculum* brings a very particular resonance to any poem or hymn concerned with the passion and death of Christ. Take, for example, the following brief passage from Chapter 1 of Livy's *History of Rome* in which the word *ferculo* occurs. Romulus, the warrior, we are told, after having killed one of the kings who opposed him, and despoiled his body, returned to Rome victorious, where 'he ascended the Capitol with the spoils of his dead foe carried before him on a frame (*ferculo*) specially constructed for the purpose. He hung the spoils there on an oak, which the shepherds looked upon as a sacred tree.'[60]

---

[58] See C. T. Lewis and C. Short, *A Latin Dictionary* (Oxford 1966) p. 735. And see also L. F. Stelten, *Dictionary of Ecclesiastical Latin* (Peabody, Massachusetts 1995) p. 100.

[59] Cited on p. 239, *The Cambridge History of Literary Criticism*, (ed.) A. Walton Litz.

[60] Livy, *The History of Rome*, Book 1, 10.

If, in a poem, a word can be said to have the right to all its echoes, surely the word *ferculo,* in the hymn for Lauds, can be thought of as evoking not only the event of the Last Supper, but also the events which followed after. And, in this context, I have in mind the manner in which Christ the King, in manifest humiliation, and yet in triumph, was led out in public procession, and raised up and hung upon 'the tree of life'.[61] Our medieval author, although undoubtedly acquainted to some extent with the major works of Roman literature,[62] may or may not have intended to recall or awaken this particular echo. But the word *ferculo* is there, all the same, in the second stanza of the hymn. And we can be sure that at least some of its many echoes and connotations survive – echoes which may be minor, perhaps, but which now form part of the work's final meaning and music.

*   *   *

I have spoken already, in general terms, of the influence on Thomas's Corpus Christi hymns of lines and phrases belonging to earlier hymns and poems. Although, in the opinion of Weisheipl, 'The three magnificent hymns of the office are not identical with any hymns known to have been previously written', nevertheless Weisheipl acknowledges that the hymn for Lauds, *Verbum supernum prodiens,* 'has many similarities with a hymn in the Cistercian liturgy for Corpus Christi.'[63] The hymn, in the Cistercian office, comprises nine stanzas divided into two hymns (Matins and Lauds) whereas, in the Aquinas version, the hymn has only six stanzas. The question of literary influence and potential borrowing was taken up and discussed at length in

---

[61] Finding the phrase *vitae ferculo* in an earlier hymn, dating from the sixth century, A. S. Walpole translates *vitae ferculo* as 'the bread of life', and notes that it is a reminiscence of 'the tree of life'. See Walpole, *Early Latin Hymns* (Cambridge 1922) p. 201.

[62] Medieval authors possessed more than a passing acquaintance with classical literature. On the subject of Aquinas's familiarity with such works, Beryl Smalley writes: 'He seldom quotes Latin classical authors, but his quotation is apt and not a mere frill when he does ... Thomas could also adduce Roman history to illustrate the waning of the Baptist's power after Christ's coming: "For this custom was observed by the ancient powers that the lesser power should not wear the insignia of his power in the presence of a greater; hence the consuls lay aside their insignia in the presence of the Dictator". See *The Gospels in the Schools, c 1100–1280.* (London 1985) p. 260.

[63] Weisheipl, p. 181.

an article by D. G. Morin in 1910.[64] It seemed clear to Morin that either the Cistercians were dependent on St Thomas or Thomas had deliberately taken over stanzas from a Cistercian liturgy in use before him.[65]

The actual manuscripts of the Cistercian *Verbum supernum prodiens*, on which Morin based his reflections, belong not to the thirteenth but to the fourteenth century, a fact which would appear to indicate that St Thomas's work predates that of the Cistercians. This view, D. G. Morin acknowledges, is one that can certainly be defended.[66] But Morin is inclined to the view, based on a number of strong arguments, that the Cistercian liturgy more likely predates that of Thomas.[67] Needless to say, any doubt still surrounding this opinion will only be resolved, once and for all, should a manuscript of the Cistercian office, predating the year 1264, ever come to light.

3. 'Give strength, bring help'

The opening stanzas of *Verbum supernum prodiens* (in the Aquinas version) although focused on some of the deepest mysteries of the Christian faith, are not addressed directly to God. They are not prayers of petition or prayers of praise, their form and character being closer to that of a theological reflection or meditation.

> The high Word
> of God
> remaining always at his Father's side,
> while proceeding forth
> to do his work on earth,
> arrived
> at his life's end.

---

[64] D. G. Morin, 'L'Office cistercien pour la Fête-Dieu comparé avec celui de saint Thomas d'Aquin', *Revue bénédictine* (April 1910) pp. 236–46.

[65] Ibid., p. 244.

[66] Ibid.

[67] Ibid., pp. 244–5. Morin also suggests that Thomas may have incorporated into his work seven of the responsories of Matins from the Cistercian Office, pp. 238–9.

Then, being by a friend
betrayed,
and about to be handed over to his
rivals
and put to death,
he chose first
to hand himself over to his disciples
on the plate of life.

In this way,
under both species,
in two-fold form, he gave himself
to us utterly,
flesh and blood like us,
so that he might thereby
feed
and answer our every need.

Being born,
he gave himself to us as our
companion.
At the Supper, he
gave himself to us as our food.
Dying,
he gave himself to us
as our ransom.
Reigning,
he now gives himself to us
as our reward.

With the stanza that follows, however, everything changes. The words of the
hymn are now being addressed directly to Christ, and instead of a relaxed and
meditative atmosphere, a new note of urgency is sounded:

O saving Victim,
you, who have opened wide

the entrance of the

sky

to all below,

our foes press hard on every side,

your aid supply,

your strength bestow.

The original Latin text doesn't speak of 'foes', as it happens, but of 'hostile wars' pressing upon us (*bella ... hostilia*). Here, then, is a more literal translation of the stanza:

O salutaris hostia,	O saving Victim, who throws
Quae caeli pandis ostium,	open the gate of heaven,
Bella premunt hostilia,	hostile wars press upon us,
Da robur, fer auxilium.	give us strength, bring us aid,

This short stanza, owing to its great simplicity and beauty, and to the number of times it has been used at the service of Benediction over the years, forms that part of the hymn which has become the best known and best loved. It is a lyric of the purest kind, and the brief image of hope which it contains is quite unforgettable – the vision, that is, of Christ throwing open the gate of heaven. The phrase 'hostile wars', when it occurs, does not refer, it seems clear, to individual enemies, but rather to a power of evil that is both faceless and impersonal – a reference, perhaps, to 'the principalities and powers' spoken of in the Epistle to the Ephesians: *For it is not against human enemies that we have to struggle, but against principalities and powers who originate the darkness in this world, the spiritual army of evil in the heavens.* Eph. 6.12. Obviously, with hostile forces of this kind ranged against us we have no hope of ever attaining salvation by our own strength. And that explains, no doubt, the two imperatives – the two *pleadings* – in the last line of the stanza: *'da robor'* and *'fer auxilium'* (give strength, bring help).

But what kind of 'strength' and 'help' can we expect to receive, here and now, from the sacrament of the Eucharist? St Thomas raises this question in the *Summa*. And, by way of reply, he notes that just as the body can be strengthened inwardly and outwardly to withstand death and sickness by taking the proper food and medicine, likewise the Eucharist, by uniting us with Christ, can help to preserve us, here and now, from the threat of 'spiritual death', and from the sickness that comes from sin. St Thomas then goes on to make a further remark about the strength we receive from the Eucharist, a claim which must surely be one of the most confident and remarkable statements ever made by Aquinas. He writes: 'Inasmuch as it [the sacrament of the Eucharist] is a sign of Christ's Passion whereby devils are conquered, it repels all attacks of the demons. Hence Chrysostom says: "Like lions breathing forth fire, thus do we depart from that table, being made terrible to the devil".'[68]

* * *

The final stanza of *Verbum supernum prodiens* consists of two things: a brief song of praise to the Holy Trinity, and a prayer that we would be given life without end '*in patria*'. This last tiny prayer can be sung with great confidence and hope since the entire purpose and meaning of Christ's life, according to the message of the hymn up to this point (a message memorably summarized in the hymn's fifth stanza) is precisely to bestow on us a reward we could never have deserved ourselves, namely, the astonishing 'ransom' won for us by Christ on the cross. And our 'reward' is nothing other than life with him in heaven without end.

(4) *Lauda Sion* Sequence for the Mass of Corpus Christi

Lauda, Sion, salvatorem,	Zion, to Your Saviour sing,
lauda ducem et pastorem,	to Your Shepherd and Your King,
in hymnis et canticis.	sing with canticle and hymn.
Quantum potes, tantum aude,	Dare with song to praise him well
quia maior omni laude,	though he does all praise excel,
nec laudare sufficis.	never cease from praising him.
Laudis thema specialis,	Wondrous theme of mortal singing,
panis vivus et vitalis	living bread and bread life-giving,

---

[68] *ST*, III q.79, a.6.

hodie proponitur.   is our theme, our task, today.

Quem in sacrae mensa coenae,   So let no one be deceived:
turbae fratrum duodenae   the living bread the Twelve received
datum non ambigitur.   is the same that we consume.

Sit laus plena, sit sonora,   Sound the anthem, clear and strong,
sit iucunda, sit decora   the fullest note, the sweetest song,
mentis iubilatio.   the very music of the breast.

Dies enim solemnis agitur,   For now there dawns a day sublime
in qua mensae prima recolitur   that brings remembrance of the time
huius institutio.   when Jesus first his table blessed.

In hac mensa novi regis,   Now the New Law's new oblation
novum Pascha novae legis   by the new King's revelation
phase vetus terminat.   ends the form of ancient rite.

Vetustatem novitas,   Now the new the old replaces,
umbram fugat veritas,   truth away the shadow chases,
noctem lux eliminat.   light dispels the gloom of night.

Quod in cena Christus gessit,   What he did at supper seated,
faciendum hoc expressit   Christ ordained to be repeated
in sui memoriam.   in his memory divine.

Docti sacris institutis,   Wherefore now, his guidance taking,
panem, vinum in salutis   bread and wine we hallow, making
consecramus hostiam.   lasting food for our salvation.

Dogma datur Christianis,   This is the truth each Christian learns,
quod in carnem transit panis   bread into flesh he turns,
et vinum in sanguinem.   wine becomes his holy blood.

Quod non capis, quod non vides,   Though we feel it not, nor see it,
animosa firmat fides,   ardent faith, which now reveals it,
praeter rerum ordinem.   all defects of sense makes good.

Sub diversis speciebus,   Here in outward signs are hidden

signis tantum et non rebus	wondrous things to sense forbidden;
latent res eximiae.	What we see are signs alone.
Caro cibus, sanguis potus,	Wine is poured and bread is broken,
manet tamen Christus totus	but in one or other token
sub utraque specie.	Christ entire we know to be.
A sumente non concisus,	Those who of this food partake
non confractus, non divisus,	neither rend the Lord nor break:
integer accipitur.	Christ is whole for all who taste.
Sumit unus, sumunt mille,	Thousand are, as one, receivers,
quantum isti, tantum ille,	one, as thousands of believers,
nec sumptus consumitur.	eat of him who cannot waste.
Sumunt boni, sumunt mali,	Both the wicked and the good
sorte tamen inaequali,	eat and drink the self-same food,
vitae vel interitus.	one to death, and one to life.
Mors est malis, vita bonis;	Though they both consume
Vide, paris sumptionis	the Lord, equal in the sacred rite,
quam sit dispar exitus.	see how they divide in fate!
Fracto demum sacramento,	When at last the bread is broken
nec vacilles, sed memento	doubt not what the Lord has spoken:
tantum esse sub fragmento,	he is present in each token;
quantum toto tegitur.	now each part contains the whole
Nulla rei fit scissura,	For the outward sign alone
signi tantum fir fractura,	may some change have undergone,
qua nec status nec statura	while the Signified stays one
signati minuitur.	and the same for evermore.
Ecce, panis Angelorum,	Look! upon the altar lies,
factus cibus viatorum,	hidden deep from human eyes,
vere panis filiorum,	bread of angels from the skies,
non mittendus canibus.	made the food of mortal man.

In figuris praesignatur,	Childrens' food to dogs denied
cum Isaac immolatur,	in wondrous prophecy described:
agnus Paschae deputatur,	in the manna from the sky, in the binding
datur manna patribus.	of the boy, in the sacrificial lamb.
Bone Pastor, panis vere,	Christ, Good Shepherd, bread
Iesu nostri miserere,	divine, show to us your mercy sign.
tu nos pasce, nos tuere,	Feed us still, still keep us thine
tu nos bona fac videre	that we may see your glory shine
in terra viventium.	in the kingdom of the good.
Tu qui cuncta scis et vales,	Source of all we have or know,
qui nos pascis hic mortales,	come and guide us here below,
tu nos ibi commensales,	make us, at your table seated,
cohaeredes et sodales	by your saints as friends be greeted,
fac santorum civium.	co-heirs at the feast of love.

Lauda Sion Salvatorem
A commentary

Lauda Sion Salvatorem, a sequence written to be sung just before the Gospel at Mass,[69] is an exhortation to 'Sion' – the community of the redeemed – to praise Christ, the great Saviour, Leader and Shepherd. Based on a number of the works attributed to Adam of St Victor,[70] *Lauda Sion* has been described, and for good reason, as 'the most theologically sophisticated' of all St Thomas's

---

[69] According to Jan-Heiner Tück the sequence was sung directly after a specifically chosen reading from the First Letter of St Paul to the Corinthians (I Cor 11.23–9). It is hard to imagine a more fitting introduction to *Lauda Sion*. The Corinthian passage contains not only a description of the institution of the Eucharist at the Last Supper, it also cites the actual words of consecration, adding: 'Until the Lord comes, therefore, every time you eat this bread and drink this cup, you are proclaiming his death.' See Tück, *Gabe der Gegenwart: Theologie und Dichtung der Eucharistie bei Thomas von Aquin*, (Freiburg 2009) p. 237.

[70] Two works in particular are worth noting: *Laudes crucis attollamus*, and the Easter sequence, *Zyma vetus expurgetur*. These works are included in *The Penguin Book of Latin Verse*, pp. 185–9 and pp. 197–201.

canticles.[71] It is hard to imagine, in fact, a hymn or sequence which could be more doctrinally Christian and Thomist. The impact of the work, however, given its incantatory power, and its bold, sonorous diction, goes far beyond that of a mere dogmatic tract in verse. From first words to final strophe, *Lauda Sion* holds our attention with the authority of a song, and makes an impact like that of great music.

Lauda, Sion, Salvatorem,	Zion, to your Saviour sing,
lauda ducem et pastorem,	to your Shepherd and your King,
in hymnis et canticis.	sing with canticle and hymn!
Quantum potes, tantum aude,	Dare with song to praise him well
quia maior omni laude,	though he does all praise excel,
nec laudare sufficis.	never cease from praising him.

When, in that last stanza, we come upon the statement about *daring* to give praise to God, the audacity to which Thomas invites us contains, of course, within it nothing whatever of human presumption or pride. It is rather that audacity which has its source in the wonderful joy and child-like enthusiasm of not being able to keep silent about the marvel of God's true nature. Thomas, in his sermon, *Lauda et laetare,* notes that there are occasions when our minds are so moved by knowledge of God, and our hearts by the transport of interior joy, there is nothing left for us to do but sing praise to God. *The peace of God,* he notes, citing Philippians, *surpasses all our thoughts* (Philippians 4.7). This point is further underlined by a quotation from Sir. 43.30: *In praising the Lord, exalt him as much as you can, for he is greater than all praise.*[72]

Lauda Sion can helpfully be divided into five sections. In the first part the entire Church is summoned to join together in joyful praise of the Blessed Sacrament (lines 1–15). In the second part reference is made to the institution

---

[71] See James McEvoy, 'St Thomas Aquinas: Poet of the Eucharist' in *The Mystery of Faith: Reflections on the Encyclical Ecclesia de Eucharistia,* (eds), J. McEvoy and M. Hogan (Dublin 2005) p. 335.

[72] The Latin text of *Laudare et laetare* (the Provisional Leonine text established by L.-J. Bataillon) has not yet been published. It has, however, already been made available for French and English translation. See Jacques Ménard (ed.) *Saint Thomas d'Aquin: Sermons* (Paris 2004) p. 80, and Mark-Robin Hoogland (ed.) *Thomas Aquinas: The Academic Sermons* (*The Fathers of the Church: Medieval Continuation,* vol. 2), (Washington 2010) p. 38.

by Christ of the eucharistic meal – the new Pasch – which believers are asked to celebrate in his memory (lines 16–30). The third part consists of a reflection on certain aspects of Catholic dogmatic teaching concerning the Eucharist (lines 31–62). The fourth part, describing the Eucharist as 'the bread of angels', draws attention to the way the Sacrament was prefigured in ancient signs and figures (lines 63–70). The fifth part consists of a brief prayer to Christ, the Good Shepherd, that in this life he would protect us and, in the next, make us sharers in the heavenly banquet (lines 71–80).

1. The grace of the new

In *Lauda Sion* St Thomas underlines over and over again the *newness* of the eucharistic meal. Christ is 'the *new* king' and, at his table, what is being celebrated is 'the *new* Pasch of the *new* Law', a meal that brings to an end, once and for all, the old ways of religion and religious practice.

Vetustatem novitas,	Now the new the old replaces,
umbram fugat veritas,	truth away the shadow chases,
noctem lux eliminat.	light dispels the gloom of night.

One detail which should not be overlooked here is the reference to the 'New Law', an event of grace which St Thomas links with the institution by Christ of 'the new Pasch'. The actual term, 'new law', occurs most memorably, of course, in St Paul. Thomas follows the Apostle in the way he speaks of the law of the ancient covenant and the grace of the New. The *New* Law, in apparent contrast to that of the Old, is not written on tablets of stone, but on the innermost hearts of men and women moved by the Spirit.[73] By emphasizing in this way the newness of the New Law, St Thomas is not for a moment intending to suggest that the God of Israel has somehow turned against his own people, and broken his covenant. 'It would be incorrect,' Jan-Heiner Tück observes, 'to construe that Thomas's intention here was to articulate a radical discontinuity

---

[73] See *Super secundum epistolam ad Corinthios lectura*, ch. 3, lect. 1, 83, in *Super epistolas s. Pauli*, vol. 1, p. 458.

between the Old and New Testament. In his understanding of the history of salvation, there is rather a firm continuity insofar as the Old Testament prefigures the salvation which is found in the coming of Christ.[74]

Believers, living now under grace, can be considered as, in some real sense, 'a law unto themselves' (*ipsi sibi sunt lex*) Rom. 2.14.[75] For the law they are moved to follow is, first and last, a law of freedom. St Thomas notes, in his Commentary on 2 Corinthians (3.17) that 'wherever the Spirit of the Lord is present, there is freedom.'[76] And he goes on to say:

> The free man is one who exists for himself (*est causa sui*), but the slave exists for the sake of the master. Therefore, whoever acts of himself acts freely, but one who is moved by another does not act freely. Therefore, one who avoids evils, not because they are evil, but because of God's command, is not free. But one who avoids evils because they are evils is free. But this is done by the Holy Spirit who perfects the human person inwardly with a good habit, so that from love that person avoids evil, as if the divine law had commanded it. Consequently, he is called free, not as though he is not subject to the divine law, but because he is inclined by a good [internal] habit to do what the divine law ordains.[77]

The word 'dogma' is not a word people are nowadays inclined to associate with freedom. But, for Thomas, 'dogma', or doctrine, in this case, represents only one thing: the wondrous, liberating truth and miracle of Christ's presence in the Eucharist.

Dogma datur Christianis,	This is the truth each Christian learns,
quod in carnem transit panis,	bread into his flesh he turns,
et vinum in sanguinem.	wine becomes his holy blood.

---

[74] See Jan-Heiner Tück, *Gabe der Gegenwart: Theologie und Dichtung der Eucharistie bei Thomas von Aquin,* pp. 244–5. We read, in a fine study by Steven C. Boguslawski OP on this subject: 'the contemporary scene in which Thomas found himself writing was shaped by an ecclesial policy toward the Jews that was becoming increasingly hostile.' Nevertheless, Boguslawski argues: 'Aquinas did not merely tolerate Jewish presence in society ... he upheld the Jews' legitimate, divinely appointed role in an overwhelmingly Christian milieu.' See *Thomas Aquinas on the Jews* (New York 2008) p. 129.

[75] See Aquinas, *Super Epistolam ad Romanos,* ch. 11, lect. 3, 217, p. 39.

[76] *Super secundum epistolam ad Corinthios lectura,* ch. 3, lect. 3, 112, p. 464.

[77] Ibid.

Quod non capis, quod non vides,	Though we feel it not, nor see it,
animosa firmat fides,	ardent faith which now reveals it,
praeter rerum ordinem.	all defects of sense makes good.

2. The necessary faith response

St Thomas, at one point in the *Summa,* asks the question, 'Is the body of Christ truly and actually in this Sacrament?', and he replies: 'The fact that the true body and blood of Christ are in this sacrament is something which cannot be apprehended by our faculties of sense, but by faith alone.'[78] So bold, in traditional Catholic teaching, is the claim made regarding Christ's presence in the Eucharist, it calls, in Aquinas's opinion, for an equally bold response in the believer. And that's why the quality of faith required for belief in the Real Presence, St Thomas links here with the striking adjective '*animosa*', an adjective which means courageous or ardent.

The man or woman of faith is not asked to give assent merely to an event in the past. The eucharistic meal contains the living presence of Christ Jesus here and now, and this saving event, which clearly belongs to both past and present, points forward also to the future, to the promised joy of the heavenly banquet. The conviction with which *Lauda Sion* speaks, or *sings*, about the impact of the grace of the Eucharist on all three times, past, present and future, is one of its great strengths. And that is also, as it happens, what distinguishes the shortest prayer ever composed by Aquinas on the Eucharist. This prayer, entitled *O sacrum convivium,* is the brief Magnificat antiphon composed by St Thomas for Second Vespers of the Feast of Corpus Christi:

> O Sacred Banquet
> in which Christ is received,
> the memory of his passion is renewed,
> the soul is filled with grace,
> and a pledge of future glory is given to us.[79]

---

[78] *ST*, III q.75, a.1.
[79] See *Officium de festo Corporis Christi,* II 2 DSG ps 7, no. 1, Busa vol. 6, p. 581.

In the *Summa theologiae* Thomas writes, 'This sacrament has a three-fold significance: one with regard to the past ... and in this respect it is called a *sacrifice*. With regard to the present ... it is called *communion* ... With regard to the future ... it is called *viaticum* because it keeps us on the way to heaven.'[80]

In a work like *Lauda Sion* what offers sanction for belief is not simply the repetition of doctrinal statements, but the sharp and bright manner in which these statements are made, the sheer memorability of the lines. Although the message being proclaimed is something wondrous, it is not a message to which we find it easy to surrender. And that's why, as Jan-Heiner Tück points out, rhymning phrases such as *Quod non capis, quod non vides / Animosa firmat fides,* 'fulfill the function of a mnemonic' and in some way 'counter the effect of the lack of verification of Christ's presence.'[81] A great work of art such as a fresco by Giotto or an oratorio by Bach can, as we know well, offer strong and immediate sanction for belief, overcoming hesitancy and even scepticism. How else can we explain the remarkable impulse which prompted Rémy de Gourmont, the French Symbolist poet, to declare after reading one of Aquinas's Eucharistic canticles: 'The inspiration of St. Thomas is fired by an unwavering genius, a genius at once strong, sure, confident and exact. What he wants to say, he speaks out boldly, and in words so lovely that even doubt grows fearful, and takes to flight.'[82]

3. Understanding 'real presence'

Inevitably, there are all kinds of questions which arise in our minds today regarding the mystery of the Real Presence. And, in the Middle Ages, there were at least as many questions raised by thinkers and theologians. When,

---

[80] *ST*, III q.73, a.4. See also III q.60, a.3.

[81] Tück, p. 276. It's almost impossible to recreate, in English translation, the immediacy and magic of the rhyming phrases we find recurring in *Lauda Sion.* G. K. Chesterton, in his book on Aquinas, remarks: 'A good translator will be the first to agree that no translation is good; or, at any rate, good enough. How are we to find eight short English words which actually stand for *Sumit unus, sumunt mille; quantum isti, tantum ille?*' See *St Thomas Aquinas* (London 1943) p. 112.

[82] Rémy de Gourmont, *Le latin mystique* (Paris 1913) pp. 274–5; cited in Étienne Gilson, *The Christian Philosophy of St Thomas Aquinas*, trans., L. K. Shook (New York 1956) p. 377.

for example, during Mass, bread is broken after the Consecration, is Christ in some way broken into parts, and thereby diminished? And, with the transformation of bread and wine into the flesh and blood of Christ, is the full Christ present in the 'bread' by itself and in the 'wine' by itself, or present only when both species are present together on the altar?

Questions of this kind are, as one might expect, raised and answered at some length by St Thomas in the *Summa theologiae*. But here, in *Lauda Sion,* no questions of this kind are mentioned. Nevertheless, the poet within Aquinas has not entirely forgotten his scholastic questions. And, at this point in the Sequence, he sets about answering a number of them one by one (strophes 13–20). The core answer he gives is always the same: hidden under the signs of bread and wine, Christ is undeniably present, and present in all his uniqueness and integrity.

Here Aquinas has clearly moved into teaching mode, and one might expect the flow of music and rhythm in the work to be in some way interrupted, or even undermined. But, strange to say, this scholastic 'interlude', while distinguished by an obvious devotion to theological accuracy, and a truly scrupulous concern for detail, strikes the ear with a melody and a rhythm that sound, if anything, more natural and more easeful than ever:

Sub diversis speciebus,	Here in outward signs are hidden
signis tantum et non rebus	wondrous things to sense forbidden;
latent res eximiae.	what we see are signs alone.
Caro cibus, sanguis potus,	Wine is poured and bread is broken,
manet tamen Christus totus	but in one or other token
sub utraque specie.	Christ entire we know to be.
A sumente non concisus,	Those who of this food partake
non confractus, non divisus,	neither rend the Lord nor break:
integer accipitur.	Christ is whole for all who taste.
Sumit unus, sumunt mille,	Thousand are, as one, receivers,
quantum isti, tantum ille,	one, as thousands of believers,
nec sumptus consumitur.	eat of him who cannot waste.

The ardent nature of St Thomas's belief in the Real Presence is made abundantly clear in the two stanzas which follow. So profound and sacred, in Thomas's view, is the privilege we enjoy by receiving the body and blood of Christ in the Eucharist, it is expected that we will make every possible effort to receive this grace worthily. Here Thomas's understanding is directly influenced by the strict warnings given by St Paul in his first Epistle to the Corinthians. There Paul speaks, in the strongest possible terms, of the peril of improper reception. He writes: *Let a man examine himself ... for anyone who eats and drinks without discerning the body eats and drinks judgment upon himself* (1 Cor. 11.28-9). St Thomas, in his Commentary on Paul, writes: 'After showing the dignity of this sacrament, the Apostle now rouses the faithful to receive it reverently. First, he indicates the peril threatening those who receive unworthily.'[83] Thomas then adds: 'because what is received sacramentally is the body of Christ and what is drunk is the blood of Christ, whoever eats this bread or drinks this cup in an unworthy manner will be guilty of profaning the body and blood of the Lord.'[84]

These statements may not sound like statements likely to find themselves included in a religious poem or canticle. But Thomas d'Aquino, like Dante Alighieri, has not the least hesitation about speaking his mind, whether in prose or in verse, when the matter is one of critical importance:

Sumunt boni, sumunt mali,	Both the wicked and the good
sorte tamen inaequali,	eat and drink the self-same food,
vitae vel interitus.	one to death, and one to life.
Mors est malis, vita bonis;	Though they both consume
Vide, paris sumptionis	the Lord, equal in the sacred rite,
quam sit dispar exitus.	see how they divide in fate!

In the early Middle Ages, after the breaking of the bread, the host was ritually divided in three distinct ways. St Thomas speaks of this custom in the *Summa*, and he quotes a few lines of verse from an anonymous author in order to

---

[83] *Super primam epistolam ad Corinthios lectura*, ch. 11, lect. 7, 687, in *Super epistolas s. Pauli*, vol. 1, p. 363.
[84] Ibid., lect. 7, 688.

describe it.[85] The fact that lines of verse are quoted in this context is, I think, worth noting. Thomas cites almost no poetry in his theological treatises, and the few examples which exist occur, almost without exception, in passages concerned with the Eucharist. Thomas explains, first of all, how that part of the eucharistic bread which is broken off, and placed in the chalice, represents Christ's risen body, and it represents also the saints who are now in glory.

The second part of the bread – the body of Christ that is consumed – represents 'those still walking upon earth because, while living upon earth [in Christ], they are united together by this sacrament.'[86] The third part, 'the part reserved on the altar until the close of the Mass, is his body hidden in the sepulcher because the bodies of the saints will be in their graves until the end of the world.'[87] Thomas then writes: 'some people have expressed [this particular idea] in verse':

Hostia dividitur in partes:	The host being rent –
tincta beatos	what is dipped, means the blest;
plene, sicca notat vivos,	what is dry, means the living;
servata sepultos.	what is kept, those at rest.[88]

The final stanzas of *Lauda Sion*, relying no longer on the language of scholastic theology, look instead to the themes and images of Scripture. At once the lines become less heavy, less conceptual. And the Eucharist is hailed, as in *Sacris solemniis*, as 'the bread of angels', a nourishment not of this earth:

Ecce, panis Angelorum,	Look! upon the altar lies,
factus cibus viatorum,	hidden deep from human eyes,
vere panis filiorum,	bread of angels from the skies,
non mittendus canibus.	made the food of mortal man.

As already noted, St Thomas, in the opening stanzas of *Lauda Sion*, drew particular attention to the newness of the eucharistic banquet. But now we

---

[85] *ST*, III q.83, a.5, ad.8.

[86] Ibid.

[87] Ibid.

[88] Ibid. This free translation of the stanza into English is taken from the Benzinger Bros. version of the *Summa* published in 1948.

are informed that the Eucharist had, in fact, been wondrously pre-figured on three occasions in the Old Testament: 'when Isaac was immolated,/when the paschal lamb was killed,/when manna was given to the fathers.' The final stanza is a prayer addressed directly to Jesus, the Good Shepherd. It is a quiet yet manifestly urgent plea for the grace of his blessing now, and in the future: grace here on earth, and grace in heaven:

Bone Pastor, panis vere,	Christ, Good Shepherd, bread
Iesu nostri miserere,	divine, show to us your mercy sign.
tu nos pasce, nos tuere,	Feed us still, still keep us thine
tu nos bona fac videre	that we may see your glory shine
in terra viventium.	in the kingdom of the good.
Tu qui cuncta scis et vales,	Source of all we have or know,
qui nos pascis hic mortales,	come and guide us here below,
tu nos ibi commensales,	make us, at your table seated,
cohaeredes et sodales	by your saints as friends be greeted,
fac santorum civium.	co-heirs at the feast of love.

These last stanzas are obviously longer than the earlier stanzas in the hymn. In fact *Lauda Sion* contains twelve double stanzas altogether: the first nine are of six lines each – divided into stanzas of three lines; the tenth and eleventh of eight; and the twelfth and thirteenth of ten. Initially the change of stanza length will come as something of a surprise to the reader. A form, a pattern, had been established for no less than fifty-four lines. That's why, when the change occurs, it's almost as if a rule had been broken. But this sudden change of stanza length, this apparent 'bending of the rule' is not unique to *Lauda Sion*. Other medieval authors quite often demonstrate the same confidence in the writing of sequences. St Thomas, like them, rather than make the poem a slave of 'rules', makes the rules serve the poem. He writes in the *Summa*: 'An artist who deliberately breaks the rules of his art [literally: sins against his art] is reckoned a better artist, having sound judgement, than the artist who, out of defective judgement, involuntarily breaks them.'[89]

---

[89] *ST*, II II q.47, a.8.

4. Poetry and dogma

Lauda Sion Salvatorum has been declared by Raby to be 'the supreme
dogmatic poem of the Middle Ages'. In his considered opinion it possesses
'an austerity and grandeur which no Latin poet of the Middle Ages ever
equaled.'[90] But can a poem be that 'dogmatic' and still remain a poem? John
Donne, the English metaphysical poet, reflecting on one occasion on the
challenge which dogma can bring to the art of verse, remarked to a friend:
'You know my uttermost when it was best, and even then I did best when I
had least truth for my subjects. In this present case, there is so much truth as it
defeats all poetry.'[91] This admission by Donne, though concerned with his own
immediate struggles as a poet, presents a not inconsiderable challenge to all
those other artists or poets who may wish to express, through art, something
of their own vision of life, their own firmly-held convictions and dogmas. And
so, once again, the question returns: can art sustain that kind of weight, and
still remain art?

This particular question is one which comes at once to mind when
considering Aquinas's *Lauda Sion Salvatorem*. None of the other hymns or
canticles by Aquinas contains so much theological or dogmatic reflection.
And yet, it has to be said, the 'poetry' in *Lauda Sion* is by no means defeated.
On the contrary. The music – the unique lyrical pattern and structure of the
work – more than holds its own with the doctrine or dogma being expressed.
Aquinas, as poet, has clearly understood that, with regard to beauty – the
creation of beauty – 'It is not sufficient ... that a work of art should be richly
charged with truth. The truth must be brought to a focus, and strike on the
mind as a simple and luminous unity.'[92] And that is precisely what has been
achieved in *Lauda Sion Salvatorem*.

---

[90] F. J. E. Raby, *A History of Christian-Latin Poetry: From the Beginnings to the Close of the Middle Ages*
(Oxford 1927) p. 408.

[91] John Donne, Letter to Sir Robert Ker (1625). Cited in J. C. H. Grierson (ed.) *Poems: John Donne*, vol.
1 (Oxford 1912), p. 288.

[92] An observation made by Albert J. Steiss when reflecting on Aquinas's theory of art and beauty. See
'Outline of a Philosophy of Art', *The Thomist*, 1940, p. 39.

Conclusion

St Thomas's celebrated theory of the three-fold criteria of beauty – wholeness (*integritas*), balance (*proportio*) and radiance (*claritas*)[93] – assumes a quite unique and manifestly beautiful expression in the making of his eucharistic canticles. In each of the poems, in the original Latin, there is a proportion, a consonance and a harmony, that immediately pleases. And there is present also, both in the eucharistic poems, and in some of the prayers attributed to Aquinas, what we might call 'a music of ideas', a consciously achieved symmetrical form, not only in the pattern of sound but also in the pattern of thought, a truly bright and balanced harmony and combination of music and reason. These are poems and canticles which undoubtedly measure up to the great claim made for them by Gerard Manley Hopkins: 'remarkable works of genius'.

---

[93] All three criteria are listed together by St Thomas in *Summa theologiae*, I, q.39, a.8.

10

Adoro te devote: *the finest prayer of Aquinas*

Godhead here in hiding, whom I do adore,
Masked by these bare shadows, shape and nothing more,
See, Lord, at thy service low lies here a heart
Lost, all lost in wonder at the God thou art.

Seeing, touching, tasting are in thee deceived;
How says trusty hearing? That shall be believed:
What God's Son has told me, take for truth I do;
Truth itself speaks truly or there's nothing true.

On the cross thy godhead made no sign to men;
Here thy very manhood steals from human ken:
Both are my confession, both are my belief,
And I pray the prayer of the dying thief.

I am not like Thomas, wounds I cannot see,
But can plainly call thee Lord and God as he.
Make this faith the deeper every day I live,
Stronger hope to hold by, greater love to give.

O thou our reminder of Christ crucified,
Living bread the life of us for whom he died,
Lend this life to me then: feed and feast my mind,
There be thou the sweetness man was meant to find.

Make the tender tale true of the Pelican;
Bathe me, Jesu Lord, in what thy bosom ran –
Blood that but one drop of has the worth to win
All the world forgiveness of its world of sin.

Jesu, whom I look at veilèd here below,
I beseech thee send me what I thirst for so,
Some day to gaze on thee face to face in light
And be blest for ever with thy glory's sight.[1]

TRANSLATION: GERARD MANLEY HOPKINS SJ

Adoro te devote
A commentary

It would be of great interest to know exactly when St Thomas composed this
quiet, radiant prayer. Although its theme is loving adoration of the Eucharist,
Adoro te devote is a work entirely separate from the Corpus Christi liturgy. We
can have no certainty, therefore, with regard to the date of its composition.
But at least this much can be said: at the time it was composed, Aquinas never
appeared more alive as a poet-theologian and man of prayer. The work is so
fresh and so unexpected it may even have marked 'a decisive moment' in his
spiritual life.[2] Its unusually personal character, and the unique beauty of its
form and content, set it apart from every other work of Aquinas, and indeed
from every work of Latin verse in the Middle Ages.

Owing no doubt to its strong eucharistic character, and because, over the
years, it has been heard sung on occasion at liturgical celebrations, *Adoro
te devote* has come to be regarded, in modern times, as a work more or less
identical with the hymns composed by Aquinas for the Feast of Corpus
Christi. A different truth emerges, however, when the earliest, surviving

---

[1] A translation by Gerard Manley Hopkins. Hopkins made a number of attempts at translating *Adoro
Te Devote*. Norman H. McKenzie includes the principal variants on pages 111–12 and 312–14 of *The
Poetical Works of Gerard Manley Hopkins* (Oxford 1990). The version cited here, with a few minor
exceptions, can be found on p. 112.
[2] See Pierre-Marie Gy, 'La relation au Christ dans l'Eucharistie selon S. Bonaventure et S. Thomas
d'Aquin', in *Sacraments de Jésus-Christ*, (ed.) J. Doré (Paris 1983) pp. 69–106.

manuscripts of the prayer and of the eucharistic hymns are consulted together. For, whereas the hymns of Corpus Christi are accompanied by individual, musical notation, as befits their character, *Adoro te devote*, in contrast, is presented simply as a prayer, an *oratio*.[3] Only after the seventeenth century, in fact, do we have evidence of this short prayer being set to music, and being changed from an individual work of devotion into a communal hymn. It was not, therefore, until a decidedly late stage in history that *Adoro te devote* began to appear in manuscript form together with its own musical notation.[4]

But if not a hymn, what can be said regarding the precise character of the work as a prayer? Fortunately, as an aid to answering this question, we have available to us the wonderfully detailed and illuminating research of Robert Wielockx. *Adoro te devote*, Wielockx explains, was composed by Aquinas as a private prayer to be recited *sotto voce* when, as so often was his practice, he chose to attend a second Mass as a non-celebrant.[5] On these occasions, according to a number of ancient sources, Thomas was in the habit, during the Canon of the Mass, of devoutly praying the second part of the *Te Deum,* from '*Tu rex glorie Christe*' to the end.[6] Wielockx has no doubt that Thomas did just that, and he suggests further that Thomas replaced the first part of the *Te Deum* with his own *oratio,* a deliberate Christological and Eucharistic substitution.[7] Instead, therefore, of the prayer being directed to all three Persons of the Trinity, St Thomas focuses his attention exclusively on Christ, and on Christ as present under the forms of bread and wine.[8]

The private use for which *Adoro te devote* was deliberately composed by St Thomas has given to this brief prayer, I have no doubt, its unique character

---

[3] See Robert Wielockx, 'La preghiera eucaristica di s.Tommaso: analisi testuale e testimonianza storica', *Atti del convegno: l'anima eucaristica di san Tommaso d'Aquino,* in *Frontiere: Rivista di filosofia e teologia,* VII (January–December 2011) pp. 329–31. Wielockx notes on page 331 that, in the best manuscript tradition, the work appears under the word *Oratio.*

[4] See A. Wilmart, 'La tradition littéraire de L'*Adoro te devote*', *Auteurs spirituels et textes dévots du moyen a͏̈ge latin* (Paris 1932) p. 373, note 1.

[5] See Wielockx, 'La preghiera eucaristica di s.Tommaso', pp. 333–4.

[6] Ibid., pp. 336–7.

[7] Ibid., p. 336.

[8] According to Wielockx St Thomas had sufficient time between the Consecration and the *Pater Noster* to recite first the *Adoro te devote* and then the second half of the *Te Deum.* Ibid., p. 336.

and tone. When recited out loud in the original Latin, and read with as much attentiveness as possible, the words of the prayer – their meaning, their music – make an impact like no other words of Aquinas. No rendering, therefore, in English translation, or indeed in any translation, can hope to convey the grace of the original. And that holds true even for the work cited earlier by Gerard Manley Hopkins. For, although it is an impressive translation by any standards, it cannot hope to match the sheer mastery and simplicity of *Adoro te devote*. The qualities of the prayer are many, and they deserve to be discussed at length. One issue, however, needs first of all to be addressed: the question of authorship. At a popular level, Aquinas has always been named as the author. But is there evidence available to support such a claim? Can we be certain that Aquinas really is the author of this remarkable prayer?

1. The question of authorship

In the early part of the twentieth century a number of challenging questions were raised by scholars with regard to the Aquinas attribution. Prominent among the scholars was the Benedictine monk, Dom André Wilmart.[9] But no less sceptical about the attribution to Aquinas, were certain Thomist theologians. One of them, E. Hugueny, argued that a phrase such as, 'Sight, touch, taste are, in you, deceived' (*fallitur*), was not a phrase Aquinas, the theologian, would ever have used.[10] In support of his opinion, Hugueny marshalled a number of texts from Aquinas's work which appear directly to contradict this particular statement.[11] More recent voices, however, argue that the word '*fallitur*' (deceived) in no way undermines the insistence by St Thomas on the fundamental inerrancy of the senses with regard to the Eucharist. For example, according to Robert Wielockx, 'the text does not

---

[9] See A. Wilmart, 'La tradition littéraire de L'*Adoro te devote*,' *Auteurs spirituels et textes dévots du moyen a ̂ge latin* (Paris 1932) pp. 361–414; first published in RTAM, 1 (1929), pp. 21–40, 149–76.

[10] See E. Hugueny, 'L'*Adoro Te* est-il de saint Thomas?' in *Archivum Fratrum Praedicatorum*, 4 (1934) pp. 221–5.

[11] For example, from the *Summa theologiae*: 'There is no deception in this sacrament'. *ST*, III q.75, a.5, ad. 2.

contradict the continuous teaching of Thomas according to which the senses are not wrong when they judge their proper object, which, as far as the Eucharist is concerned, is only the sacramental species.'[12] When, however, it comes to the actual reality of Christ's presence in the Eucharist, our five senses simply cannot grasp the mystery. And that's surely the point St Thomas is making.

With regard to internal evidence indicative of Aquinas's authorship, much could be said.[13] But, with the publication of Claire le Brun-Gouanvic's edition of Tocco's *Life* of Aquinas, the question of internal evidence is no longer, as it happens, quite so critical. For, at last, we have in our hands impressive *external* evidence relating to the question of authorship. We now know that William of Tocco, St Thomas's first biographer, included in his *Life* the full text of the work, and attributed it to Aquinas.[14] And so we find ourselves today in the privileged and happy position of being able, with confidence, to read *Adoro te devote*, knowing there can no longer be great or serious doubt that this beautiful prayer, this poem of worship and longing, this text which so compels our admiration, is indeed a work composed by Thomas Aquinas.

---

[12] See Robert Wielockx, 'Poetry and Theology in the *Adoro te devote*,' p. 158. See also Torrell, *Saint Thomas Aquinas: The Person and His Work*, pp. 195–6. Jan-Heiner Tück argues that the word *fallitur* 'need not be taken, in the strict sense of the word, to mean *deceptio*. And he notes further: 'the hymn does not state that all senses deceive, and even ascribes the point of access to the truth of the Word to the *auditus* (the sense of hearing).' See Tück, *Gabe der Gegenwart: Theologie und Dichtung der Eucharistie bei Thomas von Aquin* (Freiburg 2009) p. 259.

[13] For further examples of internal evidence, see Torrell, vol. 1, pp. 195–7. Wielockx offers three arguments in support of Aquinas's authorship, two of them regarding external evidence, and one internal evidence: (i) Of the fifty-one known texts, forty-four bear St Thomas's name, and none of the texts are ascribed to anyone other than Thomas; (ii) The most authoritative texts originate from the same geographical area, namely Naples; (iii) 'Both the poetic form (scansion, rhyming, structuring) and the theological content of the text confirm Thomasian authorship in every respect.' See 'Poetry and Theology in the *Adoro te devote*', p. 157.

[14] Tocco, *Ystoria sancti Thome de Aquino de Guillaume de Tocco*, 58, pp. 197–8. Although a manuscript of the fourteenth century claims that Thomas pronounced the prayer '*Adoro te devote*' on his death-bed, no other witnesses present at Thomas's passing made this claim. The prayer, it should be said, closely resembles in spirit the brief prayer St Thomas addressed to the Eucharist before he died, and that may well explain the confusion. What is valuable about the fourteenth century manuscript, for our purposes, is that it is yet another ancient source which links '*Adoro te devote*' with the name of Aquinas. See Wilmart, p. 390 and p. 404.

Adoro te devote

Adoro te devote, latens veritas,	You, I devoutly adore, hidden Truth, you
te que sub his formis vere latitas.	who, under these forms, are truly hidden.
Tibi se cor meum totum subicit,	My whole heart submits itself to you for,
quia te contemplans totum deficit.	in contemplating you, I am at a complete loss.
Visus, tactus, gustus in te fallitur,	Sight, touch, taste, in you are deceived;
sed auditu solo tute creditur,	hearing alone can be completely believed.
credo quicquid dixit dei filius,	I believe all the Son of God has said; nothing
nihil veritatis verbo verius.	can be more true than the Word of truth.
In cruce latebat sola deitas,	Upon the cross the Godhead alone was
sed hic latet simul et humanitas.	hidden, but here the humanity is also hidden.
Ambo vere credens atque confitens,	Truly believing and confessing both,
peto quod petivit latro poenitens.	I beg what the penitent thief begged.
Plagas sicut Thomas non intueor,	I do not see wounds, as Thomas did,
Deum tamen meum te confiteor.	but I confess you as my God.
Fac me tibi semper magis credere,	Make me believe ever more in you,
in te spem habere, te diligere.	having hope in you, and loving you.
O memoriale mortis domini,	O memorial of the death of the Lord,
panis vivus vitam prestans homini.	living bread that gives life to man,
Presta michi semper de te vivere,	Allow me always to live for you, and allow
et te michi semper dulce sapere.	me to taste your sweetness always.
Pie pellicane, Ihesu domine,	O kind pelican, Lord Jesus, cleanse me,
me immundum munda tuo sanguine.	who am unclean, in your blood,
Cuius una stilla salvum facere,	One drop of which would be enough to save
totum mundum posset omni scelere.	the whole world of all its defilement.
Ihesu, quem velatum nunc aspicio,	Jesus, whom I now gaze at veiled, when
quando fiet illud quod tam sicio?	shall that which I so desire come to pass?
Vt te revelata cernens facie,	So that seeing you, your face revealed, I may
visu sim beatus tue glorie.[15]	be blessed with the vision of your glory.

---

[15] Critical text of the prayer based on examination by Robert Wielockx of the surviving manuscripts. See Wielockx, 'Poetry and Theology in the *Adoro te devote*', *Christ among the Medieval Dominicans*, p. 172.

2. A poem of the Eucharist

Once Aquinas is regarded as the actual or likely author of *Adoro te devote*, one question immediately arises: what was it that inspired him to compose a work of this kind? Why, among all his other works, is there no other prayer, no other canticle, which reveals such a deep, personal faith, and which contains such a depth of longing? The most obvious answer to this question is that Aquinas is not attempting here to compose a prayer for communal use, a hymn which will, in time, form part of the sacred Liturgy. No, his intention is, in a sense, more modest: it is to compose a short poem, a work of private devotion, which will help him to concentrate on the mystery of Christ's presence in the Eucharist during Mass.

The fact that it is the Eucharist and not some other sacrament, or other mystery of the faith, which is the subject of this unique work, is no accident. For, whereas the other sacraments contain something of the power of Christ's presence, here in this sacrament uniquely, according to Thomas, *the entire Christ* is present.[16] Here, as nowhere else on earth, he comes in the fullness of his person.

When, as happens on many occasions in his work, St Thomas speaks of the Eucharist, he speaks of it with an almost unique enthusiasm. The Eucharist, he declares, is 'the greatest of all the sacraments,'[17] 'the sign of supreme charity,'[18] and 'the upholder of our hope'.[19] It is 'the common spiritual good of the whole Church'[20] and, for those among us who are believers, it is a celebration far more wonderful than a mere memorial of Christ's Passion. For, by the grace of this sacrament, we are united to the saving power of the Passion and, as a result, receive 'a pledge of future glory'.[21]

In the *Summa*, when writing directly on the theme of the Eucharist, Thomas

---

[16] *ST*, III q.76, a.1. And see also III q.65, a.3.
[17] *ST*, III q.65, a.3.
[18] *ST*, III q.75, a.1.
[19] Ibid.
[20] *ST*, III q.65, a.3, ad 1.
[21] A phrase from the prayer, 'O sacrum convivium', a tiny Magnificat antiphon composed by St Thomas for the liturgy of Corpus Christi. See Busa, vol 6, p. 581.

explains how the blood and water which flowed from the side of Christ are symbols of the sacraments. What was once achieved by the Passion of Christ, for the salvation of the world, is now being wonderfully poured out for us in the Eucharist.[22] In another place, taking up the words in St John's Gospel, *Immediately there came out blood and water* (Jn. 19.34), Thomas, echoing a statement of St John Chrysostom, writes: 'Since the sacred mysteries derive their origin from that source, when you approach the awe-inspiring chalice, approach it as if you were about to drink from Christ's own side.'[23]

Reading a text like this may help us to understand why St Thomas was drawn not only to contemplate with wonder and silent awe the mystery of the Eucharist, but was drawn also to compose a thing of words, a poem of homage to the mystery. Speaking, on one occasion, about what inspires the making of verse or music or painting, W. H. Auden remarked:

> The impulse to create a work of art is felt when, in certain persons, the passive awe provoked by sacred beings or events is transformed into a desire to express that awe in a rite of worship or homage, and to be fit homage, this rite must be beautiful … In poetry the rite is verbal; it pays homage by naming.[24]

St Thomas, of course, understands that mere verbal homage is never enough. 'Praise with the lips is useless,' he declares, 'if it does not come from the heart.'[25] Nevertheless, in the context of prayerful worship, Thomas makes it clear that spoken words also have their importance. 'The outward praise of the lips,' he notes, 'arouses the inward fervour of those who praise.'[26] And so here, we can say, in *Adoro te devote*, St Thomas, both as devout believer and as poet, pays homage to the Eucharist by naming the mystery. His words, of course, do not expect to grasp, for a moment, the wondrous truth they are attempting

---

[22] *ST*, III q.62, a.6.

[23] *ST*, III q.79, a.1.

[24] W. H. Auden, 'Making, Knowing and Judging,' in *The Dyer's Hand and Other Essays* (New York 1962) p. 57.

[25] *ST*, II II q.91, a.1, ad 2.

[26] Ibid. Compare Augustine, *Confessions*, Bk 11, 1: 'By setting down these words, I fire my own heart and the hearts of my readers with love of you [God] … I have said before, and I shall say again, I write this book for love of your love.'

to describe. Theirs is a language of prayer and of surrender, a language more of enchantment than science, a canticle of deep and pure desire: a loving worship.

3. The structure of the prayer

One of the most distinctive characteristics of *Adoro te devote* is the quality of its end rhymes. Lines 1–14 end in consonants, and lines 15–28 end in vowels, a striking detail which immediately draws attention to the fact that, at an external level at least, *Adoro te devote* divides into two equal and distinct parts. But this division is not something merely technical or external. I intend later to indicate that it corresponds, in fact, to a fundamental pattern, a basic meditative structure in the prayer which has not, surprisingly, been noted before now by commentators. What, fortunately, we do have available to us already – thanks to the scholarly work of Robert Wielockx – is an illuminating analysis of both the poetic and the theological structures of *Adoro te*.

With regard to poetic structure, for example, Wielockx notes that lines 1–2 and lines 9–10 have the same end rhyme (*-itas*). The matching effect of these lines is to make them appear as a kind of frame (what Wielockx calls an 'inclusion'[27]) around lines 3–8. These lines, 3–8, consist of three distinct double-lines which make separate statements, each statement of critical importance to St Thomas as a man of faith. And that may well explain why the six lines have been set apart, within the prayer, in a distinct frame, as it were. Here are the lines in question:

Tibi se cor meum totum subicit,	My whole heart submits itself to you for,
quia te contemplans totum deficit.	in contemplating you, I am at a complete loss.
Visus, tactus, gustus in te fallitur,	Sight, touch, taste, in you are deceived;
sed auditu solo tute creditur,	hearing alone can be completely believed.
credo quicquid dixit dei filius,	I believe all the Son of God has said; nothing
nihil veritatis verbo verius.	can be more true than the Word of truth.

---

[27] Other examples of 'inclusion' can be found in the second part of the prayer. See Wielockx, 'Poetry and Theology in the *Adoro te devote*', p. 162.

According to Wielockx, these three distichs, or double lines, refer first of all, to 'the insufficiency of the highest rational faculties,' second, to 'the deficiency of the senses' and, third, to 'the capacity of faith to attain all truth.'[28] And these themes we find repeated in a number of the other hymns of Aquinas.[29] It would appear, therefore, that the poetic structure of the work has been deliberately shaped by St Thomas to underpin the theological structure and meaning of the prayer.

*   *   *

One helpful way to understand *Adoro te devote* is to see it in relation to certain prayers which, in the Middle Ages, grew up around the rite of the elevation of the sacred host, a rite or ceremony which took place immediately after the consecration. The prayers in question were private, popular prayers, decidedly 'less solemn' than official liturgical prayers, and quite often possessed, according to Marie-Dominique Chenu, of 'a striking originality.'[30] But the period of time in which the elevation took place was far too brief for the recitation of a prayer such as *Adoro te devote*. Accordingly, whereas it may well have begun at the moment of the elevation, the prayer would have had to continue on, *sotto voce*, for at least some part of the Canon.[31]

In order fully to understand the opening words of the prayer – their directness, their contemplative immediacy – we need to think of them as words spoken by a man kneeling in the presence of the raised Host immediately after the consecration. They are words of loving adoration. A lifetime of reflection and meditation on the mystery of the Eucharist finds here its most moving and most memorable expression. It is an event, we can say, of both form and vision, a miracle of creative attention. Rilke, the German poet, was surely not mistaken when he remarked: 'If a thing is to speak to you, you must for a certain time regard it as the only thing that exists, the unique

---

[28] Ibid., p. 164.
[29] Ibid.
[30] M.-D. Chenu, *Introduction à l'étude de Saint Thomas d'Aquin* (Paris 1950) p. 296.
[31] See Wilmart, 'La tradition littéraire', p. 378, note 13.

phenomenon that your diligent and exclusive love has placed at the centre of the universe.'[32]

Adoro te deuote, latens veritas,[33]	You, I devoutly adore, hidden Truth, you
te que sub his formis vere latitas.	who, under these forms, are truly hidden.

This prayer is not simply addressed to the Eucharist; it is a prayer addressed to Christ present in the Eucharist. And it is a statement of faith, a canticle of paradox. For the God to whom it is addressed remains unseen under the forms of bread and wine: Christ utterly present, utterly hidden. Here, within the sacramental order, faith not vision is the believer's most immediate and most profound contact with God, a point strongly emphasized in the opening stanzas of the prayer. When, however, the work begins to draw to a close, St Thomas, daring to lift his gaze above and beyond the limits of this world, expresses an unforgettably deep and heart-felt longing to see God face to face.

Ihesu, quem velatum nunc aspicio,	Jesus, whom I now gaze at veiled, when shall
quando fiet illud quod tam sicio?	that which I so desire come to pass?
Vt te revelata cernens facie,	So that seeing you, your face revealed, I may
visu sim beatus tue glorie.	be blessed with the vision of your glory.

This vision, so much desired, is given as a pledge in the Eucharist. But its promise, its great blessing, is never completely realized in this life. Our thirst remains. For no matter how much our faith may appear to strengthen or develop, a 'veil' of some kind still covers the face of Christ Jesus. This acknowledgement, within the prayer, of the enormous challenge to faith which the divine 'hiddenness' presents is, without question, one of the prayer's most distinctive characteristics. According to Robert Wielockx, 'The tension between faith and the sacramental order, on the one hand, and the beatific vision and resurrection, on the other, is the main theological idea involved in the overall structure of the *Adoro te devote*.'[34]

---

[32] Rainer Maria Rilke, Letter to a Young Girl, in *Selected Letters: 1902–1926*, trans., R. F. C. Hull (London 1946) pp. 324–5.

[33] Although we have become familiar with the Latin phrase '*latens deitas*', St Thomas's original phrase was '*latens veritas*'. See Wielockx, 'Poetry and Theology', p. 172.

[34] Wielockx, 'Poetry and Theology', p. 165. From its opening words, according to Olivier-Thomas

Faith is not vision. Nevertheless, in this life, faith is the most effective way by which we gain access to Christ. In *Adoro te devote* four steps are clearly indicated by which growth in faith is seen to depend.[35] In the first place, in order that belief in Christ may be awakened, what is required is *hearing* (*auditu creditur*). The hidden truth (*latens veritas*), Thomas makes clear, simply cannot be apprehended by any of the other senses. So faith depends on an objective word received or heard from an authoritative source that comes from *outside*. But it also requires something else as well: an individual and free response from *within*, a personal declaration. And that is, as it happens, the voice we hear speaking in the next sentence:

> *Credo quicquid dixit dei filius,*   I believe all the Son of God has said; nothing
> *nihil veritatis verbo verius.*   can be more true than the Word of truth.[36]

In passing, it is worth noting here the delightful play on words in the second half of this sentence, '*nihil veritatis verbo verius*', a trick or grace of style which might almost be considered a signature of St Thomas. Commenting on this particular phrase, and on other similar phrases in Aquinas's work, Walter Ong writes: 'These are capital passages. They illustrate how word-play can grow directly out of distinctly Christian doctrine and be put to effective literary use. It is a mistaken notion of a past age disowned by current criticism to think that word-play must involve only abstract notions and must be deficient in emotional drive.'[37]

The third reference to faith draws attention to both the humanity and divinity of Christ. Whereas, on the cross, the divinity of Christ was concealed from sight, his humanity was visible for all to see, his *broken* humanity. But now,

---

Venard, the prayer makes clear that 'the miracle, the mystery of the presence of God in the Eucharist', cannot be grasped with the light of sense or the light of intelligence. 'It is by another light,' he says, 'an obscure light like the luminous cloud of which Exodus speaks ... by which we are able to understand a little this great mystery: the light of faith.' See *Pagina sacra: Le passage de l'Écriture sainte à l'écriture théologie* (Paris 2009) p. 664.

[35] These 'four steps' are described by Wielockx in 'Poetry and Theology ', pp. 165–7.

[36] In a free translation of these lines, Richard Crashaw emphasizes the importance of the individual response of faith to the saving words of Revelation: 'Faith is my force. Faith strength affords/to keep pace with those powerful words./And words more sure, more sweet, than they/love could not think, truth could not say.' See '*Adoro te*' in *The Poems, English, Latin and Greek of Richard Crashaw,* (ed.) L. C. Martin (Oxford 1927) p. 292.

[37] Walter Ong, 'Wit and Mystery: A Revaluation', *Speculum* 22 (July 1947) p. 318.

in the sacrament of the Eucharist, both the humanity and divinity remain utterly concealed. All that is visible on the altar are the elements of bread and wine. And yet, strengthened by the gift of faith, St Thomas is able, without hesitation, to confess belief in both the human and divine presence of Jesus in the Eucharist:

In cruce latebat sola deitas,	Upon the cross the Godhead alone was
sed hic latet simul et humanitas.	hidden, but here the humanity is also hidden.
Ambo vere credens atque confitens,	Truly believing and confessing both,
peto quod petivit latro poenitens.	I beg what the penitent thief begged.
Plagas sicut Thomas non intueor,	I do not see wounds, as Thomas did,
Deum tamen meum te confiteor.	but I confess you as my God.

The thief, crucified beside Jesus on the cross, witnessed only the broken humanity of God, but he possessed the bold and astonishing faith to cry out, 'Jesus, remember me when you come into your kingdom!' That cry implied some kind of belief in the divinity of Christ, and it is with that cry, with that belief, St Thomas chooses to identify.

In the two lines which follow there is a brief reference to the faith-experience of St Thomas the Apostle. It marks one of the most eloquent and compelling passages in the prayer. Thomas, known as Doubting Thomas, was the Apostle who demanded visible proof of the resurrection of Jesus: *Unless I see the holes that the nails made in his hands and can put my finger into the holes they made, and unless I can put my hand into his side, I refuse to believe* (Jn. 20.26-28). Jesus subsequently appeared to Thomas. The encounter is recorded in St John's Gospel: *He spoke to Thomas, 'Put your finger here; look, here are my hands. Give me your hand; put it into my side. Doubt no longer but believe.' Thomas said, 'My Lord and my God'* (Jn. 20.27-8). By saying these words, the Doubter, Aquinas tells us in his commentary on the Gospel, gave clear expression to 'a true faith', and thereby became a *good theologian*: 'He professed the humanity of Christ when he said, *my Lord* ... And he professed the divinity of Christ when he said, and *my God*.'[38]

---

[38] *Commentary on the Gospel of St John,* vol. 2, ch. 20, lect. 6, 2562, trans., F. R. Larcher (Petersham, Massachusetts 1999) p. 620.

* * *

The reference to Doubting Thomas concludes the first part of the prayer, the first fourteen lines. The second part of the prayer, as we have already noted, is different from the first with regard to end-rhymes. All fourteen lines end with a vowel, whereas the fourteen lines of the first part end with a consonant. But why is *Adoro te devote* divided in this way? Is it possible that the character of the second half of the prayer is so significantly different from the first that a change in rhyme-endings came about almost automatically? Or did St Thomas, in fact, deliberately make this change, intending to highlight the difference between the two parts? In whatever way this question is answered, the division between the two halves of *Adoro te devote* corresponds, I believe, to a fundamental difference between the two sections.

One point not noted so far by commentators is the fact that the entire second part of *Adoro te devote* takes the form of *asking*. It is a prayer, or a series of prayers, of petition. The original impulse towards asking was, of course, prompted by the brief references to the Good Thief and to Doubting Thomas at the close of the first section. But, for the rest, the first part of the prayer is different from the second. It is, at core, we can say, an act of simple meditation on the mystery of the Eucharist. So, in *Adoro te*, we have, first of all, a prayer of reflection or adoration (lines 1–14) and then a prayer of petition (lines 15–28).

This two-fold pattern, manifest here in *Adoro te devote*, is repeated in no less than three of St Thomas's great eucharistic hymns: *Sacris solemniis*, *Verbum supernum prodiens*, and *Lauda Sion*.[39] It is a pattern which serves to underline the central place Thomas gives, in his theology, to the prayer of asking. Like no one else in his generation, St Thomas was concerned to highlight the importance of this simple yet profound form of Gospel prayer. On this subject Simon Tugwell writes: 'It fell to the lot of Thomas to construct what is surely far and away the clearest and most coherent treatise on prayer

---

[39] It is perhaps worth noting here that, in *Lauda Sion*, when the prayer changes into the mode of petition, the first four end-rhymes all end in vowels: '*Bone Pastor, panis vere,/Iesu, nostri miserere:/Tu nos pasce, nos tuere,/Tu nos bona fac videre/In terra viventium.*

since Origen. And he achieves much of his clarity by insisting on a very precise understanding of prayer as petition.'[40]

The second section of the prayer opens with a final reference to faith. This marks what we might call the fourth 'step' of authentic progress in faith. St Thomas asks that his personal belief in Christ be strengthened and, at the same time, he asks for the blessing of the two other theological virtues, hope and love:

> *Fac me tibi semper magis credere,*   Make me believe ever more in you,
> *in te spem habere, te diligere.*   having hope in you, and loving you.

It's impossible not to be struck by the direct, personal voice of need and of desire that, in this second section, makes itself heard over and over again. I am thinking in particular of the following petition which, in a quite remarkable way, combines the utter desperation of need with the most absolute trust and confidence in God. I know of no more humble statement ever composed by Thomas Aquinas.

> *Pie pellicane, Ihesu domine,*   O true pelican, Lord Jesus, cleanse me,
> *me immundum munda tuo sanguine,*   who am unclean, in your blood,
> *Cuius una stilla saluum facere,*   One drop of which would be enough to save
> *totum mundum posset omni scelere.*   the whole world of all its defilement.

The image of Christ as a pelican can be found in medieval paintings, frescos and stained glass. The bird was believed to wound itself in order, with its own life-blood, to feed its young. It became, therefore, a symbol of Christ's death on the cross, and of his amazing sacrificial love for humanity.[41] That sacrifice has, of course, been made present in the symbols of bread and wine in the

---

[40] See Simon Tugwell, *Albert and Thomas: Selected Writings* (New York 1988) p. 275.
[41] The idea in the prayer namely that 'one drop of [Christ's blood] would be enough to save the whole world of its defilement' was inspired by a phrase often attributed to St Bernard of Clairvaux. Thomas liked to repeat the phrase in a number of his works. In one place, for example, attributing the phrase to Bernard, he writes: '*Minima gutta sanguinis Christi suffecisset ad redemptionem humani generis*' (The smallest drop of Christ's blood would have been enough to have redeemed all humankind). See *Questiones quodlibertales*, II q.1, a.2.

Eucharist. And it is the former, the bread, which is the focus of the following petition:

> *O memoriale mortis domini,*   O memorial of the death of the Lord,
> *panis vivus vitam prestans homini.* living bread that gives life to man,
> *Presta michi semper de te vivere,*   allow me always to live for you, and allow
> *et te michi semper dulce sapere.*   me to taste your sweetness always.

In the first section of the prayer there was a particular emphasis on truth, but here the emphasis is on *life*: living in and for Christ.[42] The bread that the believer has been given to eat – the living bread of Christ's body – is nothing less than a pledge of eternal life: the tiny word *'semper'* (always) carrying considerable weight here of both meaning and emotion. The contemplative intimacy suggested by the sentence, 'Allow me always to live for you, and allow me to taste your sweetness always', merits particular attention. The desire behind the sentence springs, of course, from a heart transformed by faith, hope and love. But it is faith, first of all, which, according to Thomas, makes possible real intimacy with God. In his *Commentary on the Sentences*, he writes: 'The first union of the soul with God is achieved by faith, and that's because, by faith, the soul is in some sense espoused to God, as it says in Hosea 2.20: *I will espouse you to myself in faith.'*[43]

The view expressed here is one St Thomas shared with his contemporaries, but what is unusual and distinctive about the quotation is the reference to Hosea. Apparently none of Thomas's contemporaries cited this particular text of Hosea in this particular context.[44] And that's a point worth noting. I say this because when, in *Adoro te devote*, St Thomas expresses his desire for a deeper faith and a deeper communion with God, and includes in his prayer the following two brief petitions, *'fac me tibi semper magis credere'* (make me believe in you ever more), and *'te michi semper dulcis sapere'* (allow me to taste your sweetness always), he would appear to be echoing the very text from

---

[42] See Wielockx, 'Poetry and Theology', p. 166.

[43] *In Quartum librum Sententiarum*, dist. 39, a.6, ad 2, Parma vol. 7, p. 1028.

[44] This point is made by Wielockx, 'Poetry and Theology', pp. 167–8.

Hosea we have been considering: *'sponsabo te michi in fide'* (I will espouse you to myself in faith).[45]

J.-P. Torrell, impressed by these small links and echoes, concludes: 'So it is quite possible that, in writing this verse, Thomas remembered Hosea and the theme of God's espousals with his people, a theme that would later be developed with such strength in the mystical tradition. Thomas, with his customary discretion, and without the least display, inserts himself in this [mystical] line.'[46]

* * *

On one occasion, reflecting back on what it was like to enjoy close and fraternal contact with Aquinas, a Dominican contemporary remarked: 'it was a refreshment to the spirit merely to live with him and to be able from time to time to speak with him.'[47] Of course, that kind of direct, intimate conversation is no longer possible. Nevertheless, with regard to prayer, we do have surprising access to what might be called the actual speaking voice of the saint: Aquinas not merely talking *about* prayer in the abstract, but actually praying. The man, the 'good theologian', overheard as it were, in the very act of prayer and meditation.

Conclusion
Aquinas: a discreet mystic

One of the reasons why it has seemed fitting to end this study of Aquinas with a reflection on *Adoro te devote* is because the prayer contains, in an exemplary form, many of the most impressive characteristics of Aquinas as poet and man of prayer. *Adoro te* is the work of a theologian – that goes without saying – but its author is not only a profound thinker, he is also a very considerable

---

[45] In the Latin Vulgate the text from Hosea reads: *'Sponsabo te michi in sempiternum'* (I will espouse you to myself forever).

[46] Torrell, 'Adoro te: La plus belle prière de saint Thomas', in *La vie spirituelle*, vol. 152, no. 726 (March 1998) p. 32.

[47] *Fontes vitae*, 33, p. 200; Foster, p. 52.

artist, and a man of the deepest humility. The sacred host before which he bows down with living faith, and to which he gives full and loving attention, contains, in sacramental form, the real presence of Christ Jesus. And every thought expressed in the prayer, every word spoken, suggests a surrender of both heart and mind. The author of *Adoro te devote* is a man of faith and prayer, a theologian on his knees.

Over the past few hundred years, theology has tended to become such a specialized activity – such an exclusively *intellectual* activity – it has risked losing contact with living faith experience and with the life of devotion. Few of its practitioners have been able, in practise, to combine the strenuous task of thinking with the spontaneous grace and passion of devotion. As a result, theology has begun to seem dry and abstract, an academic discipline unrelated to the search for holiness or to a path of spirituality. And, at the same time, there has been another casualty – perhaps an even greater one – and that is the life of humble devotion. Deprived of contact with the sanity and challenge of a robust intellectual tradition, devotion has suffered, all too often, by degenerating into forms of false or exaggerated piety or into a mere sentimentalism. No doubt, for that reason, Hans Urs von Baltahasar felt constrained to remark in 1984: 'I insist on the inseparability between theology and spirituality, their separation being the worst disaster that ever occurred in the history of the Church.'[48]

Almost all of Aquinas's work was composed in an academic context and, as a result, the contemplative element in his thought is not the element that most immediately impresses. But should the reader of Aquinas be given the chance or opportunity to study the work at greater depth, it soon becomes clear how fundamental to Aquinas's vision as a theologian is the life of prayer and contemplation. Rather, therefore, than a wall of separation existing between theology and spirituality, what the work in fact reveals is an unmistakable conjunction of mind and heart, of passion and intelligence, of deep reflection and loving adoration.

---

[48] See 'Address of Hans Urs von Balthasar,' in *L'Osservatore Romano* (English edition), 23 July 1984, p. 8. The address was given by von Balthasar on 25 June 1984, after he had received the 'International Paul VI Prize' in the presence of Pope John Paul II.

In *Adoro te devote* there are two particular individuals with whose prayer Thomas chooses to identify, and both are humble Gospel figures: Thomas the Doubter and the Dying Thief. That act of instinctive identification on the part of Aquinas speaks volumes about his understanding of Christian prayer. Although *Adoro te* is itself an act of the most profound adoration, no prayer, in Thomas's understanding, ever loses contact with the stark reality of human need. Every prayer, in a sense, is a prayer of asking. That said, however, although our human need – our *miseria* – is indeed revealed in prayer, there is something far more important revealed at the same time, and that is of course the *misericordia*, the loving mercy of God. For that reason the texts most frequently used in the liturgy by the Church, as St Thomas points out, are the psalms composed by David (a man 'who obtained pardon after sin') and the letters written by St Paul (a man who likewise 'obtained mercy'), 'so that, by these examples, sinners might be aroused to hope.'[49]

When St Thomas comes to comment on these two biblical texts, one from the Old and one from the New Testament, he has a lot to say, as we have discovered, about the true meaning and practice of prayer. Most of what he says on the subject, however, has not been commented on by readers before now, and that's a pity. I say this because, apart from the magnificent question number 83 in the Second Part of *Summa*, and an early reflection on the subject in his *Commentary on the Sentences*,[50] there are no other sections in his work which offer such a breadth and depth of insight and wisdom regarding the subject of prayer. And, what's more, this wisdom is communicated, for the most part, in a more open, more relaxed manner than is the case with the somewhat severe, plain style of the *Summa* – a fact which serves to make Aquinas, in these commentaries, more immediately accessible to us as spiritual Master.

Not all of Aquinas's works were composed in an academic context. The great eucharistic hymns, for example, were composed for a liturgical feast of the Church, and the prayers attributed to Aquinas were written, we may presume, for his own private use. The most remarkable of these prayers is

---

[49] Prologue, 6, *Super epistolas s. Pauli lectura*, Marietti edition (Rome 1953) p. 2.
[50] See *Commentary on the Sentences*, Bk 4, dist. 15, q. 4.

Adoro te devote, a prayer which is by far the most moving, contemplative work ever composed on the Eucharist. That Aquinas was not only a great saint but also a mystic in the strict sense of the word was something taken for granted by all the early biographies. Rare phenomena such as the gift of tears, prophecy, visions and mystical locutions are reported again and again. But the core of St Thomas's contemplative life was revealed, I would say, not so much in these extraordinary phenomena but rather in his manifest love of God, and in his sheer delight in wisdom.

St Thomas knew God not merely by theological formulae but by what he calls 'the experience of divine goodness'. He writes: 'God is not far from us, nor outside us, but rather he is in us, as Jeremiah 14 says: *You are in us, O Lord.* Thus the experience of the divine goodness is called tasting.'[51] In the end, of course, St Thomas remains silent about the inner workings of his own contemplative experience. He is, in that sense, we can say, a discreet mystic. 'Thomas,' Josef Pieper reminds us, 'wishes to make plain, not his own inner state, but his insight into a given subject.'[52] The end result is a mysticism which is never expressed in fascinating psychological or psycho-spiritual experiences, but is rather made wonderfully manifest in inspired works of wisdom.

Aquinas was a Christian mystic not in spite of being a theologian, but *because* he was a theologian of a particular kind, a '*bonus teologus*', a man wholly dedicated to the contemplation of truth and to the proclamation of the Gospel. His 'wings' of contemplation, to use one of his own images, were those of 'a dove' of contemplation, not those of 'a raven'.[53] His life of contemplation was never for himself alone. He was a 'dove' of kindness and, unlike the selfish 'raven', never forgot the needs of others, but was always concerned to bring to them the fruits of his contemplation. Thomas, in the last months of his life, experienced, we know, moments of unimaginable ecstasy. But this privilege of prayer, this ecstasy, was not that of a mere psychological enthusiasm. It was rather, we can believe, as the overwhelming evidence of his life of prayer makes manifest, an ecstasy of love and of devoted service.

---

[51] Psalm XXXIII, *In Psalmos,* p. 266.
[52] Josef Pieper, *Guide to Thomas Aquinas,* p. 109.
[53] Psalm LIV: 5, Busa Vol 6, p. 129.

*   *   *

Once, when paraphrasing a sentence of St Paul, Thomas betrayed something of his own deep contemplative spirit, and something also of his own burning, apostolic desire for the good of others. The lines have already been quoted in an earlier chapter, but since they alert us, with clear authority, to the 'unknown Thomas' with whose identity and vision this book has been largely concerned, I will take the liberty here of quoting them once again. Thomas writes: 'I long for you to be in the very heart [literally 'in the entrails'] of Christ Jesus, that is, in order that you may love him intimately, and that you may be loved by him; for human life consists in this.'[54]

---

[54] *Super epistolam ad Philippenses lectura*, ch. 1, lect. 2, 15, in *Super epistolas*, vol. 2, p. 93.

Appendix 1

Four prayers attributed to Aquinas: original Latin text[1]

(1) Prayer for wise ordering

Concede michi misericors Deus que tibi placita sunt ardenter concupiscere, prudenter investigare, veraciter agnoscere, et perfecte implere. Ad laudem et gloriam nominis tui ordina statum meum, et quod a me requiris tribue ut sciam, et da exequi sicut ut oportet et expedit animae meae. Via mea, Domine, ad te tuta sit, recta et consummata, non deficiens inter prospera et adversa, ut in prosperis tibi gratiam referam et in adversis servem patientiam, ut in illis non extollar, et in istis non deprimar; de nullo gaudeam nisi quod promoveat me apud te, nec de aliquo doleam nisi quod abducat a te; nulli placere appetam vel displicere timeam nisi te. Vilescant michi omnia transitoria propter te, et cara sint michi omnia tua et tu Deus super quam omnia. Tedeat me omnis gaudii quod est sine te, nec cupiam aliquid quod est extra te. Delecte me labor qui est pro te, et tediosa sit michi omnis quies que non est in te. Frequenter da me cor meum ad te dirigere, et in defectionem meam cum emendationis proposito

---

[1] The Latin text of The Prayer for Wise Ordering is taken from Claire le Brun-Gouanvic's 1996 edition of William of Tocco's *Ystoria sancti Thome de Aquino*, p. 156. The text of the other three prayers is taken from the 1980 Busa edition of Aquinas's work, vol. 6 (*Reportationes*) p. 584. The Latin texts in Busa and le Brun-Gouanvic, it should be noted, differ in some minor respects from the text of the earlier 1953 Marietti edition of Aquinas's work.

dolendo pensare. Fac me, Deus meus, humilem sine fictionem, ylarem sine dissolutione, tristem sine deiectione, maturum sine graviture, agilem sine levitate, veracem sine duplicitate, te timentem sine desperatione, sperentem sine praesumptione, proximum corrigere sine simulatione, ipsum edificare verbo et exemplo sine elatione, obedientem sine contraditione, patientem sine murmuratione. Da michi, dulcissime Deus, cor pervigil quod nulla abducat a te curiosa cogitatio. Da nobile quod nulla deorsum trahat indigna affectio; da invictum quod nulla fatiget tribulatio; et da liberum quod nulla sibi vendicet violenta temptatio; et da rectum quod nulla obliquet sinistra intentio. Largire michi, Domine Deus meus, intellectum te cognoscentem, diligentiam te quaerentem, sapientiam te invenientem, conversationem tibi placentem, perseverantiam te fideliter expectantem, et fiduciam te finaliter amplectentem: tuis penis hic confligi per penitentiam, tuis beneficiis uti in via per gratiam, et tuis gaudiis in primis in patria frui per gloriam. Amen.

(2) Prayer for virtues

O Deus omnipotens, omnia sciens, principio et fine carens, qui es virtutum donator et conservator, digneris me stabilire solido fidei fundamento, et tueri inexpugnabili spei clypeo, atque decorare nuptiali charitatis vestimento; da mihi per justitiam tibi subesse, per prudentiam insidias diaboli cavere, per temperantiam medium tenere, per fortitudinem adversa patienter tolerare; da bonum quod non habeo, ab habentibus humiliter quaerere; malum culpae quod feci, veraciter accusare, malum poenae quod sustineo, aequanimiter ferre: bono proximi non invidere; de bonis tuis semper gratias agere: habitu, incessu, et motu disciplinam semper servare; linguam a vaniloquio restringere, pedes a discursu cohibere: oculos a vago visu comprimere; aures a rumoribus separare: vultum humiliter inclinare: mentem in caelestia levare: transitoria contemnere: te tantummodo desiderare; carnem domare: conscientiam expurgare; sanctos honorare: te digne laudare: in bono proficere: et bonos actus fine sancto terminare. Planta in me, Domine, virtutes, ut circa divina sim devotus, circa humana officia providus, circa usum proprii corporis nulli onerosus.

Da mihi, Domine, ferventem contritionem, puram confessionem, perfectam satisfactionem. Ordinare me digneris interius per bonam vitam; ut faciam quod deceat, et quod mihi proficiat ad meritum, et reliquis proximis ad exemplum. Da mihi ut nunquam ea quae fiunt insipienter appetam: et quae fiunt accidiose fastidiam; ne contingat inchoanda ante tempus appetere, aut inchoata ante consummationem deserere. Amen.

(3) Prayer of praise and thanksgiving

Laudo, glorifico, benedico te, Deus meus, propter immensa indigno mihi praestita beneficia. Laudo clementiam tuam me diu expectantem, dulcedinem tuam ulcisci simulantem, pietatem tuam vocantem, benignitatem suscipientem, misericordiam peccata remittentem, bonitatem supra merita impendentem, patientiam injuriae non recordantem, humilitatem consolantem, patientiam protegentem, aeternitatem conservantem, veritatem remunerantem. Quid dicam, Deus meus, de tua ineffabili largitate? Tu enim vocas fugientem, suscipis revertentem, adjuvas titubantem, laetificas desperantem, stimulas negligentem, armas pugnantem, coronas triumphantem, peccatorem post poenitentiam non spernis et injuriae non memineris, a multis liberas periculis, ad poenitentiam cor emollis, terres suppliciis, allicis promissis, castigas flagellis, angelico ministerio custodis, ministras temporalia, reservas nobis aeterna, hortaris dignitate creationis, invitas clementia redemptionis, promittis praemia remunerationis, pro quibus omnibus laudes referre non sufficio. Majestati tuae gratias ago propter immensae bonitatis tuae abundantiam, ut semper in me gratiam multiplices, et multiplicatam conserves, et conservatam remuneres. Amen.

(4) Prayer for the attainment of heaven

Te Deum totius consolationis invoco, qui nihil in nobis praeter tua dona cernis, ut mihi post hujus vitae terminum donare digneris cognitionem primae veritatis, fruitionem divinae majestatis. Da etiam corpori meo, largissime remunerator, claritatis pulchritudinem, agilitatis promptitudinem, subtilitatis aptitudinem, impassibilitatis fortitudinem.

Apponas istis affluentiam divitiarum, influentiam delitiarum, confluentiam bonorum, ut gaudere possim supra me de tua consolatione, infra de loci amoenitate, intra de corporis et animae glorificatione, juxta de angelorum et hominum delectabili associatione.

Consequatur apud te, clementissime Pater, in eo rationalis sapientiae illustrationem, concupiscibilis desiderabilium adeptionem, irascibilis triumphi laudem, ubi est, apud te evasio periculorum, distinctio mansionum, concordia voluntatum, ubi est amoenitas vernalis, luciditas aestivalis, ubertas autumnalis, et requies hiemalis. Da, Domine Deus, vitam sine morte, gaudium sine dolore, ubi est summa libertas, libera securitas, secura tranquillitas, jucunda felicitas, felix aeternitas, aeterna beatitudo, veritatis visio, atque laudatio, Deus. Amen.

Appendix 2

The Corpus Christi hymns with literal translation

Pange lingua

Pange, lingua, gloriosi
corporis mysterium,
sanguinisque pretiosi,
quem in mundi pretium,
fructus ventris generosi
rex effudit gentium.

Sing, O tongue, the mystery
of the glorious body,
and of the precious blood,
which the King of the Gentiles,
the fruit of a noble womb,
shed for the ransom of the world.

Nobis datus, nobis natus
ex intacta virgine,
et in mundo conversatus,
sparso verbi semine,
sui moras incolatus
miro claudit ordine.

Given for us, born for us,
from a chaste Virgin,
having dwelt in the world,
sowing the seed of the Word,
he closed in wondrous manner
the period of his earthly stay.

In supremae nocte coenae
recumbens cum fratribus,
observata lege plene
cibis in legalibus,
cibum turbae duodenae
se dat suis manibus.

On the night of the Last Supper
reclining with his brothers,
having fully observed the law
with regard to legal foods,
to the group of twelve he gives
himself as food with his own hands.

Verbum caro panen verum	The Word incarnate makes flesh
verbo carnem efficit,	true bread by a word, and the blood
fitque sanguis Christi merum,	of Christ becomes true wine;
et si sensus deficit,	and, if sense is deficient
ad firmandum cor sincerum	to confirm the sincere heart,
sola fides sufficit.	faith alone suffices.
Tantum ergo sacramentum	Let us therefore, prostrate,
veneremur cernui,	adore such a great sacrament,
et antiquum documentum	and let the old teaching
novo cedat ritui,	yield to the new rite;
praestet fides supplementum	let faith stand forward to supply
sensuum defectui.	the deficiency of the senses.
Genitori genitoque	To the Begetter and the Begotten
laus et jubilatio,	be praise and jubilation,
salus, honor, virtus quoque	salvation, honour, and strength,
sit et benedictio,	and blessing also,
procendentis ab utroque	and to the One proceeding
compar sit laudatio.	from both be equal praise.

Sacris solemniis

Sacris solemniis	To the sacred rites
iuncta sint gaudia	let joys be joined,
et ex praecordiis	and let praises sound
sonent praeconia,	from inmost hearts;
recedant vetera,	let ancient things recede,
nova sint omnia,	let all things be new:
corda, voces, et opera.	hearts, voices, and works.
Noctis recolitur	The night of the Last Supper
cena novissima,	is recalled, on which,
qua Christus creditur	it is believed, Christ gave
agnum et azyma	to the disciples, lamb
dedisse fratribus	and unleavened bread, according

Iuxta legitima	to the fixed practices
priscis indulta patribus.	prescribed by the ancient fathers.
Post agnum typicum	After the symbolic lamb [was eaten],
expletis epulis,	and the great meal ended,
corpus dominicum	the body of the Lord
datum discipulis	was given to the disciples,
sic totum omnibus	given with his own hands, in its
quod totum singulis,	entirety to all,
eius fatemur manibus.	and entire to each one.
Dedit fragilibus	To those who were fragile
corporis ferculum,	he gave the support of his body,
dedit et tristibus	and to those who were sad
sanguinis poculum,	he gave the chalice of his blood,
dicens: accipite	saying: Receive the cup
quod trado, vasculum,	which I am handing to you;
omnes ex eo bibite.	all of you drink from it.
Sic sacrificium	Thus he instituted this sacrifice,
istud instituit,	and willed
cuius officium	that the care of it
committi voluit	be entrusted to priests alone,
solis presbyteris,	whose office it is
quibus sic congruit,	first to consume it themselves,
ut sumant et dent ceteris.	and then to give it to others.
Panis angelicus	The angelic bread
fit panis hominum,	becomes the bread of men;
dat panis caelicus	the heavenly bread
figuris terminum;	makes an end of figures.
O res mirabilis!	O wondrous thing!
Manducat Dominum	The poor, the servant,
pauper, servus, et humilis.	and the lowly, consume the Lord.
Te, trina deitas	O Godhead, One in Three,

unaque, poscimus,　　　we beseech you

sicut nos visitas,　　　that you would visit us,

sicut te colimus:　　　as we adore you;

per tuas semitas　　　lead us along your paths

duc nos, quo tendimus　　　where we direct our course

ad lucem, quam inhabitas.　　　to the light in which you dwell.

Verbum supernum prodiens

Verbum supernum prodiens　　　The heavenly Word proceeding forth

Nec Patris linquens dexteram,　　　and yet not leaving the right hand

Ad opus suum exiens,　　　of the Father, going to his work,

Venit ad vitae vesperam.　　　has reached the evening of life.

In mortem a discipulo　　　Before having to be handed over

Suis tradendum aemulis,　　　to his rivals by a disciple, and put

Prius in vitae ferculo　　　to death, he first handed himself over

Se tradidit discipulis.　　　to his disciples on the plate of life.

Quibus sub bina specie　　　To them, under a twofold species

Carnem dedit et sanguinem,　　　he gave his flesh and blood

Ut duplicis substantiae　　　that he might feed the whole man

Totum cibaret hominem.　　　made up of twofold substance.

Se nascens dedit socium,　　　By his birth he gave himself as our

Convescens in edulium;　　　companion, at the Supper as our

Se moriens in pretium,　　　food, dying as our ransom; reigning

Se regnans dat in praemium.　　　he gives himself as our reward.

O salutaris hostia,　　　O saving Victim, who throws

Quae caeli pandis ostium,　　　open the gate of heaven,

Bella premunt hostilia,　　　hostile wars press upon us,

Da robur, fer auxilium.　　　give us strength, bring us aid,

Uni trinoque Domino　　　Eternal glory be

Sit sempiterna gloria,　　　to the One and Triune Lord.

Qui vitam sine termino
Nobis donet in patria.

May he grant us life
without end in the fatherland.

Lauda Sion

Lauda, Sion, salvatorem,
lauda ducem et pastorem,
in hymnis et canticis.

Praise, Sion, the Saviour,
praise the Leader and Shepherd
in hymns and canticles.

Quantum potes, tantum aude,
quia maior omni laude,
nec laudare sufficis.

As much as you can, as much
as you dare, for he is above
all praise; indeed no praise
is sufficient.

Laudis thema specialis,
panis vivus et vitalis
hodie proponitur.

Today there is proposed
to us a special theme
of praise: the Bread both living
and life-giving.

Quem in sacrae mensa coenae,
turbae fratrum duodenae
datum non ambigitur.

Which – it is not to be doubted –
was given to the twelve-fold
band of brothers at the table
of the holy Supper.

Sit laus plena, sit sonora,
sit iucunda, sit decora
mentis iubilatio.

Let praise be full and resounding;
let the jubilation of the soul
be joyous and fitting.

Dies enim solemnis agitur,
in qua mensae prima recolitur
huius institutio.

For a solemn day is being observed
upon which is commemorated
the first institution of the table.

In hac mensa novi regis,
novum Pascha novae legis
phase vetus terminat.

At this table of the new King
the new Pasch of the New Law
brings to an end the ancient Pasch.

Vetustatem novitas,

The new [supplants] the old,

umbram fugat veritas,	truth puts shadow to flight,
noctem lux eliminat.	light banishes night.
Quod in cena Christus gessit,	What Christ did at the supper
faciendum hoc expressit	he required to be done
in sui memoriam.	in memory of him.
Docti sacris institutis,	Taught by the sacred precepts,
panem, vinum in salutis	we consecrate bread and wine
consecramus hostiam.	into the Victim of salvation.
Dogma datur Christianis,	This is the dogma given
quod in carnem transit panis	to Christians: bread changes
et vinum in sanguinem.	into flesh, and wine into blood.
Quod non capis, quod non vides,	What you don't understand,
animosa firmat fides,	what you don't see, ardent
praeter rerum ordinem.	faith confirms beyond
	the order of things.
Sub diversis speciebus,	Under different species, different
signis tantum et non rebus	in signs [externals] only,
latent res eximiae.	and not in fact, wondrous things
	lie hidden.
Caro cibus, sanguis potus,	Flesh is food, blood is drink;
manet tamen Christus totus	nevertheless Christ remains entire
sub utraque specie.	under one or other species.
A sumente non concisus,	The whole [Christ] is received
non confractus, non divisus,	by the recipient – uncut,
integer accipitur.	unbroken, undivided.
Sumit unus, sumunt mille,	One person receives [him], a
quantum isti, tantum ille,	thousand receive [him], the one
nec sumptus consumitur.	as much as much as the thousand.
	And though consumed, he is
	not diminished.

Sumunt boni, sumunt mali, *sorte tamen inaequali,* *vitae vel interitus.*	The good and the wicked both receive [him], but with the unlike fate of life or of death.
Mors est malis, vita bonis; *Vide, paris sumptionis* *quam sit dispar exitus.*	Death to the bad, life to the good. Behold, of a like reception, how the end itself can differ!
Fracto demum sacramento, *nec vacilles, sed memento* *tantum esse sub fragmento,* *quantum toto tegitur.*	When the sacrament at length is broken, have no doubts, but remember that as much is hidden in a fragment as is contained in the whole.
Nulla rei fit scissura, *signi tantum fir fractura,* *qua nec status nec statura* *signati minuitur.*	There is no dividing the reality, only a breaking of the sign; and, by the breaking, neither the status nor stature of the One signified is diminished.
Ecce, panis Angelorum, *factus cibus viatorum,* *vere panis filiorum,* *non mittendus canibus.*	Behold the bread of angels is made the food of [earthly] pilgrims; truly it is the bread of children; it should not be cast to dogs.
In figuris praesignatur, *cum Isaac immolatur,* *agnus Paschae deputatur,* *datur manna patribus.*	It was prefigured in types: when Isaac was immolated, when the paschal lamb was killed, when manna was given to the fathers.
Bone Pastor, panis vere, *Iesu nostri miserere,* *tu nos pasce, nos tuere,* *tu nos bona fac videre* *in terra viventium.*	Good Shepherd, true bread, Jesus, have mercy on us, feed us and protect us, allow us to see good things in the land of the living.

Tu qui cuncta scis et vales,
qui nos pascis hic mortales,
tu nos ibi commensales,
cohaeredes et sodales
fac santorum civium.

You who know all things, and can do all things, you who feed us mortals here, make us fellow-guests there, co-heirs and companions of the holy citizens [of heaven].

Index